The Fictional Minds of Modernism

The Fictional Minds of Modernism

Narrative Cognition from Henry James to Christopher Isherwood

Edited by
Ricardo Miguel-Alfonso

BLOOMSBURY ACADEMIC
NEW YORK • LONDON • OXFORD • NEW DELHI • SYDNEY

BLOOMSBURY ACADEMIC
Bloomsbury Publishing Inc
1385 Broadway, New York, NY 10018, USA
50 Bedford Square, London, WC1B 3DP, UK
29 Earlsfort Terrace, Dublin 2, Ireland

BLOOMSBURY, BLOOMSBURY ACADEMIC and the Diana logo are trademarks of
Bloomsbury Publishing Plc

First published in the United States of America 2020
This paperback edition published in 2021

Copyright © Ricardo Miguel-Alfonso, 2020

Cover design by Eleanor Rose | Cover image: Detail from Composition, 1922, Eliezer (El) Markowich Lissitzky (1890-1941) © Museum of Modern Art, New York, USA / Bridgeman Images

All rights reserved. No part of this publication may be reproduced or transmitted in any form or by any means, electronic or mechanical, including photocopying, recording, or any information storage or retrieval system, without prior permission in writing from the publishers.

Bloomsbury Publishing Inc does not have any control over, or responsibility for, any third-party websites referred to or in this book. All internet addresses given in this book were correct at the time of going to press. The author and publisher regret any inconvenience caused if addresses have changed or sites have ceased to exist, but can accept no responsibility for any such changes.

Library of Congress Cataloging-in-Publication Data
Names: Miguel-Alfonso, Ricardo, editor.
Title: The fictional minds of modernism: narrative cognition from Henry James to Christopher Isherwood / edited by Ricardo Miguel-Alfonso.
Description: New York: Bloomsbury Academic, 2020. | Includes bibliographical references and index. | Summary: "Rethinks the ways that modernist narratives may be read as resources for understanding cognition and theory of mind"–Provided by publisher.
Identifiers: LCCN 2019037313 (print) | LCCN 2019037314 (ebook) | ISBN 9781501359774 (hardback) | ISBN 9781501359781 (epub) | ISBN 9781501359798 (pdf)
Subjects: LCSH: English fiction–20th century–History and criticism. | Psychology in literature. | Consciousness in literature. | Narration (Rhetoric) | Modernism (Literature)–Great Britain.
Classification: LCC PR888.P75 F53 2020 (print) | LCC PR888.P75 (ebook) | DDC 823/.009112–dc23
LC record available at https://lccn.loc.gov/2019037313
LC ebook record available at https://lccn.loc.gov/2019037314

ISBN: HB: 978-1-5013-5977-4
PB: 978-1-5013-7370-1
ePDF: 978-1-5013-5979-8
eBook: 978-1-5013-5978-1

Typeset by Deanta Global Publishing Services, Chennai, India

To find out more about our authors and books visit www.bloomsbury.com and sign up for our newsletters.

Contents

Foreword: Cognitivism and Modernist Narrative Acts:
    Our Arrival *Frederick Luis Aldama*   vi

1   Introduction *Ricardo Miguel-Alfonso*   1
2   On the Cognitive Value of Modernist Narratives *Jukka Mikkonen*   17
3   Metaphor and the Place of Mind in Three Modernist
     Novels *Marco Caracciolo*   31
4   Narratives of the Mind: Henry James's "The Private Life,"
     Locke's Private Language, Wittgenstein's Public Privacy,
     and the Emergence of a Modernist Language of
     Mental Life *Garry L. Hagberg*   53
5   Henry James and the Crypto-Psychological Novel: Remarks on the
     Mindfulness of *The Awkward Age* *José Antonio Álvarez-Amorós*   85
6   The Mind, "a Room of One's Own": An Epiphanic Moment in
     Virginia Woolf *José Ángel García-Landa*   109
7   Complexities of Social Cognition in Dorothy Richardson's
     Pointed Roofs *Patrick Colm Hogan*   133
8   Atmospheric Changes: Proust, Mind-Reading, and
     Errancy *Paul Sheehan*   157
9   Weimar Cognitive Theory: Modernist Narrativity and
     the Metaphysics of Frame Stories (After *Caligari* and
     Kracauer) *David LaRocca*   179
10 Reading Minds in Christopher Isherwood's
     The Berlin Stories *Janine Utell*   205

Notes on Editor and Contributors   227
Index   231

Foreword

Cognitivism and Modernist Narrative Acts: Our Arrival

Frederick Luis Aldama

In 2010, the University of Texas Press published *Toward a Cognitive Theory of Narrative Acts,* drawing together new work in this developing field. With Ricardo's expertly curated volume here, we leave the "toward" gesture behind. Instead, we can celebrate our arrival. Indeed, the scholars and their myriad of empirical approaches are neither a gesture *toward* something nor a reaction against something else. They exist as knowledge built on a solidly planted and arrived cognitivist research program.

The impulse in this volume is generative. Of course, to enrich our understanding of narrative—and in this case, a particular iteration of narrative classified as modernist—we must consider it as a product of our making. In this sense, it's a product of our non-dualist mind/bodies as grown *together* within the time and place of the real, interconnected world: physical, cultural, social, biological, and so on. That is, to deepen our understanding of narrative we must follow a research program that at once sees clearly that they grow from intermental exchange in time and place and therefore necessitate the exploration of the mind/body as one. Indeed, for the emergence of new knowledge to happen, one must necessarily bring a comprehensive and integrative approach—cognitivism—to the empirical study of narrative.

The scholarship herein sidesteps subjective opinion and raw speculation in favor of establishing a research program that moves forward through a series of checks and balances within the respective area of scholarly inquiry. It also focuses on modernist narratives; those "man-made objects" derived from "act of the mind" (Ricardo) that are built to satisfy "motivations of all sorts" as well as that announce their own recreative artifice; that make new our perception, thought, and feeling all while delighting in the artifice of their distillation and reconstruction of mind/bodies in the world. That is, the scholarship herein sheds light not only on how we *make* and how we *cocreate* narratives, but also on how we generate what I call elsewhere the ever-creative and recursive function of the generative device of the discourse.

With its laser sharp focus on modernist narratives, the scholarship herein also offers a more complex understanding of narrative than erstwhile mimesis-only models. Not only do we come to understand how creators of modernist narratives give shape to experience and meaning but also why we stand back in aesthetic awe, asking ourselves: How did they manage to pull this off?

In the spirit of the volume's expansive research program, I would also like to suggestively, albeit briefly, sketch the borders of texts considered within the modernist canon. Indeed, to do so let me first evoke Goethe's 1827 articulation of the concept of *world literature*. With this centrally in mind, we see that modernist literature is at once grown within specific national soils but where their circulation (and with it their formal narrative devices) is worldly. Already during Goethe's time and certainly in full swing in the early twentieth century with Modernism, we see the growing of literature as a chain of linkages across authors, translators, and readers from Europe across Asia, Oceania, Africa, and the Americas. Indeed, the product of modernist authors reading and learning from one another on a global scale was a cultural phenomenon never seen before: a budding poet like T. S. Eliot in 1915 and a fantastically creative genius like James Joyce in 1922 could borrow the "interior monologue" technique from Édouard Dujardin's then-unknown novel *Les lauriers sont coupés* and have it transformed and perfected by authors everywhere. We see poetic forms crisscrossing oceans with José Martí (Cuba) and Rubén Darío (Nicaragua) and Juan Ramón Jiménez (Spain). We see all variety of narratives cross-pollinations between Bertolt Brecht (Germany) and Yasunari Kawabata (Japan). Authors were learning from other authors from across the planet. They were teaching readers to read new and elaborate narrative techniques—and on a planetary basis. Everything in literature and art became a *world-shared* cultural phenomenon. As a result of linkages and worldly contact zones that transcended borders, nationalities, and cultural national traditions, these authors and artists from around the world came to be identified by categories such as Modernism.

Modernist narratives came to embody the worldly impulse of literature coinciding with the growing of the field of brain histology. For instance, in 1873 the Italian biologist and pathologist Camillo Golgi invented a staining technique called *reazione nera* (black reaction) that provided for the first time a very clear and well-contrasted picture of neurons and offered to observation the virtually complete morphology of brain cells. For his work on the central nervous system,

Golgi received the Nobel Prize in Physiology or Medicine in 1906, together with the great Spanish biologist Santiago Ramón y Cajal, a genius in the interpretation of the microscopic images of neurons. During the modernist period we have the first steps toward an empirical study of the mind/brain along with the whole nervous system, and the coming into its own of the global phenomenon of modernist literature.

What better way to celebrate our arrival in a cognitivist study of narrative than to focus on modernist narrative fictions. The significant and cutting-edge scholarship that makes up *Modernist Narrative and Its Fictional Minds* resoundingly demonstrates that the exploration of the many forms of aesthetic production and reception is advancing at a swift pace. With the most solid and innovative of scientific research in hand, these scholars deepen our knowledge of aesthetic creativity and aesthetic experience—and on a planetary scale. They establish once and for all that Modernism is more than the gateway to great art. It is and has remained the major road to the realization of world literature and a worldly science.

Note on Sources

Unless otherwise stated, italics in the quotes is in the original.

1

Introduction

Ricardo Miguel-Alfonso

In 1966, Roland Barthes famously opened one of his essays by declaring that "there are countless forms of narrative in the world," forms that materialize in "a prodigious variety of genres, each of which branches out into a variety of media, as if all substances could be relied upon to accommodate man's stories."[1] As a statement about the importance of narrative for human life, Barthes's words reflect a universal human need that has become increasingly clear in modern times. The centrality of narrative as a way to articulate and explain the meaning of the real world, from its most basic aspects to its most complex structures, is today the focus of studies of different kinds and from a variety of theoretical standpoints. The formalist approaches of the early twentieth century, such as structuralism or stylistics, have been gradually replaced by more comprehensive and integrative theories, notably cognitivism, which seek to provide descriptions and elucidations of the world-making abilities (in the broadest sense of the term) of the human mind. This is why terms such as "cognitive aesthetics" or "virtual narratives" have become common currency in studies of art and literary theory. The recent works of David Herman, Alan Palmer, Brian Richardson, Patrick Colm Hogan, and Lisa Zunshine, among many others, testify to this renewed interest.

A theory of such narrative forms is supposed to encompass and explain most, if not all, human attempts to communicate at a verbal level. And since communication is always preceded by a singular act of mind, whatever its purpose, studying narrative becomes essential for our understanding of the mind itself. Recollection, desire, judgment, manipulation . . ., all of them are structured and communicated according to narrative patterns, as are other more complex emotions and intentions. In this sense, there is a close connection between narrative and the expression of mind, the former being the natural vehicle of the latter both in the real world and in artistic, fictional compositions.

This expression of a subject's consciousness is what we have traditionally called the author's "vision." Its interpretation has always constituted the starting point—and, for some critics, the ultimate objective—of literary criticism, since it comprises the writer's broadly political, religious, and philosophical ideas. The analysis of narrative reconstructs these ideas by revealing the way in which they are organized and expressed.

The mind is, therefore, the origin of narrative constructions as much as of everything else in the world of human inventions. From computers to philosophical treatises and short stories, the mind is the necessary starting point of any creation. All man-made objects derive from acts of the mind that seek to satisfy motivations of all sorts, from love to entertainment and from curiosity to bewilderment. And narratives are no less "artifacts" than any physical object. The motivations of the mind are obviously varied, perhaps even limitless, but most of them find their natural outlet in language, and this is particularly true of stories. This does not mean that objects and stories are equivalent. In fact, we can safely say, against popular belief, that a certain narrative organization precedes even the creation of any object, however big or small. The complex act of mind involved in the conception and design of an object of any kind often implies a previous narrative, however simple, of how that object in particular has to be constructed in order to be effective (even recipes and do-it-yourself instructions are written in narrative form). This means that rather than preceding thinking, narrative works simultaneously with it by organizing it and giving it its final expression. Otherwise, there would be no coherence.

Stories, as Jonathan Gottschall has recently argued, are an essential part of our comprehension of the world and the transmission of knowledge, to such an extent that our capacity to create them can be said to constitute one of our most primary instincts as human beings.[2] Stories seem to work very much like the physical objects we create, that is, by satisfying some specific necessity or lack. But although both of them fulfill this requisite, again there is no equivalence between them. The needs that a story can satisfy are mostly intellectual and affective rather than biological, and still all of them are a crucial part of human history. As Terence Cave has recently argued, literature (in all its complexity and variety) is central to human life because it provides readers with "affordances." Affordances, a term Cave takes from the American psychologist James J. Gibson, are "the potential *uses* an object or feature of the environment offers to a living creature."[3] This object can be created by necessity or adapted from another, more primitive one, but its function is to make it easier to adapt to the ecosystem and to solve problems and overcome obstacles. From the cultural point of view, language is the first and most crucial of these affordances. Literature is what we may call a "second-degree affordance" in that it uses language to reflect on reality (and also on the potentials of language itself). In other words, literature is one of the virtually limitless scenarios that the ecosystem offers us to try out our beliefs, judgments, and, in general, ideas.

There is a common agreement among scholars of both linguistics and literature that the role of narrative in human life is that of bestowing order and meaning on the otherwise-random phenomena among which we live. Yana Popova, to use one recent example, claims that narrative "organizes particular events (mostly human motives and actions) through establishing a necessary connection or a causal link between them."[4] This causal relation has been the epistemological basis not only of fictionwriting but also of other humanistic disciplines such as history or philosophy. In the literary field, especially when it comes to the novel and the short story, this has been not just a desire but a compositional principle in itself. With notable exceptions, the quest for mimetic realism has been a constant aspiration for both literary writers and critics from Aristotle to the realist and naturalist literature of the late nineteenth and the early twentieth centuries. The underlying assumption in the privileging of "realism" and "objectivity" in storytelling has to do with the pursuit for truth, a philosophical and moral criterion that often has little to do with fiction. As Jerome Bruner has argued, "Unlike constructions generated by logical and scientific procedures... narrative constructions can only achieve 'verisimilitude.' Narratives, then, are a version of reality whose acceptability is governed by convention and 'narrative necessity' rather than by empirical verification and logical requiredness."[5] But a certain degree of correspondence with reality remains the ideal of fiction writing *as a product of the human mind*.

For many decades now, narratology has studied not only the nature and structure of narrative—fictional or otherwise—but also its influence on our perception of reality, its relevance for other disciplines, and its place within the general human sciences. In so doing, it has attempted to systematize the many different ways in which storytelling accounts for how we organize our perceptions of reality. A linear, cause-effect relation has been the usual theoretical pattern to interpret how we make sense of real phenomena. Barring overtly self-conscious works—from classics such as Cervantes's *Don Quijote* and Sterne's *Tristram Shandy* to contemporary works by Jorge Luis Borges, John Barth, Robert Coover, or Julio Cortázar, among many others—the "realist" interpretation of narrative has been taken to be a natural epistemological condition of reading. In many literary theories, from structuralism to the new historicism, this has become an unquestioned a-priori principle.

Since our understanding often works by establishing causal relations among phenomena, we have applied the same principle to narrative; and since narrative is a central instrument for the comprehension of the outer world, we have assumed that a literary text must necessarily follow the same pattern; that is, it must be organized according to the same principles that govern our thinking about the real world. The classical idea of mimesis is the product of this assumption. But it is important to remember here that the origins of the relations in a fictional work are also mental, and therefore the study of narration must take into account the mind that produces a story. The study of narrative, or literature in general, cannot be divorced from authorial intention, historical situatedness, or cultural influences, but only the former can give us access into the creative undertaking that a narrative involves. In this sense, a story is first and foremost an encounter between minds, and it is so in two interrelated senses: on the one hand, it is articulated on the dialogic relation between the characters' voices, which provides the most immediate information (or lack thereof) we need to interpret it; on the other, and this is equally fundamental, a story also records the primordial encounter between the author's consciousness and what we may call "the consciousness of his world." Popova has argued that narrative is a form of thinking that shapes "our understanding of other people and their actions."[6] Similarly, novelist David Lodge claims that literature, especially the novel, "creates fictional models of what it is like to be a human being, moving through space and time."[7] Therefore, to say that our mind has a natural ability for world-making implies that it has the capacity to imagine minds and voices other than the author's and can keep a dialogue among them.

These and other definitions stress the role of narrative in creating lifelike worlds that help us evaluate our own. The fact that these worlds are fictional makes no substantial difference when it comes to their understanding, since they are nearly always modeled on real-life minds (science fiction and horror fiction are notable exceptions, even though their relation to the historical world is often present, although it remains implicit rather than explicit). The reader's perception of the characters' minds rests on his or her previous experience in the real world, an experience that appears in his or her mind as an ideal narrative against which the reader has to match other narratives. This is why the most recent approaches to the reading of narrative stress its *enactive* nature. According to the enactivist approach, texts acquire their full meaning when our patterns of consciousness attribution in the real world are transferred to the act of reading, the only difference between their respective contexts being that "[the character's] originating experience . . . is created by readers in their interaction with the text."[8] This is what we may call a dialogic relation, one in which our experience of the world finds a natural (because analogous) correlate in a constructed fictional world. Reading, therefore, becomes a process of recognition, identification, and—in most cases—criticism by dissent.

To study narrative, therefore, is to explore the workings of the human mind from the stage of pure perception to the articulation of structures of knowledge, opinion, and judgment. And to study fictional narratives means to a large extent to find out to what extent those workings apply to the reality we know, whether past or present. The "ideology" of a text (in the broadest sense of the term) is always a reflection of the author's mental structures. And here "reflection" does not mean a mimetic copy but a particular vision of it. This is why the term "realism" appears out of date, and it is more appropriate to regard narrative as a fundamental form of "critical realism," that is, not as a way of providing factual representations but rather as a way of revealing what Patrick Colm Hogan has labeled "distortions."[9] These distortions constitute the actual substance of literary narrative, and not the mere re-presentation of the external world. As we will see later, modernist fiction took this predicament to an extreme.

Understood this way, the work of narrative is to both embody and provide cognitive knowledge. But this knowledge cannot be isolated as just a product of one author's particular mind. Embedded in that mind are intuitions, ideas, emotions, and value judgments of different kinds. The mind is essentially a subjective construction, but it cannot be understood only from within. The historical and cultural context in which people move modifies constantly their perception of the "ecosystem" they inhabit. A person's narrative, whether mental or written, is many times an account of the symbiosis between his or her mind and the world. David Herman has explained this exchange in the following terms: "Storytelling practices take their place within a wider array of cultural institutions, norms, and procedures, technological innovations, and embodied engagements with built as well as natural environments that provide crucial scaffolding for intelligent behavior."[10] While institutions shape the human mind, the human mind engenders narratives that provide a critical view of those institutions. This is one of the most complex kinds of "intelligent behavior" that Herman mentions, for it requires not only a mature and balanced vision of the world but also the mastery of language, the skill to appeal to the reader, a certain set of ideals, the ability to provoke thinking, and so on.

The ideological misrepresentations Hogan mentions have to be disclosed by foregrounding the problems of interpretation of language *as language*. Since narratives are an integral part of a culture and its values, the way to understand the latter is to work through the texture of the former and find the meaning that underlies the vision they embody. And since any vision of the world is ideological in the broadest sense of the term, narrative provides us—by contrast—with access not only to a writer's mind-set but also to his or her world's ideology. It is not infrequent that personal values are explicitly put forward in a story, even in those that appear to be more "mimetic" or realistic," but we must remember that artworks, whether or not narratives, are intentional structures, and therefore their thematization of a certain vision of the world always lurks underneath their language. In fact, language itself embodies that vision by simultaneously verbalizing it and giving it meaning. Unlike other narratives, literary narratives present versions of the world that include specifically how meaning is constructed *in that world*. Social, sexual, racial, educational, generational, and many other differences and conflicts become enmeshed with subjective and personal views and desires, and that net of interlocked values and intentions becomes the true substance of stories. John Gibson has expressed this cognitive significance in the following terms: "[Literature provides] a complexity of vision, a finely textured presentation of human activity and circumstance.... We find that in literature ... already known regions of reality tend to suggest deeper levels of meaning and hint at broader patterns of aboutness and significance."[11] This "aboutness" is always geographically and historically situated, or, in other words, a product of culture.

A "textured" form is what makes literature self-referential and draws our attention toward the very idea of "mere representation" as suspicious. It is the role of narrative to give meaning to experience, to organize and categorize it; in the case of literary narrative, its function extends to the articulation of critical representations of the complexity of that experience. It is not just a view of life but an inquiry into what that life means that makes for a successful story. Even though the compositional mechanisms of all narratives may be basically the same, literary narrative is a "second-degree" narrative. But it is always a narrative about the culture to which it belongs; or, in other words, it is a "socially, culturally, and materially embedded instrument of mind."[12]

The study of consciousness in fiction is not essentially different from that of human consciousness—which is important especially in the literature written since the eighteenth century. The modern revolution of the Enlightenment in philosophy and art emphasized the value of subjectivism in the study of human understanding and placed great importance on subjectivity. British Empiricism was fundamental in promoting the practical and subject-oriented nature of knowledge, including artistic taste. The shift from universality to particularity, to put it in very broad terms, had consequences for both the theory and practice of literature, one of the most salient examples being the rise of the novelistic genre. Since then, narrative fiction has moved gradually from mimetic realism to the deconstruction of form, structure, genre, and time. Modernism is no doubt the major example of this historical tendency.[13]

In order to understand fictional consciousness, the role of narrative disruption is as important as can be consistency, closure, or completeness. As Lisa Zunshine has explained, "Narratives that challenge their readers' theory of mind by their unusual and difficult representations of fictional consciousness may offer valuable insights on the workings of our consciousness, which is anything but predictable, orderly, and simple."[14] This is important for what we may call "methodological" reasons. One of the greatest interests of the cognitive study of literature, which manifests itself in different theories of mind, is the possibility of harmonizing the scientific analysis of mind and the humanities by finding a common root in their respective ways of approaching consciousness. Before achieving such unity between the natural and the human sciences, we must be able to explain not only how narrative works in its most traditional sense—that is, how much coherence and realism it is capable of producing—but also how it can be dislocated and ultimately called into question. Possibilities are as important as limits. In the end, realism is but a concept that we project onto literary "artifacts" in order to assimilate them into our rational, systematic vision of reality. This is why it is important to go back to where many of the most far-reaching transformations in narrative construction emerged.

The Modernist Challenge to Fictional Minds

In order to understand the implications of modernist literature for the theoretical ideas of mind and narrative, we must begin with a fundamental consideration about the very nature of language. My remarks so far have taken it for granted that there is a clear correspondence between an ordered narrative and the order of reality—or, in other words, that language is a transparent medium that carries an unequivocal meaning to be found outside the subject. It has been a long time since we know that this is not necessarily true. It is not even *often* true. However much we wish to believe that words are transparent when it comes to what we call their "literal" meaning (which means that we take words and their referents have an objective, even causal relationship), their combination in a narrative is never a sum of the parts, and certainly not the sum of their referential meanings combined. This is why the interpretation of narrative is not the interpretation of its units, but of the whole they help to construct. Narrative interpretation must look into the mechanisms of narrative itself *as a constructive process*, paying attention to the forms of attention and surprise it elicits in readers. And this is especially true of works, such as modernist ones, whose degree of formal sophistication sometimes makes it difficult for readers to recognize the most basic traits of a story, thwarting our primary reading expectations by using increasingly complicated structures. When this happens, we must look not so much at the opacity of words but to interpret their density in a given narrative. As Jerome Bruner argues, "It is not textual or referential ambiguity that compels interpretive activity in narrative comprehension, but narrative itself."[15] Instead of dividing the text into components and isolating them from the whole to see how they work as discrete units, criticism must reveal the whole network of stylistic choices that make up a narrative and the relations among them.

In other words, what happens when the compositional strategies of a literary narrative do not just mirror the changes in a culture but rather become their embodiment? How does literary criticism proceed when interpretation is not a matter of finding how "ideologically disfunctional distortions"[16] are represented but rather how they have become the text's own fabric? To what extent can a text go beyond representation and become a symbol of its historical and cultural age? These are important questions in order to understand the art and the literature of Modernism, questions that this collection is intended to address.

Although Virginia Woolf famously declared in 1924 that Modernism had begun sometime "in or around December 1910," some of its formal disruptions date back to the 1880s and 1890s, when new artistic movements such as impressionism had fostered new ways of conceiving narrativity as a representational and explanatory tool. In this sense, the notion of Modernism that guides this collection goes back to the pioneering work of Henry James and extends to the more formally challenging and readerly unsettling compositions of the so-called high modernists. In chronological terms, we are talking about the period between the 1890s and the end of the Second World War. However close to the accepted critical standard, this is obviously an arbitrary choice, since the limits of Modernism become increasingly unclear as we approach the postmodern era. This is important to clarify because, although there have been critics for whom there is no clear distinction between Modernism and postmodernism, it is during the former when the most fundamental challenges to mind theory emerged in the realm of narrative. Postmodernism is, in the end, an extension and formal intensification of them.

Understood in this way, the modernist emphasis on discontinuity, fragmentation, and abstraction leads artists and critics of this period to rethink the ways in which we understand narrative linearity and, as a consequence, the very configuration of human consciousness. To interrogate the logical structure and imitative power of narrative was a way of questioning the very nature of reality, especially the ways in which subjects construct their respective worldviews and how these relate to different practices of storytelling. As Thomas Pavel has recently argued, modernist works "use great quantities of rough-hewn narrative matter or of sophisticated digressions for a relentless depiction of the breakdown of connections between the individual and the world."[17] The first and most crucial of these ruptures is represented by the relentless questioning of the relationship between mind, language, and reality. Examples of this aspiration abound in varying degrees of complexity, from openly metaliterary stories (e.g., James Joyce's *Ulysses*) to works about the general configuration of historical consciousness (e.g., Gertrude Stein's *The Making of Americans*). This radical questioning reaches beyond the literary field and into the humanities in general, from philosophy to art to history. In fact, underlying the philosophy of Modernism is a thorough critical exploration of the very idea of the human and the assumptions that surround this notion since at least the early modern age. Mind and language are but two of them. The consequence, as Paul Sheehan argues, is "a turn away from the human as a *given* towards the human as a *problem*."[18]

There are, however, different ways to understand this fundamental rethinking of the correlation between the mind and the world. Alan Palmer, for example, has suggested that the representation of mind in many modernist narratives reveals a profound break in the continuity of thought and external behavior and the ensuing loss of the capacity for social interaction.[19] In this view, the modernist mind is often reduced to the realm of inner speech or highly conscious verbal thinking, whereas the minds of characters in other, more "classical" periods are construed as "whole" minds, that is, as minds comprising—apart from a more or less conscious flow of language—large sets of nonverbal states either transient, like moods, desires, emotions, intentions, purposes, and motives, or stable, like beliefs, attitudes, judgments, and character traits. Obviously, the textual channels that convey such different types of consciousnesses also change. The default mode in classical narrative is not direct or free indirect thought, but rather thought report, or, more accurately, what Palmer calls "contextual thought report," that is, a type of narratorial discourse that combines the presentation of verbal thought, nonverbal states of mind, action, and behavior, as though emphasizing the already-fragile boundaries between thinking and acting which will become heavily obtrusive in modernist fiction.[20] The problem here is one of resolution: if minds are constructed and represented as largely nonverbal wholes, then actions, body language, and external gestures can be decoded into states of mind with an acceptable level of accuracy and thus facilitate social interaction; but if they are essentially verbal artifacts, they remain sealed off to social, public efforts to interpret them and normalize behavioral expectations. In this sense, the modernist mind intensifies the abstract, intellectualist character and position of the impressionist artist and enhances the work's textual self-consciousness and its interpretive difficulty.[21]

David Herman, on the other hand, has recently put forward an alternative view to Palmer's. If modernist fiction is for Palmer the locus of the internalist mind, severed from action and teleology, Herman argues the contrary—that minds in modernist fiction "at once shape and are shaped by larger experiential environments, via the particular affordances or opportunities for action that those environments provide."[22] For him, the mind in modernist narrative reaches beyond the self, is a distributed mind, and is alien to the internalism of Cartesian cartographies that divorced the mind from the external world. Herman thus opposes the critical commonplace that modernist fiction participated in a psychological inward turn and developed new strategies to delve into psychological depths and argues instead "that modernist narratives can both be illuminated by and help illuminate postcognitivist accounts of the mind as inextricably embedded in contexts for action and interaction."[23] To make his point, he uses enactivist frameworks that oppose and supersede the old, Cartesian geographies of mind that drastically separate the realms of mind and body. He explicitly attacks the existence of an upward scale from the mind inside to the world outside, and attempts to replace the internal-external continuum with another based on the inevitable interaction of mind and world—that which goes from a tight coupling between an intelligent agent and his surrounding environment to a loose coupling between both. This coupling is always present, only the degree varies.

Herman also reviews typical internalist perspectives of how mind is created and represented in modernist fiction, that is, the inward turn of narrative and the presentation of worlds not as they are but as they are experienced. He rather proposes an underexplored approach: "Though modernist narratives did in fact depart from realist protocols, this departure involved not an inward turning but rather a foregrounding of the inextricable interconnection between 'inner' and 'outer' domains,"[24] that is, a supersession of the Cartesian ontological divide between both. In other words, what modernist narratives actually achieved was not to engage psychological depths, but rather spread the mind abroad to show how it was intertwined with worldly circumstances: "By contrast, my argument is that modernist narratives figure a different geography of mind; in place of Cartesian mappings of the mental as a bracketed-off internal space, these texts allow the mind to be imagined as a kind of distributional flow, interwoven with rather than separated from situations, events, and processes in the world."[25] So he calls for a revision of the internalist models of consciousness representation that, for him, are called into question by modernist narratives.

A good example of these concerns is provided by Gertrude Stein's recently republished lectures on narration, a work intended both to explain and to disrupt preconceived notions of narrative, from novels to newspapers to personal letters. Stein's text plays with the very basic conventions of the genre from the beginning, and it does so in order to embody in itself the changes that modernist aesthetics has brought on traditional literary forms: in other words, it is a modernist explanation of Modernism. For Stein, narration is basically a verbal construction that seeks to tell a story by means of specific words, words that cannot be changed unless we want to transform the story altogether. Stories are reified in their respective words and their grammar, to such an extent that they become objects. As she explains it in her characteristic style,

> That narrative is going to be made that the story they have to tell is going to be told that the nation which lives in a land that has made it that nation will have to tell its story in its own way about that there can be no doubt, the story must be told will be told can be told but they will tell this story they tell this story using the exactly same words that were made to tell an entirely different story and the way it is being done the pressure being put upon the same words to make them

move in an entirely different way is most exciting, it excites the words it excites us who use them.[26]

The excitement of modernist art and narrative lies in its relentless search for other words, for another style that unsettles our expectations about stories and keeps language in fluid movement, somehow separating it from its original meaning and taking it into new expressive regions.

> And so we have this situation, a settled language because a language is settled after it does not change any more that is as to words and grammar, and it being written so completely written all the time it inevitably cannot change much and yet the pressure upon these words to make them do something that they did not do for those who made that language come to exist is a very interesting thing to watch.[27]

The first strategy in this unsettling of narrative—and, with it, our perception of the world—is to undo the cause-effect relation between phenomena, to show the inconsistency of separating parts that are inextricably united in the same process. "Narrative," she argues, "has been the telling of anything because there has been always has been a feeling that something followed another thing that there was succession in happening."[28] Her own style dramatizes the urge to break barriers between paragraphs, sentences, and grammatical units. In fact, "sentences and paragraphs need not necessarily go on existing."[29]

Although Stein does not explore the issue specifically, to assert the continuity between mind and world is the ultimate objective of this series of deconstructions. In fact, it is the very epistemological principle of modernist narrative as a whole, as this collection tries to reveal in different contexts. The demonstration of such continuity is intended to give equal importance to mind, body, and world without privileging one over the others. As Marianne DeKoven has argued,

> It would be impossible, and a serious distortion of the modernist text, to claim that it resolves its dualisms in favor of one term over the other. Instead, the text enacts precisely the modernist moment of simultaneity, of dualism that seeks neither a unitary resolution (one term over the other) nor a transcendent third term, a dialectical synthesis, but rather a simultaneity that, from within dualism, imagines an alternative to it: not an obliteration or replacement of dualism—I would argue that all modes of doing away with dualism are ultimately versions of dialectical synthesis—but an alternative to it that maintains difference while denying hierarchy.[30]

Difference without hierarchy implies, among other things, that interpretation cannot—at least not objectively—endow a certain voice or character with authority as a source of knowledge. In fact, unlike in the traditional metaphor of the mirror, narratives must embody the uncertainty that we—both as human beings and as readers—experience when it comes to explaining the world we live in. Confusion, doubt, alarm, skepticism . . . , these are not only "real-world" states of mind but also actual epistemological tools whose application to literary interpretation yields a more complete and nuanced understanding of ourselves.

> The sub-text of every fiction is perception itself, we might argue—that is, reading, writing, interpretation, and the making meaning of texts, words, language, experience. All readers have to press their imagination to new efforts in order to arouse themselves to the vision that the characters in each fiction are not only models and anti-models for us in our lives. More immediately and more effectively, they shine out as models of us as readers—passive readers, alert readers, recalcitrant readers, naive readers: every type of reading and response may be mirrored—represented—as these works of fiction parody, ironise, and metaphorise the experiences of coming face to face with the "Reality" that is ourselves—in all its disguises and variations.[31]

In the end, our response to the texture and the difficulty of a literary work, especially a modernist one, dramatize (rather than represents) the complexity of the reality that has produced that work. If we understand character and mind in a "substantialist" way, as many contemporary readers and critics of modernist narrative did in their time, the gap between the text and the reader will be unbridgeable. As Omri Moses has argued in the context of modernist art, character (and his or her mind) cannot be taken as having "fixed, intractable, and repetitive psychological content that is not readily responsive to the immediate conditions imposed by a situation."[32] The mind is in constant flux, and this fluidity generates its own particular forms of attention and response. These forms materialize in language, which includes doubt, perspectivism, undecidability, and even communicative failure.

The contributors to this book generally line up with Herman's idea about the continuity between self and world and the ensuing inseparability of mind and representation. Our aim is to explore how modernist narratives offer insights into the historical world as a subject of knowledge rather than a mere object of contemplation. Through the analysis of a variety of international novels, short stories, and films we want to demonstrate that the so-called inward turn of modernist narratives constitutes, in fact, a reflection of the necessary interaction between *mind*, *self*, and *world* that constitutes knowledge, and therefore excludes any radical split among any of these three categories. In other words, each of the chapters examines the cognitive value of modernist narrative in a different context (and genre) by showing how the perception of objects and of other people is a relational activity that requires an awareness of the ultimately constant flux of reality. In order not to impose one single version of mind theory, each one of the contributors has chosen his or her own as a starting point for his or her theoretical or analytical exploration. The four more "theoretical" chapters (although two of them also engage in readings of specific authors) lead the way in this sense. Their purpose is to show how the modernist transformation of mental representation in fiction emerged in the works of both philosophers (Ludwig Wittgenstein) and literary writers (Henry James and Virginia Woolf). In doing so, they are meant to establish the frame of reference for the rest of the chapters to explore in more detail its consequences for a variety of narrative works and genres. The choice of writers is as inclusive and varied as the scope of a collection makes it possible, which is necessarily limited once we take into account that Modernism encompasses—and deeply transforms—virtually every narrative genre while at the same time helps to consolidate other, more recent ones (cinema and graphic novels). Of course, other important names have been left out because of obvious space limitations. In any case, we offer here a study of some of the major contributors to the modernist challenge to the notion and practice of "fictional minds" in a variety of genres between its inception in the work of Henry James and its consolidation in the first four decades of the twentieth century.

Notes

1. Roland Barthes, "Introduction to the Structural Analysis of Narrative," trans. Lionel Duisit, *New Literary History* 6 (1975): 237.
2. See Jonathan Gottschall, *The Storytelling Animal: How Stories Make Us Human* (Boston: Houghton Mifflin, 2016).
3. Terence Cave, *Thinking with Literature: Towards a Cognitive Criticism* (Oxford: Oxford University Press, 2016), 48.
4. Yana Popova, *Stories, Meaning and Experience* (London: Routledge, 2006), 51.
5. Jerome Bruner, "The Narrative Construction of Reality," *Critical Inquiry* 18.1 (1991): 5.

6 Popova, *Stories, Meaning and Experience*, 78.
7 David Lodge, *Consciousness and the Novel* (London: Secker and Warburg, 2002), 14.
8 Marco Caracciolo, *The Experientiality of Narrative: An Enactivist Approach* (Berlin: Walter de Gruyter, 2014), 129.
9 Patrick Colm Hogan, Ulysses *and the Poetics of Cognition* (New York: Routledge, 2014), 9.
10 David Herman, *Storytelling and the Sciences of Mind* (Cambridge, MA: MIT Press, 2013), 230.
11 John Gibson, *Fiction and the Weave of Life* (Oxford: Oxford University Press, 2007), 142.
12 Herman, *Storytelling and the Sciences of Mind*, 230.
13 Obviously, not everybody agrees with this general characterization. For some critics, especially in the context of British literary theory and criticism, modernist experimentation was but an exception in a long tradition of straightforward realist writing.
14 Lisa Zunshine, *Why We Read Fiction: The Theory of Mind and the Novel* (Baltimore: Johns Hopkins University Press, 2006), 42.
15 Bruner, "The Narrative Construction of Reality," 9.
16 Hogan, Ulysses *and the Poetics of Meaning*, 9.
17 Thomas Pavel, *The Lives of the Novel: A History* (Princeton, NJ: Princeton University Press, 2013), 286.
18 Paul Sheehan, *Modernism, Narrative and Humanism* (Cambridge: Cambridge University Press, 2002), 181.
19 See Alan Palmer, *Fictional Minds* (Lincoln: University of Nebraska Press, 2004) and *Social Minds in the Novel* (Columbus: Ohio State University Press, 2010).
20 Palmer, *Fictional Minds*, 209–10.
21 Jesse Matz, *Literary Impressionism and Modernist Aesthetics* (Cambridge: Cambridge University Press, 2001), 9–11.
22 David Herman, "1880–1945: Re-Minding Modernism," in *The Emergence of Mind: Representations of Consciousness in Narrative Discourse in English*, ed. David Herman (Lincoln: University of Nebraska Press, 2011), 249–50.
23 Ibid., 249.
24 Ibid., 253.
25 Ibid., 255.
26 Gertrude Stein, *Narration: Four Lectures* (1935; rpt. Chicago: University of Chicago Press, 2010), 7.
27 Ibid., 9.
28 Ibid., 18.

29 Ibid., 22.
30 Marianne DeKoven, *Rich and Strange: Gender, History, Modernism* (Princeton, NJ: Princeton University Press, 1991), 25.
31 Kathleen M. Wheeler, *"Modernist" Women Writers and Narrative Art* (London: Macmillan, 1994), 184–85.
32 Omri Moses, *Out of Character: Modernism, Vitalism, Psychic Life* (Stanford, CA: Stanford University Press, 2014), 5.

2

On the Cognitive Value of Modernist Narratives

Jukka Mikkonen

Introduction

The cognitive value of literature—whether literary works can contribute to our understanding of ourselves and reality—is one of the perennial problems in philosophical aesthetics and key questions in analytic philosophy of art. In addition, empirical psychology has recently become interested in the question, and partly because of the rise of cognitive scientific approaches in the humanities, the question has also returned to literary studies.

When studying literature's ability to enlarge our understanding, the focus has traditionally been on the works' mimetic dimension: literary works are taken to offer us experiential knowledge—knowledge of what it is like to be in a certain situation or to see the world from a certain point (or points) of view, for instance. Recently, it has been fashionable in philosophy, psychology, and cognitive literary studies to approach the cognitive value of literature in terms of the theory of mind. It is proposed that reading fictional literature is about inferring fictional states of minds and, further, that this activity could improve readers' ability to understand the mental states of others and, perhaps, workings of the human mind at large.

Conversely, many have argued that literary minds are qualitatively different from real human minds and the mimetic way of reading literary works does great aesthetic violence to them. Moreover, analytic philosophy of art—which has explored the topic for over a half a century—has investigated the cognitive gains of art typically in terms of, or derived from, truth and resemblance, favoring examples drawn from realist literature. Such an approach seems problematic in Modernism where an author ponders, "What is reality? And who are the judges of reality?"[1]

Yet, modernist fiction is characteristically "epistemological," as Brian McHale famously describes it. McHale argues that modernist fictions foreground questions, such as "What is there to be known?; Who knows it?; How do they know it, and with what degree of certainty?"[2] Likewise, Alan Palmer thinks that modernist works are "oriented toward the investigation of such issues as perception and cognition, perspective, the subjective experience of time, and the circulation and reliability of knowledge."[3] David Herman, too, maintains that modernist narratives illuminate "the degree to which perceiving, acting, and thinking are inextricably interlinked, with the constant cross-circulation among these activities accounting for intelligent agents' enactment of a world."[4] Precisely the modernists' interest on these fundamental issues, together with the philosophical and psychological erudition of many of its representatives, makes it tempting to approach certain modernist narratives as literary-philosophical explorations.

This chapter examines the assumed cognitive value of modernist narratives from a philosophical point of view. In particular, I am interested if we can learn about the workings of the mind in reading modernist narratives. If not, could modernist narratives contribute to cognition some other way?

Modernism and the Mind

Narratology has long celebrated third-person narrators for their ability to give us access to fictional characters' minds. "Epic fiction is the sole epistemological instance where . . . subjectivity . . . of a third-person *qua* third-person can be portrayed," Käte Hamburger proposed in the 1950s.[5] Later, Dorrit Cohn spoke of third-person narrators' "unnatural power to see into their characters' inner lives,"[6] and Marie-Laure Ryan of narrators' "supernatural ability of reading into foreign minds."[7] Correspondingly, Monika Fludernik states that "fiction at one point discovers that it . . . can present consciousness extensively as if reading people's minds."[8]

The epistemic accessibility of fictional minds has later become a subject of dispute in narrative theory, but the idea of the resemblance between real and literary minds and the reader's ability to enter a character's mind lives strong in cognitive literary studies, for instance. The idea that the way we interpret literary minds is akin to how we interpret other people in our everyday encounters is a standard assumption in cognitive approaches to literature. Theory of mind, a psychological concept describing our comprehension of others' minds, has been particularly influential in explaining our engagement with literary narratives; the critic Lisa Zunshine claims that "ToM makes literature as we know it possible,"[9] whereas the philosopher Gregory Currie proposes that "mentalizing" (a term he prefers over ToM), the understanding of mental states and the capacity to reason about them, lies in the core of literary interpretation.[10] Alan Palmer, in turn, thinks that "in essence, narrative is the description of fictional mental functioning."[11] He claims that "one of the pleasures of reading novels is the enjoyment of being told what a variety of fictional people are thinking. . . . This is a relief from the business of real life, much of which requires the ability to decode accurately the behavior of others."[12] Later, Palmer has emphasized the externalist perspective to the mind, yet maintaining that "readers enter storyworlds primarily by attempting to follow the workings of the fictional minds contained in them."[13]

It is a commonplace that modernist narratives deal with "inner experience" and the "representation of the mind." Palmer, for instance, claims that "the modernist novel is still based on a belief in truth and reality" and that modernist authors "attempt to record as faithfully as possible the workings of fictional minds."[14] David Herman questions the idea of the *inward turn* in Modernism but asserts that modernist narratives characteristically deal with the representation of the mind:

> The upshot of modernist experimentation was not to plumb psychological depths, but to spread the mind abroad—to suggest that human psychology has the profile it does because of the extent to which it is interwoven with worldly circumstances. The mind does not reside within; instead, it emerges through humans' dynamic interdependencies with the social and material environments they seek to navigate.[15]

Sure enough, modernist literature was greatly affected by developments in psychology, such as Ernst Mach's theory of subjective experience, William James's view of the stream of thought or consciousness, Henri Bergson's view of immediate experience, Sigmund Freud's idea of the unconsciousness, and so on.[16] Many critics underline that modern psychology and the modernist movement in literature were intertwined.[17] Moreover, psychological theories were not only an inspiration for authors but, for many writers, also the exploration of human experience was a programmatic pursuit. In her essay "Modern Fiction" (1925), Virginia Woolf proposes how writers could come "closer to life":

> Let us record the atoms as they fall upon the mind in the order in which they fall, let us trace the pattern, however disconnected and incoherent in appearance, which each sight or incident scores upon the consciousness. Let us not take it for granted that life exists more fully in what is commonly thought big than in what is commonly thought small.[18]

In a passage from the same essay cited ad nauseam, and repeated now again, Woolf proposes:

> Examine for a moment an ordinary mind on an ordinary day. The mind receives a myriad impressions—trivial, fantastic, evanescent, or engraved with the sharpness of steel. From all sides they come, an incessant shower of innumerable atoms; and as they fall, as they shape themselves into the life of Monday or Tuesday, the accent falls differently from of old; the moment of importance came not here but there; so that, if a writer were a free man and not a slave, if he could write what he chose, not what he must, if he could base his work upon his own feeling and not upon convention, there would be no plot, no comedy, no tragedy, no love interest or catastrophe in the accepted style, and perhaps not a single button sewn on as the Bond Street tailors would have it. Life is not a series of gig lamps symmetrically arranged; life is a luminous halo, a semi-transparent envelope surrounding us from the beginning of consciousness to the end. Is it not the task of the novelist to convey this varying, this unknown and uncircumscribed spirit, whatever aberration or complexity it may display, with as little mixture of the alien and external as possible? We are not pleading merely for courage and sincerity; we are suggesting that the proper stuff of fiction is a little other than custom would have us believe it.[19]

Referring to Woolf's program, one could defend the mimetic approach to Modernism and claim that this movement considered itself truer to life and reflected people's experience with their environment: it was the world, or the human character, that had changed. Eric Auerbach, for one, praised Woolf for her talent in capturing the modern epoch.[20] He admires Woolf's *To the Lighthouse* precisely for its lifelikeness and acuity:

> What realistic depth is achieved in every individual occurrence, for example the measuring of the stocking! Aspects of the occurrence come to the fore, and links to other occurrences, which, before this time, had hardly been sensed,

which had never been clearly seen and attended to, and yet they are determining factors in our real lives.[21]

There is plenty of genetic evidence available for one who argues that the moderns aimed to give their readers an insight into the human mind. Virginia Woolf says that in *Mrs. Dalloway* she intended to "adumbrate . . . a study of insanity & suicide: the world seen by the sane & the insane side by side—something like that."[22] Many think she succeeded. One critic says that in the work Woolf gives us a "convincing portrait of schizophrenic breakdown,"[23] whereas another proposes that *Mrs Dalloway*'s passages on Septimus Smith "allow the reader to experience thoughts, psychological problems, and mental illnesses he or she *does not normally have access to*."[24] Indeed, many think that fictional narratives have not only cognitive value but also an advantage. Monika Fludernik asserts that fiction "provides readers with experiences that they cannot have on their own—and this constitutes the fascination of all narratives"; as an example, she tells us how "in the wake of the interior monologue . . . it has become quite fashionable to present the moment of a protagonist's death through his/her mind."[25] In addition to depicting particular minds, it is repeatedly said that modernist narratives are particularly well suited in illuminating different ways to conceive the world. In such a view, the modernist novel is thought as an epistemological lesson in subjectivism, skepticism, or relativism.

Looking for minds in literature is not an odd enterprise. We spontaneously look for intentional mindful agency in all sorts of actions and representations. Further, many authors definitely put great effort in the psychological interest (or plausibility, if you like) of their works. Then again, we are eager to see minds and persons everywhere. We attribute (inappropriate) human-like intentions (desires) to nonhuman animals, such as dogs and birds, and (more or less playfully) even to plants (a stubborn tree). How about minds in literature?

We will run into difficult epistemological problems if we limit ourselves to the mimetic approach. There is a long way from literary experience to actual knowledge of what it is like to be in a certain situation, for example. Of course, literary works may make great insights into human mind, but then again, a depiction may be impressive and convincing and yet erroneous or misguided (if assessed for its truth). Perhaps Mrs. Woolf is not a real expert of schizophrenia, or any other sort of mental disorder. Moreover, that we gain a feeling of a real experience in reading a work of fiction ought not to make us reduce literary interpretation to human psychological models. Literary narratives operate on both real-world and literary "parameters" and have both a "mimetic" and a "poetic" dimension: they have a humanly interesting content (the mimetic dimension) that they give an artistic rendering (the poetic dimension).[26] And it is the poetic dimension that sets certain reservations for the cognitivist approach.[27]

The External Perspective

In the philosophy of literature, a distinction is regularly drawn between our two fundamental ways of thinking and speaking of fictional works. Kendall Walton says that "players of games of make-believe"—which includes readers of fiction—both *participate* in the fictions (make-believe, imagination, immersion, transportation) and *observe* them, that is, look at the properties that generate the imaginings.[28] For him, this "dual standpoint" is "one of the most fundamental and important features of the human institution of fiction."[29] Peter Lamarque and Stein Haugom Olsen also distinguish between "internal" and "external" perspectives to fictions. From the internal perspective, they say, we project ourselves into the "world" of the work and reflect the characters as *persons*; from the external perspective, in turn, we identify the *fictional characters* and acknowledge their artificiality.[30] In actual literary experience, we assumedly employ both the perspectives and shift our focus between them without noticing it much. Also, one might expect that the intensity of imagining or the extent of "external considerations" is both genre- and reader-relative. Still, the distinction is crucial for our understanding of fiction. The perspectives regulate, for instance, the criteria we apply to the characters: from the internal point of view, fictional characters may be "arrogant" or "mean," just like real people, whereas from the external perspective they have literary-critical properties such as "being stereotypical," "symbolizing the futility of life," and so on.[31] Lamarque claims that

> although from an internal perspective characters often act and live their lives according to ordinary principles of choice and cause, when viewed, externally, as artefacts in a work of art they become subject to radically different kinds of explanation. Why do they act as they do? Perhaps because they *must* act that way to meet aesthetic, structural and genre-based demands for works of that kind. Perhaps their actions have a symbolic function or a function connected with the development of a theme or because they represent a "polarity" with another character.[32]

The idea is not limited to that an artistic genre determines the "logic" or "rationality" of the story; rather, it is that the content of a literary work is essentially tied to its texture.[33] How do we distinguish between individual minds in literature? Not all cognitive activity is verbal, and we should ask, for instance, whether the narrator depicts thoughts that the character has verbalized himself or herself or whether the narrator verbalizes the character's perceptions and feelings. And how sincere, or subjective, the narrator is? Characteristic for literature is that these questions often remain open. Moreover, it is fascinating to sense discrepancy between the narrator and a character, for instance.[34] Dorrit Cohn, for one, remarks that authors like Woolf are "for some reason unwilling to entrust the presentation of the inner life to the character's own verbal competence"; instead, in *Mrs. Dalloway* and *To the Lighthouse* we find searches "through complicated landscapes of the mind, syntactically too complex to be attributed to inner speech."[35] In like manner, Lanier Anderson thinks that "the idiom of Woolf's depiction of Clarissa is elevated—*so* exalted, in fact, that it can occasionally seem unwarranted by the underlying thoughts over which its words are poured."[36]

Further, Anderson illustrates how Woolf's artistic representation transcends our normal cognitive parameters by making dynamic links between the consciousnesses of the characters:

> Whereas Zunshine highlights a (relatively familiar) phenomenon of "vertical" integration of mental attitudes that are *about* others' attitudes, and thus take those further attitudes as objects to form a nested hierarchy representing the social situation [form: Richard sees that Lady Bruton knows that Miss Brush thinks that Hugh's beliefs about the sentiments of the *Times* editors are bunkum], by contrast, what is demanded in the jaunt around London is a facility for navigating "horizontal" connections joining the thoughts of one person to those of another so as to permit the smooth flow of consciousness across different minds. Such horizontal connections are unfamiliar from everyday life. After all, the possibility of consciously transitioning from one person's thought to another's *in real life* (as opposed to in the fictional world) would seem to depend on the truth of something like Clarissa's implausible thesis that consciousness can extend from one mind into another, flowing across the juncture created by common attention.[37]

Nevertheless, Anderson remarks that "horizontal mental linkage is not a feature of ordinary social existence, so its mastery will not build up our socially useful 'Machiavellian intelligence' [as evolutionary psychologists sometimes dub the capacity Zunshine highlights]."[38] This leads us to a further point, namely, that literary minds are products of textual artifice and appreciated partly for their artificiality. Lamarque asserts that

> the whole modernist movement in art amounted to a challenge at a fundamental level to the idea of representing reality. At its best modernism exhibited the plurality of worlds, private and public, in contrast to some single "objective" world given in experience. Once representation itself had been exposed as a kind of artifice it was natural for artists to highlight the artifice of their own media.[39]

If we abandon the mimetic approach to literary cognition, is there anything left? Could literary narratives enhance cognition after our acknowledging their artificiality and the dissimilarities between real-world and literary experiences? Is there value in literary narratives deviating from the natural norms?

Cognitive Enrichment, Imaginative Flexibility?

In arguing for the value of stories in constructing reality, the psychologist Jerome Bruner proposes that

> the innovative storyteller . . . may go beyond the conventional scripts, leading people to see human happenings in a fresh way, indeed, in a way they had never before "noticed" or even dreamed. The shift from Hesiod to Homer, the advent of "inner adventure" in Laurence Sterne's *Tristram Shandy*, the advent of Flaubert's perspectivalism, or Joyce's epiphanizing of banalities—these are all innovations that probably shaped our narrative versions of everyday reality as well as changed the course of literary history, the two perhaps being not that different.[40]

The view that literary narratives could enrich our cognitive frames or scripts has become popular in cognitive narratology. Fludernik, for one, maintains that through repeated use, "non-natural narrational frames" become "naturalized": second-person narration and a dying person's interior monologue, for example, have lost their "surprise factor" and become "natural frames," part of our cognitive stock.[41] Some think that the new frames that literary works have on offer do not limit to literary interpretation but may be valuable for our thought in general. Jan Alber, for instance, claims that "one should study literary fiction because it allows us to transcend ourselves and to experience scenarios and situations which are strictly speaking impossible in the real world."[42] Of Alber's particular interest are "unnatural" scenarios and events, which "significantly widen the cognitive horizon of human awareness; they challenge our limited perspective on the world and invite us to address questions that we do not normally address."[43]

Alber maintains that literary narratives could generate *new* cognitive frames by blending scripts (animals, corpses, or inanimate objects as narrators)[44] or they could *enrich* our existing frames by stretching them "beyond real-world possibilities until the parameters include the strange phenomena with which we are confronted."[45] In addition to providing readers new frames and enhancing their existing frames, Alber thinks that the "unnatural scenarios of literary fiction are particularly well designed to *make us more open and more flexible* because they urge us to deal with radical forms of otherness or strangeness."[46] According to him, flexibility of imagination characteristically links to growth in ethical understanding (openness and tolerance).

I am very sympathetic to the view that literary narratives could widen our "mental universe"[47] or "the cognitive horizon of human awareness."[48] But I also think that the mere repetition of these ideas leads us in danger of establishing a *religion* of literature. The pompous claims are not proportional to their supporting evidence—no matter how evidence is understood—and at times look even like dogmas. It is unclear if literary works actually produce changes such as those described. While the comprehension of a literary work often requires us to adjust or modify our cognitive apparatus, to "blend schemes," for example, it is not known if the conceptual adjustments required in the interpretation of the work carry over the literary experience and affect the reader's actual cognitive mechanisms.

The matter is also extremely difficult to study. Yet, *some* evidence for the cognitivist's claims is needed. How could we have even some support for the assertion of such changes *commonly* taking place as a result of a *literary* response? This is a real worry; the claims are problematic also because they imply that all conceptual changes would automatically be for the good (which they are not).[49] What if *Mrs. Dalloway* rather distorts our understanding of reality? A professional critic could, of course, offer his or her readers a *prescriptive* reading of the work, arguing that the readers would improve their conceptual understanding, would they follow the proposed interpretation. Still, one would expect a suggestion how the matter could be approached and where to look for evidence of the assumed conceptual changes.[50]

While the methodological questions are pressing, the theory needs to be improved too. It is far from clear *how* our gaining new or enhanced cognitive frames (e.g., the "naturalization" of a dying person's interior monologue) from literary works actually enriches our understanding of our lifeworld. How does our engagement with Clarissa Dalloway's perfectly unnatural "extended mind" improves our social cognition? The same requirement goes for the idea of "imaginative stretching." Imagining logical impossibilities is great intellectual fun—as in Borges's stories, for instance—but what do we gain, so to say, from imagining them? The idea of ethical openness is fascinating but suspicious in light of philosophical study on our "imaginative resistance" to morally deviant views in fiction.

Conclusion

We have two fundamental ways of thinking and speaking of fictional works. We may engage with them imaginatively and explore them as artifacts. Theories of the cognitive value of literary fiction have generally focused on either of these two perspectives. In the "mimetic" tradition, theories have built on the idea that literary works provide us a lifelike experience from which we learn. The problem is that in reducing the cognitive value of literature to the gaining of experiential knowledge we endorse naïve realism and treat art as a mirror of life. Besides, the mimetic approach fails in capturing what is distinctive and special in literature. In the "poetic" tradition, in turn, the value significance of literature has been linked to literature's distinctive features, such as foregrounding and defamiliarization thus caused. The problem of these views is their falling short in illuminating the proper "cognitive" payoff. Also, there is the question of their generalizability, as there are very little distinctively "literary features" uniting works of literature. Moreover, theories in both traditions have offered very little support for their claims. A comprehensive model of literary cognition ought to acknowledge the "dual standpoint" of fiction and demonstrate how literary works could be cognitively valuable with regard to both their "natural" experientiality and their literary artificiality.

In this chapter, I have been partly playing the devil's advocate. I would not conclude from the critical anti-cognitivist remarks that literary works (or here, modernist narratives) cannot have significant cognitive value. Rather, I think that the remarks should push the cognitivist, such as myself, to come up with more comprehensive and nuanced accounts of literary interpretation and cognition. I am very sympathetic to the idea of the cognitive value of literature; what I wish for is a rigorous study of it.

Notes

1 Virginia Woolf, "Mr. Bennett and Mrs. Brown" (1924), in *Essentials of the Theory of Fiction*, ed. Michael J. Hoffman and Patrick D. Murphy (Durham, NC: Duke University Press, 1996), 31.
2 Brian McHale, *Postmodernist Fiction* (London: Routledge, 1987), 9; emphasis in the original.
3 Alan Palmer, "1945–: Ontologies of Consciousness," in *The Emergence of Mind: Representations of Consciousness in Narrative Discourse in English*, ed. David Herman (Lincoln: University of Nebraska Press, 2011), 276.
4 David Herman, "1880–1945: Re-minding Modernism," in *The Emergence of Mind*, ed. Herman, 264.
5 Käte Hamburger, *The Logic of Literature* (1973; Bloomington: Indiana University Press, 1993), 83; emphasis removed.
6 Dorrit Cohn, *The Distinction of Fiction* (Baltimore: Johns Hopkins University Press, 1999), 106.
7 Marie-Laure Ryan, *Possible Worlds, Artificial Intelligence, and Narrative Theory* (Bloomington: Indiana University Press, 1991), 67.
8 Monika Fludernik, *Towards a "Natural" Narratology* (New York: Routledge, 1996), 48.
9 Lisa Zunshine, *Why We Read Fiction* (Columbus: Ohio State University Press, 2003), 5. In addition to competing models of Theory of Mind (ToM; theory-theory and simulation theory), it is disputed whether interpersonal understanding requires ToM at all.
10 See Gregory Currie, "Literature and Theory of Mind," in *The Routledge Companion to Philosophy and Literature*, ed. Noël Carroll and John Gibson (New York: Routledge, 2016).
11 Alan Palmer, *Fictional Minds* (Lincoln: University of Nebraska Press, 2004), 12.
12 Ibid., 10. Palmer also remarks that much of our knowledge about fictional minds depends on hypotheses and conjectures which we base on the characters' actions (246).
13 In "1945–: Ontologies of Consciousness," Palmer does not claim that fictional minds are identical to real minds; rather, he thinks that fictional minds are semiotic constructs that are similar to real minds.
14 Ibid., 275.
15 Herman, "1880–1945: Re-minding Modernism," 253–54.
16 Joshua Gang aptly remarks that "modernism was not psychologically monolithic; instead, an array of psychological theories—including behaviorism, structuralism, and psychoanalysis—circulated simultaneously and competed against each other." Joshua Gang, "Mindless Modernism," *Novel* 46 (2013): 117.

17 See, for example, Perry Meisel, *The Literary Freud* (London: Routledge, 2007), esp. chapter 4. Virginia Woolf's interests in theories of knowledge and language are also well known. For the connections between her literary work and philosophical theories of her time, see, for example, Jaakko Hintikka, "Virginia Woolf and Our Knowledge of the External World," *Journal of Aesthetics and Art Criticism* 38 (1979): 5–14; Ann Banfield, *The Phantom Table: Woolf, Fry, Russell and the Epistemology of Modernism* (Cambridge: Cambridge University Press, 2000); and Megan Quigley, "Modern Novel and Vagueness," *Modernism/Modernity* 15 (2008): 101–29.

18 Virginia Woolf, "Modern Fiction" (1925), in Woolf, *Selected Essays*, ed. David Bradshaw (Oxford: Oxford University Press, 2008), 8.

19 Ibid., 9. According to Woolf, modern writers' interest "lies very likely in the dark places of psychology. At once, therefore, the accent falls a little differently; the emphasis is upon something hitherto ignored; at once a different outline of form becomes necessary, difficult for us to grasp, incomprehensible to our predecessors" (11).

20 The assumed cognitive value of modernist narratives ought not to be limited to their ability to reveal individual minds. Modernist narratives illuminate a cultural understanding of the world, as Auerbach remarks in his chapter on Woolf; a related view is to look at Joyce's *Finnegans Wake* reflecting the scientific understanding of his time, a worldview affected by psychoanalysis and quantum physics, for instance.

21 Erich Auerbach, *Mimesis: The Representation of Reality in Western Literature*, trans. Willard R. Trask (Princeton, NJ: Princeton University Press, 1953), 552.

22 Virginia Woolf, *The Diary of Virginia Woolf*, Vol. 2: *1920–1923*, ed. Anne Olivier Bell (London: Hogarth Press, 1978), 207.

23 Suzette Henke, cited in Jan Alber, "The Ethical Implications of Unnatural Scenarios," in *Why Study Literature?*, ed. Jan Alber et al. (Aarhus: Aarhus University Press, 2011), 221.

24 Alber, "The Ethical Implications of Unnatural Scenarios," 220; emphasis added.

25 Monika Fludernik, "Natural Narratology and Cognitive Parameters," in *Narrative Theory and the Cognitive Sciences*, ed. David Herman (Stanford, CA: CSLI, 2003), 256.

26 See Peter Lamarque and Stein Haugom Olsen, *Truth, Fiction, and Literature: A Philosophical Perspective* (Oxford: Clarendon Press, 1994), 261–65.

27 By "cognitivism" I mean the philosophical view, which holds that artworks may provide their audiences significant knowledge and insight concerning matters of human interest. The position should not be confused with cognitive scientific study of literature.

28 Kendall L. Walton, *Mimesis as Make-Believe* (Cambridge, MA: Harvard University Press, 1990), 49–50.

29 Kendall L. Walton, "How Remote Are Fictional Worlds from the Real World?" *Journal of Aesthetics and Art Criticism* 37 (1978): 21.

30 In *Truth, Fiction, and Literature*, Lamarque and Olsen also emphasize the value of the dual standpoint, claiming that "being 'caught up' in fictional worlds and at the same time recognizing their fictionality involves a delicate balance—even a tension—which certainly accounts for much of the pleasure and value of imaginative works of art" (144).

31 Lamarque and Olsen, *Truth, Fiction, and Literature*, 146.

32 Peter Lamarque, *The Opacity of Narrative* (Totowa, NJ: Rowman and Littlefield, 2014), ix; emphasis in original.

33 When drawing, say, a philosophically interesting setting or insight from fiction, one is led to ask its worldly extension. Lamarque and Olsen maintain that abstract ideas in literature are based on the narrator's perspectival descriptions and essentially connected with the fictional particulars, so that transferring the ideas to another (nonliterary) context trivializes them. See Lamarque and Olsen, *Truth, Fiction, and Literature*, 454.

34 Maria Mäkelä, for one, argues that literary narratives do not reveal their characters' minds but rather, foreground and thematize the telling and hide the underlying experience. In her view, literature is characteristically ambiguous, seemingly objective descriptions turn out to be subjective, and the origin of a thought always remains vague. See her "Cycles of Narrative Necessity: Suspect Tellers and the Textuality of Fictional Minds," in *Stories and Minds: Cognitive Approaches to Literary Narrative*, ed. Lars Bernaerts, Dirk de Geest, Luc Herma, and Bart Vervaeck (Lincoln: University of Nebraska Press, 2013), 129–51.

35 Dorrit Cohn, *Transparent Minds: Narrative Modes for Presenting Consciousness in Fiction* (Princeton, NJ: Princeton University Press, 1978), 44. Representation is, of course, tied to artistic conventions. As Cohn puts it, "The monologues of *Ulysses* may be regarded as a particularly clear instances of the historical dimension of realism Roman Jakobson defined in his essay 'On Realism in Art': the revolutionary artist deforms the existing artistic canons for the sake of closer imitation of reality; the conservative public misunderstands the deformation of the canon as a distortion of reality. The first generation of *Ulysses* readers, conditioned by a long tradition of monologues modeled on dialogues, could only have experienced Bloom's and Stephen's mental productions as radical departures from realistic representation. . . . Today's reader is more likely than his grandparents to take Joyce's conception of verbal thought for granted, to accept the notion that it differs from communicative speech in a number of significant respects, and to accept the monologues of *Ulysses* as supremely convincing achievements of formal mimeticism" (92–93).

36 R. Lanier Anderson, "Is Clarissa Dalloway Special?" forthcoming in *Philosophy and Literature*.
37 Ibid.; emphasis in the original.
38 Ibid.
39 Lamarque, *Opacity of Narrative*, 38.
40 Jerome Bruner, "The Narrative Construction of Reality," *Critical Inquiry* 18 (1991): 12.
41 See Fludernik, "Natural Narrative and Cognitive Parameters," 256. In *Towards a "Natural" Narratology*, Fludernik also claims that "by the time of Joyce's and Woolf's depiction of minds in their plenitude, these authors could build on cognitive parameters which were well in place and available for use: readers had considerable training in tuning in on such non-natural mind reading within a natural frame" (172).
42 Alber, "The Ethical Implications of Unnatural Scenarios," 211.
43 Ibid., 227. "Unnatural" may be taken to include so-called omniscient narrators and other elements that are present in all sort of "realist" narratives too.
44 Jan Alber, "Impossible Storyworlds—And What to Do with Them," *StoryWorlds: A Journal of Narrative Studies* 1 (2009): 82.
45 Ibid., 82–83, 91–93; see also Alber, "The Ethical Implications of Unnatural Scenarios," pp. 222–24.
46 Alber, "The Ethical Implications of Unnatural Scenarios," 232; emphasis added.
47 Alber's term ("Impossible Storyworlds," 93).
48 Alber's term ("The Ethical Implications of Unnatural Scenarios," 227).
49 See Peter Lamarque, *The Philosophy of Literature* (Oxford: Blackwell, 2009), 250; Gregory Currie, "On Getting Out of the Armchair to Do Aesthetics," in *Philosophical Methodology: The Armchair or the Laboratory?*, ed. Matthew C. Haug (New York: Routledge, 2014), 443.
50 For different approaches to evidence, see Jukka Mikkonen, "On Studying the Cognitive Value of Literature," *Journal of Aesthetics and Art Criticism* 73 (2015): 273–82.

3

Metaphor and the Place of Mind in Three Modernist Novels

Marco Caracciolo

Introduction

It is almost a critical commonplace to say that modernist writers paid meticulous attention to consciousness and its gamut of subjective states. David Herman's chapter in his edited collection *The Emergence of Mind* offers a reconceptualization of this view. Herman critiques the idea that modernist fiction performs an "inward turn,"[1] arguing that this phrase, as found in scholarship on Modernism,[2] is bound up with a Cartesian dichotomy between mind and world: it reflects "a Cartesian geography of the mental, whereby the mind constitutes an interior space separated off from the world at large."[3] By contrast, discussing Virginia Woolf's *Mrs. Dalloway*, Herman suggests that "Woolf's protagonist [Clarissa Dalloway] resists situating self and other, mind and world, along an internal-external polarity."[4]

Herman's approach is remarkably astute, and in many ways his interest in the continuum between mental states and the physical world informs this chapter as well. Yet Herman's equation between Cartesian dualism and the inner versus outer polarity raises questions. Howard Robinson explains Descartes's position as follows: "Descartes was a *substance dualist*. He believed that there were two kinds of substance: matter, of which the essential property is that it is spatially extended; and mind, of which the essential property is that it thinks."[5] If the mind exists on a separate plane from the world of material things, if it is *not* spatially extended, then there is no reason to see it as being "inside" anything. Thus, from a Cartesian perspective, any talk of the mind being "internal" is necessarily metaphorical: opposing the "inner life" of the mind to the external world involves laying out in space what is not, or at least not straightforwardly, spatial in nature.

Far from being restricted to the technical language of philosophy, spatial metaphors for mind are embedded in what philosophers call "folk psychology,"[6] or our prescientific understanding of how the mind works. We see the mind as a container for ideas, for instance, or we describe a difficult decision as a conflict between different "parts" of us. Adopting these metaphors does not imply any deep commitment to Cartesian dualism. In fact, this kind of metaphorical language is not purely arbitrary: it has its roots in our experience of the body as the material, and spatial, locus of mental processes. As contemporary researchers working under the heading of embodied cognition have argued, perceptual experience implicates the spatiotemporal positioning of our bodies,[7] just as emotional experience coincides with embodied feelings.[8] These are sensations inside (or at least close to) our bodies, so that spatial metaphors are to some extent motivated, and they could be read in an anti-Cartesian way as well: they could suggest a fundamental continuity, if not identity, between physical events in our bodies and apparently immaterial psychological events.

Herman is right to say that modernist fiction, by and large, undermines dualistic assumptions about the mind. But he does not acknowledge the fundamentally metaphorical nature of the "Cartesian geography" he seeks to deconstruct, and he—consequently—downplays the complex relationship between modernist fiction, metaphors for mental processes, and particular conceptions of mental functioning. This relationship lies at the core of this chapter: metaphor, I claim, can raise pointed questions about the place of mind, or how our feelings and thoughts sit vis-à-vis the physical world. I thus focus on how, in modernist fiction, metaphors and similes cut across dichotomies between mind and matter, performing—through the creativity of literary language—a critique of Cartesian dualism. I will show this critique at work in three modernist novels: Kate Chopin's *The Awakening* (1899), a landmark of Southern US literature and feminist writing; *Con gli occhi chiusi* (*Eyes Shut*, 1919) by Federigo Tozzi, an Italian author writing at the intersection of late nineteenth-century "verismo" (a movement closely related to Émile Zola's naturalism) and Modernism; and Virginia Woolf's modernist masterpiece *Mrs. Dalloway* (1925). These novels explore the rift between their characters and social reality, through the protagonist's quest for emancipation (Chopin), incapacity to act (Tozzi), or psychiatric disorder (Woolf). While they do not, of course, span the whole range of modernist writing, I consider these authors exemplary in their use of creative metaphors for mind—and I find this convergence on metaphor even more suggestive in light of the authors' disparate geographical and linguistic background.

In *The Vanishing Subject*, Judith Ryan traces the modernist rejection of Cartesian models to the empiricist psychologies that emerged in the second half of the nineteenth century.[9] Ryan focuses on seminal work by Franz Brentano (*Psychology from an Empirical Standpoint*, 1874), Ernst Mach (*Contributions to the Analysis of Sensations*, 1886), and William James (*The Principles of Psychology*, 1890), showing that these thinkers shaped—directly or indirectly—modernist writers' engagement with the mind. In particular, Ryan suggests, these theorists converged on the idea that "the familiar distinction between subject and object was no longer tenable, or at the very least it meant that it was tenable in a different way from that which had been supposed."[10] In a dualistic framework, if mind and matter are different substances, then subjectivity must also be distinguished from the mere existence of inanimate objects. By contrast, as both Herman and Ryan contend, modernist fiction unsettles the boundary between mind and material world, exposing their fundamental interrelatedness.

It is no coincidence, then, that modernist writers tend to place the body front and center. Scholars of Modernism have frequently acknowledged this centrality of the body: "The modernist crisis of representation became, for many artists, a crisis of embodiment," writes Susan McCabe.[11] Recent discussions of literary Modernism—for instance, Julie Taylor's *Djuna Barnes and Affective Modernism* or Kirsty Martin's *Rhythms of Sympathy*[12]—have similarly focused on the somatic nature of the modes of consciousness probed by modernist writing. These claims bear immediate relevance to my discussion in this chapter: foregrounding the embodied nature of mental processes is one way of destabilizing the separation between mind and world, because our bodies are material entities through and through. If we can show that mental experience emerges from bodily events, then we have already gone a long way toward undermining Cartesian dualism. William James famously argued for this continuity between mind and body in the domain of emotional experience: "Our feeling of [bodily] changes as they occur *is* the emotion," he writes in an influential essay.[13] As part of their critique of dualism, the modernist narratives I will examine in this chapter capitalize on James's intuition about the embodiment of mind; but they also extend it *beyond* emotion, to other modes of consciousness and thinking. Metaphor is an important means of forging a link between material (bodily) and mental events, as we will see.

In the contemporary mind sciences, embodied approaches to cognition have revisited the intuitions of empiricist thinkers such as James. Antonio Damasio, for instance, sees in James a forerunner of his "somatic marker hypothesis."[14] More generally, the anti-Cartesian assumptions of many researchers working in today's mind sciences are closely reminiscent of the empiricist Zeitgeist that pervades modernist fiction. This explains the pertinence of modernist writers in today's world, and also why Modernism is a key reference point for the contemporary "neuronovel."[15] I will return to this point in the conclusion. The next section will prepare my case studies by expanding on the link between embodiment, metaphor, and folk psychology.

Mind and Metaphor

We understand abstract things by comparing them to concrete things that we can directly perceive. This idea—known as "experientialism"[16]—has become one of the tenets of cognitive linguistics, in the wake of George Lakoff and Mark Johnson's influential *Metaphors We Live By*.[17] This view of cognition places a premium on metaphor not just as a linguistic (and literary) device but as a cognitive tool allowing humans to project bodily patterns *beyond* basic scenarios of physical interaction with the world.[18] Thus, when we say that a truce is "a step forward in the peace process," we are comparing two scenarios that point to different sematic domains: a single bodily action (a step) and a relatively immaterial happening, the truce, that condenses events (talks between and within the parties, etc.) unfolding over a certain time period. As a conventionalized metaphor, the "step forward" captures what the speaker thinks is significant about the truce in a form that reflects our everyday, embodied engagement with physical reality.

Just like the concept "truce," the workings of the mind—one's own, or other people's—also have a certain abstract quality. Surely, we can experience some of our own mental states and events through introspection. But very little of what happens in our brains is conscious,[19] and even our consciousness is far from the clarity and stability of our interactions with the material world. This elusiveness of our psychological life explains the need for metaphorical language bridging mental processes with physical reality. Once we have turned mental events into quasi-physical ones, we can better understand how they are connected in temporal and causal terms. Historically, this kind of association has been pervasive in twentieth-century psychology. Dedre Gentner and Jonathan Grudin have investigated patterns of metaphor usage in a corpus of scientific articles published in the journal *Psychological Review* from 1894 to 1975.[20] They conclude that the most frequent metaphors fall into four categories, which they call "animate-being," "neural," "spatial," and "systems." They also observe an increase in systems metaphors (which "liken some mental phenomenon to a system of lawfully constrained interactions among elements")[21] over the years, at the expense of organic, animate-being metaphors.

However interesting this analysis, the link between metaphor and psychology runs much deeper than Gentner and Grudin show. In fact, even as *scientific* psychology has embraced metaphors, these have already been part of *folk* psychology, or (as seen in the previous section) our everyday understanding of the mind. John Barnden has explored this idea systematically in his typology of what he calls "common-sense metaphors of mind."[22] He distinguishes between three categories, "cognizing as physically sensing," "mind as physical space," and "ideas as physical objects." A sentence such as "Martin had a blurred view of the problem" is an example of the first category, in that it associates comprehension with sight. "In one part of his mind, Bob was thinking about the party" illustrates the second category. The "Cartesian geography" discussed by Herman also belongs to this category, since it conceptualizes the mind as a container: what is "inside" the mind are the experiences and beliefs that make up people's subjectivity. Finally, in Barnden's third category, the mind's contents are compared to physical objects and phenomena, as in "Veronica had caught hold of the idea."[23] Barnden also identifies a few subcategories: for instance, "mind as physical space" includes both "ideas as internal utterances" and "mind parts as persons."[24]

Barnden's typology works differently from Gentner and Grudin's: it aims to capture not the exact semantic fields involved in the metaphors, but different kinds of association between the mental and the physical world. Yet both inventories converge on the idea that, through metaphor, we map mental objects and events onto physical ones. I will call metaphorical language that operates along these lines "physicalist metaphors for mind," a term first used by Kearns.[25] Combining Barnden's and Gentner and Grudin's models yields the following typology of physicalist metaphors:

Mental activity is seen as . . . (1) sensory activity
(2) occurring in physical space
(3) involving material . . . . (3a) agents
(3b) processes (natural)
(3c) entities (organic)
(3d) entities (inorganic)

The first two items correspond to Barnden's "cognizing as physically sensing" and "mind as physical space," respectively. The third item is more complex, because it covers Gentner and Grudin's "animate-being," "neural," and "systems" metaphors. In (3a) mental states are compared to animate creatures, for example, because they seem to have their own intentionality (a traumatic memory can spring on us like a dangerous animal). In (3b) mental activity is compared to a natural process, such as waves or the weather (a traumatic memory as a cloud passing over the sun). In (3c) mind is metaphorically linked to organic matter (a traumatic memory as a scar, or as a raw nerve—this is an expansion of Gentner and Grudin's "neural" type). Finally, in (3d) metaphor forges a connection between the mind and inanimate matter (a traumatic memory as a button or switch—a switchboard being one of the examples of Gentner and Grudin's "systemic" type). In many, if not most, cases, metaphors for mental processes involve a combination of types (1), (2), and (3).

It is important to realize what these metaphors imply. In Barnden's words, "There is no a priori reason to think that a metaphorical description captures some scientific truth about the mind."[26] This applies to the problem of mind-matter dualism, too. Metaphorical comparisons between, for example, mind and space, or mind and material processes, are typically used in an agnostic way, without suggesting anything about the *actual* relationship between mind and matter. In other instances, and this is the case in the novels I analyze later, metaphors can raise questions about how subjectivity emerges from material realities—questions that may, in turn, *challenge* dualistic assumptions.[27] Whether this takes place or not depends on two factors: the context in which a particular metaphor is deployed and the degree of conventionality of the metaphor itself—that is, the extent to which it departs from standard language for human psychology. More specifically, the more novel and elaborate a metaphor for mind is, the more likely it is to be taken at face value in its bringing together the domain of the mental and the domain of the physical. Lakoff and Turner have studied the ways in which literary metaphor may build on and extend metaphorical mappings found in everyday discourse.[28] Of the possible functions that they identify, I am especially interested in what they call "questioning": a metaphor used in a literary context may question a *shallow* reading of folk-psychological metaphors for mind—that is, a reading in which the mind-matter association preserves a dualistic flavor.

A lot hinges on the context in which metaphors appear, as I said. The modernist novels I will examine in the following sections are particularly effective at undermining dualism because they deploy two related metaphorical strategies: on the one hand, they fully exploit the potential of physicalist metaphors for mind, often combining types (1), (2), and (3) in creative ways; on the other hand, and crucially, they ascribe mentalistic qualities to the inanimate world, "reversing" the mapping at work in physicalist metaphors (or swapping their source and target domains, to use the more technical terminology of cognitive linguistics). The upshot is that, in my case studies, mental and material realities seem to meet halfway—a strategy that undermines dualistic views by creating a strong sense of interconnectedness between human subjectivity and the physical world.

This hypothesis has an important precedent: Michael Kearns's *Metaphors of Mind in Fiction and Psychology*, which is to this day the most comprehensive study of the relation between folk-psychological metaphors for mind and literary writing.[29] Kearns focuses on the nineteenth century, tracing the development of new metaphors for mental processes, particularly "web-of-relations and mind-in-landscape [metaphors]. Both have to do with the increasingly prominent concept mind-as-a-living-being, which by the end of the nineteenth century achieved an acceptance approaching that of mind-as-entity."[30] In my terminology, "web-of-relations" and "mind-in-landscape" metaphors are subtypes of (2), since they both imply a spatial extension of mind. "Mind-as-living-being" corresponds to type (3a), "mind-as-entity" to (3d). My study of metaphor in modernist fiction picks up where Kearns leaves off, at the end of the nineteenth century, when—as argued by Ryan—empiricist psychologies cast doubt on the separation between subjectivity and the physical world.

Into the Abysses: Kate Chopin's *The Awakening*

Set in Louisiana, Kate Chopin's novel *The Awakening* (1899) centers on the quest for self-emancipation of its female protagonist. The narrative of Edna Pontellier's revolt against the strictures of marriage is clearly indebted to French literature of the late nineteenth century, particularly Gustave Flaubert's *Madame Bovary* and Guy de Maupassant's short stories.[31] Yet, by portraying the awakening of the protagonist's feminist self-consciousness, the novel foreshadows another kind of awakening: namely, the emergence, at the turn of the century, of a modernist sensibility. "The complex oscillations in narrative point of view... make this a founding work of Modernism," writes Marianne DeKoven.[32] Chopin's narrative focuses on Edna's shifting evaluations as she comes to question her marriage with Mr. Pontellier, a member of New Orleans's French-speaking Creole élite. Yet the narrator is also able to step back from the character and carefully unravel the social structures that oppress Edna—hence DeKoven's "complex oscillations."

Of particular interest, for our purposes, is the narrator's exploration of the widening rift between Edna and society, an exploration conducted in a deeply affective mode. In the first pages of the novel, Edna's estrangement from her husband is signaled by a sense of vague unease and anxiety, which does not have a clear-cut object yet: it is not, for instance, irritation at or resentment against her husband; it is just, as the narrator explicitly points out, "a mood."[33] Philosopher Matthew Ratcliffe's account of mood can shed light on Edna's psychology.[34] For Ratcliffe, who draws on the phenomenological tradition, mood is a matter of what he calls "existential feelings," or a subject's affective orientation toward the world. These feelings have two defining features: "First of all, they are not directed at specific objects or situations but are background orientations through which experience as a whole is structured. Second, they are *bodily feelings*" (*A* 38; emphasis in the original). Put otherwise, existential feelings cut below distinctions between subjective consciousness and external objects; thus, as Ratcliffe explicitly notes, they raise an embodied challenge to Cartesian dualism.

It is significant, then, that the language with which Chopin describes the protagonist's existential feelings is highly metaphorical. For instance, this is the context in which the word "mood" makes its first appearance in the novel: "An indescribable oppression, which seemed to generate in some unfamiliar part of her consciousness, filled her whole being with a vague anguish. It was like a shadow, like a mist passing across her soul's summer day. It was strange and unfamiliar; it was a mood" (*A* 8). This is a remarkable passage, which combines several of the metaphorical types examined in the previous section. First, the mind is spatialized ("part of her consciousness"), and the narrator focuses on how Edna's anguish spreads from this unfamiliar "part" through her "whole being"—an instance of type (2) mapping. The second half of the quotation enriches the spatial metaphor with a reference to natural processes (type 3b), imagining Edna's psychology as a "summer day" where the sun is blocked by a "shadow" or "mist." The character's existential feelings reach toward the nonhuman world.

But the nonhuman world is also seen through a metaphorical lens. The novel's first part is set on Grand Isle, an island off the Louisiana coast. Thematically, the ocean plays a central role in these pages. Edna is not a good swimmer, and she is at the same time afraid of, and attracted to, the sea: "The voice of the sea is seductive; never ceasing, whispering, clamoring, murmuring, inviting the soul to wander for a spell in abysses of solitude; to lose itself in mazes of inward contemplation. The voice of the sea speaks to the soul. The touch of the sea is sensuous, enfolding the body in its soft, close embrace" (*A* 16). The first sentence anthropomorphizes the sea, metaphorically comparing its appeal to a "voice." The second part of the quotation reverses the picture as soon as the external qualities of this voice—expressed by the accumulating gerunds—are introjected: the invitation is not to explore the depths of the sea but the "abysses" of human psychology. The physical world and "inward contemplation" are brought together, as if the boundary between them was thin and permeable—a demonstration of how literary language can use the spatial metaphor of the inner against the grain of mind-matter dualism. On Grand Isle, Edna identifies with the nonhuman spaces of the sea, an identification that both gives expression to her existential feelings and enables her to "awaken" to the grim realities of her marriage.

However, as soon as Edna leaves the seaside house for the city, New Orleans, the metaphors for mind change significantly. Types (2) and (3b) are superseded by (3d) metaphors involving inanimate objects, for instance, something mechanically "snapping" in the following passage: "I feel as if I had been wound up to a certain pitch—too tight—and something inside of me had snapped" (*A* 102). But the most significant metaphors by far involve clothes: "She was becoming herself and daily casting aside that fictitious self which we assume like a garment with which to appear before the world" (*A* 64); "All the tearing emotion of the last few hours seemed to fall away from her like a somber, uncomfortable garment, which she had but to loosen to be rid of" (*A* 124). As a barrier between the body and the external world, the garment reifies the dualistic boundary that Edna's attraction to the sea had negated; further, it is an object associated—symbolically—with the social constraints that marriage imposes on Edna. The fact that here an inauthentic side of Edna's personality and excessive, "tearing emotion" are seen as pieces of clothing evokes the possibility of psychological change, of finding herself by shedding the unwanted layers of her psyche. Yet the choice of this inanimate object to model her existential feelings also suggests that the comforting embrace of the sea is, in this part of the novel (and of the storyworld), less available than it was on Grand Isle. Only the experience of music prompts metaphors reminiscent of the sea: "The music grew strange and fantastic—turbulent, insistent, plaintive and soft with entreaty. The shadows grew deeper. The music filled the room. It floated out upon the night, over the housetops, the crescent of the river, losing itself in the silence of the upper air" (*A* 71). Music captures Edna's attention just as the sea invited inward contemplation—by taking her out of her immediate situation, toward the nonhuman world of the river and "upper air."

The storyworld of *The Awakening* is thus structured around an opposition between the sea/island and the city, with each of them evoking a particular set of metaphors for mental processes. This strategy gives rise to what Benjamin Biebuyck and Gunther Martens call a metaphorical "paranarrative"[35]—a coherent series of metaphorical associations that enrich and complicate the main narrative (in this case, Edna's story of self-discovery). When Robert, Edna's lover on Grand Isle, returns to the city, spatial metaphors for mind start surfacing again: "She found in [Robert's] eyes, when he looked at her for one silent moment, the same tender caress, . . . which had penetrated to the sleeping places of her soul and awakened them [on Grand Isle]" (*A* 108). But here Edna finds herself in an intractable impasse, because society does not allow her to realize her love for Robert: the garment-like emotions associated with the city—and with human intercourse—cannot be taken off. The only solution is, then, to change metaphorical regime and retreat into the nonhuman embrace of the sea. This is precisely what happens in the final episode of the novel, in which Edna literally sheds her clothes and commits suicide by losing herself in "the touch of the sea, [which enfolds] the body in its soft, close embrace" (*A* 127). Edna's suicide is not only a rejection of the values of a male-dominated society but also the affirmation of a quintessentially modernist conception of mind—one in which inner, psychic realities are connected in subtle and yet potent ways to an anthropomorphized nature, with the body and its affects serving as a bridge toward the nonhuman. This ending is the result of a double logic, narrative *and* metaphorical, where physicalist language for mental processes does not only contribute to characterization or consciousness representation but is also instrumental in carrying the story forward.

Movement without Action: Federigo Tozzi's *Eyes Shut*

Giacomo Debenedetti was the first Italian critic to call attention to the modernity of Federigo Tozzi's *Eyes Shut*, reading it alongside seminal works by James Joyce and Marcel Proust.[36] Set in rural Tuscany and focusing on the experiences of an adolescent, Pietro, Tozzi's novel is suspended between the stark materialism of Italian verismo and a more modernist sensibility. Pietro is the son of a greedy and brutal innkeeper, Domenico; unlike his father, Pietro is introverted, distracted, inept at physical labor. He falls in love with Ghisola, the daughter of one of his father's workers, but their relationship is obstructed both by Domenico's disapproval and by Pietro's incapacity to control and express his tumultuous emotional life. As Eduardo Saccone suggests in his reading of the novel, Pietro is marked by a feeling of detachment or disconnection from reality—a feeling epitomized by the recurrent gesture of closing his eyes.[37] The novel centers on Pietro's inability to speak the language in which all other characters are fluent—namely, the language of purposive, goal-oriented action: Domenico "wanted [Pietro] to go afield, attend to the pruning of the vines and all the other jobs, like he did. But Pietro didn't seem to see or hear anything."[38] After moving to Florence to attend school, Pietro finds no interest in books or in spending time with his fellow students: all he can do is lie "on the bed with his eyes shut" (*ES* 104). This strategy destabilizes the link, central to plot, between the protagonist's mental states and narrative-advancing actions:[39] as the narrator puts it, Pietro's inner life "always got on top" (*ES* 45)—or, more literally, "superimposed itself" upon the world of action.[40]

As in *The Awakening*, the protagonist's social isolation does not result in a split between mind and matter, because Tozzi's description of Pietro's mental states is deeply embodied and materialistic. Unlike Edna in *The Awakening*, however, Pietro's psychology does not trace a clear trajectory in the course of the narrative; there is no budding self-consciousness leading to a tragic finale, but only restlessness and anxiety persisting throughout the novel. Even the ending of *Eyes Shut* portrays a psychological event: having realized that Ghisola betrayed him (something that was obvious to all other characters, and to the reader), Pietro falls out of love with her. The protagonist's existential feelings are carefully teased out by the narrator—typically, in highly metaphorical passages. While Chopin's storyworld builds on the dynamic tension between two ways of conceptualizing the mind in its relation to the physical world (types 2 and 3b vs. 3d), Tozzi offers variations on two metaphors for mind *without contrasting them*: they are my types (2) and (3d), spatial metaphors and objectifying metaphors.

The link between these metaphors is provided by Tozzi's signature kinetic style: in exploring Pietro's psychology, the narrator consistently evokes what psycholinguist Rolf Zwaan would call "experiential traces" associated with motion, which lend a strong embodied quality to these descriptions.[41] Yet the movement involved by Tozzi's psychological language is not the goal-oriented movement of action; it is nervous, jittery, aimless motion. Consider the following passage:

> [Pietro] made attempts to subdue his fits of melancholy but couldn't put them from his mind at will. Sometimes he was jolted out of them and then his mind went into a confused and turbid state. . . . He had the illusion it was assuming enormous proportions, so that his thoughts went astray in it and produced unexpected echoes, as in a large hall. . . . One minute he seemed to possess himself completely, the next less, and these shifts unsettled him, giving him dizzy spells. (*ES* 25)

The clearest expression of type (2) metaphor is in the central portion, where the mind assumes "enormous proportions" and is compared to "a large hall." But within this spatial framework, mental states become involuntary physical movements: melancholy comes in "fits," which "jolt" Pietro and send his thoughts "astray," making him feel "dizzy." These movements blur the boundary between internal space and external reality, because inner tensions result in sensory responses directed at the physical world ("dizzy spells").

The following passage develops this theme, combining type (2) with type (3d) metaphors through the image of a T-square: "He sat long hours with his head in his hands, fancying he was working, with anxiety crisscrossed and cut at all angles by bad temper and low spirits, as by lines ruled with a t-square" (*ES* 103). The kinetic dimension is here implicit in the final mention of the "lines," which evoke the embodied gesture of drawing. Further, the narrator registers variations in Pietro's existential feelings by conflating phenomenology with a lifeless object—a proto-existentialist device that conveys the unsettling strangeness of the character's anxiety, as if the character found an extraneous object within the folds of his psychology. Another passage spells out the existential strangeness at the heart of Pietro's mind, once again combining a kinetic trace with an inanimate substance, in this case a liquid: "A familiar ache dashed his brain like a cold jet that never let him get anything done. His very existence seemed strange to him" (*ES* 61–62).

The strangeness is also projected onto the natural landscape and inanimate objects that surround Pietro. Tozzi's novel repeatedly juxtaposes the protagonist's existential impasse with the harsh landscapes of Tuscany, for instance, in this description of Florence:

> All at once a gap between two houses, then other houses that grip each other and hold on tight, pressing and sinking, then rising and turning to vanish from view behind houses that have a quite different rhythm and come from the opposite side. Paths climbing uphill but these too stop short or turn into a broad irregular fan of spokes, quite flat or out of shape, where houses perch precariously, sideways, crossways, any way they happen to or are able to, being pushed by others that give the effect of trying to find a place to settle in, each for itself. (*ES* 135–36)

This passage is rich in what cognitive linguist Leonard Talmy would call "fictive motion"[42]—a common trope in which motion is attributed to inanimate, static entities. Phrases such as "the houses vanish from view" and "paths climbing uphill" are relatively standard examples of fictive motion because they reflect the movements of an implicit or hypothetical subject, who turns his or her gaze away from the houses or climbs an uphill path. Tozzi's spatial description pushes this linguistic strategy to the extreme: the houses seem to come to life with a quasi-animate physicality, clenching and jostling as if "trying to find a place to settle in." This metaphorical struggle provides an objective correlative—in the terminology of an influential modernist, T. S. Eliot[43]—for the psychological struggles and commotions that result in Pietro's incapacity to act.

Not only are inanimate objects such as the T-square and the cold jet spliced into the character's mind, but this mind is reflected and extended outward, in psychologizing descriptions of the inanimate world. The upshot is that the spatialized (and objectified) landscape of Pietro's psychology and the anthropomorphized setting become interlocked—with kinetic traces mediating and easing the process: whether he turns his attention inward or outward, Tozzi's narrator sees movement that is all the more unsettling because it does not fulfill a precise narrative function. Even as it severs the link between the protagonist's psychology and narrative action, Tozzi's novel does *not* embrace mind-matter dualism, because its metaphorical, dynamic style brings together human subjectivity and the materiality of the nonhuman world.

Madness and Materialism: Virginia Woolf's *Mrs. Dalloway*

Compared to the inchoate Modernism of both Chopin and Tozzi—whose novels are, as we have seen, intimately bound up with nineteenth-century models—Woolf's *Mrs. Dalloway* falls squarely into the modernist canon. While Chopin and Tozzi restrict the narrative perspective to a protagonist at odds with the social world, Woolf paints on a larger canvas: she places the titular Mrs. (Clarissa) Dalloway center stage while probing the minds of several other characters, particularly Septimus Warren Smith (a shell-shocked Great War veteran) and Peter Walsh (Clarissa's long-time friend). The narrator follows these characters' trajectories through London on a single day: Clarissa is making the final preparations for the high-class party that she is throwing in the evening; Septimus is struggling with mental illness, which leads to his suicide at the end of the day; and Peter, who has just returned from India, looks back on his life and his relationship with Clarissa.

Because the narrative is focalized through multiple characters, metaphors for mental processes contribute to the individual "mind style" of Clarissa, Septimus, and Peter.[44] But what these characters share is at least as important as what distinguishes them; at different moments of the day, they all develop a subtle sense of the interconnectedness of things—an insight into how human subjectivity and the world of inanimate things and natural processes are intertwined. Woolf thus brings to the fore, at the level of the protagonists' conscious awareness, the realization that Chopin and Tozzi left embedded in metaphors for mind. Martin analyzes this sense of interconnectedness with the nonhuman world under the heading of "atmosphere."[45] Here is how it emerges in Clarissa's mind:

> [Somehow] in the streets of London, on the ebb and flow of things, here, there, she survived, Peter survived, lived in each other, she being part, she was positive, of the trees at home; of the house there, ugly, rambling all to bits and pieces as it was; part of people she had never met; being laid out like a mist between the people she knew best, who lifted her on their branches as she had seen the trees lift the mist.[46]

Subjectivity ("she") becomes a diffuse, atmospheric quality that seeps into material objects ("trees," the "house") and other subjects ("part of people"). The self is not just *extended* into the space of perception and social interaction while remaining centered on an experiencing subject;[47] on the contrary, subjectivity physically mingles and blends with the world, presenting a particularly radical challenge for dualist epistemologies. This is what the passage achieves by combining a spatial metaphor with my type (3b), because the most prominent metaphor for Clarissa's atmospheric selfhood is a natural process, the "mist."

A similar insight emerges in a later scene, in which Peter falls asleep on a bench in Regent's Park. In the dream sequence that follows, the woman sitting next to him is transfigured into a creature "made of sky and branches . . . , [who] had risen from the troubled sea . . . as a shape might be sucked up out of the waves to shower down from her magnificent hands compassion, comprehension, absolution" (*MD* 63). Here the evoked space is an oneiric one, not (as in Clarissa's passage) the real streets of London. But Peter's imagination, just like Clarissa's, works toward undermining the distinction between a human subject and natural elements, such as the sky, the sea, and trees.

However, the most explicit statement of human-nonhuman interconnectedness can be found in one of the sections focusing on Septimus:

> But they beckoned; leaves were alive; trees were alive. And the leaves being connected by millions of fibres with his own body, there on the seat, fanned it up and down; when the branch stretched he, too, made that statement. The sparrows fluttering, rising, and falling in jagged fountains were part of the pattern; the white and blue, barred with black branches. (*MD* 24)

At first glance, this passage conveys a delusion of physical linkage between Septimus's body and the natural world. Yet there is method in Septimus's psychotic imagination. While Clarissa evokes the lyrical, but also fundamentally vague, metaphor of the "self as mist," and Peter only blends human subjectivity and natural processes in a dream vision, Septimus has an unflinchingly materialistic perspective on the world: for him, the leaves are "connected by millions of fibres with his own body." Likewise, a few lines before this passage Septimus had compared a human voice to a "grasshopper's, which rasped his spine deliciously and sent running up into his brain waves of sound which, concussing, broke" (*MD* 24). Later he will mention "a brain made sensitive by eons of evolution" and "nerve fibers" (*MD* 74). Mental processes are reduced to physical happenings in a brain and body shaped by evolutionary history. Therefore, Septimus may be the most mentally troubled of the novel's characters, but he is also the only one to fully face up to the material nature of mind: how mind emerges from, and can ultimately be reduced to, inanimate matter—our bodies—arranged in a sufficiently complex way. In other words, Septimus is struggling with the so-called hard problem of consciousness,[48] which concerns the relationship between our mental life and physical substance. He gives a radically physicalist (i.e., anti-Cartesian) answer to the problem: consciousness is, at best, an epiphenomenon, and all that exists is raw matter—the matter that his own body joins when he throws himself out of the window of his apartment.

If we now shift our attention to the use of physicalist metaphors in passages focalized through Clarissa, Peter, and Septimus, an intriguing fact stands out: while Woolf's description of mental processes is indeed rich in metaphorical language, metaphors are much less frequent in the Septimus sections. Clarissa, for instance, sees a strong emotion as a monster lurking "in the depths of that leaf-encumbered forest, the soul" (*MD* 13); her attempts to identify the cause of a sudden bout of unhappiness are compared to searching for an object lost in "the grass" of her mind, where one has to part "the tall blades very carefully" (*MD* 132). Peter experiences grief rising "like a moon looked at from a terrace" (*MD* 46); he later feels "as if inside his brain by another hand strings were pulled, shutters moved" (*MD* 57). All these are elaborate metaphors and similes combining type (2) with types (3c) and (3d), respectively: spatial metaphors that envision mental functioning in terms of organic matter (the forest and the grass) or inanimate entities (the moon, strings, and shutters).

No such metaphors appear in the stream of Septimus's consciousness: at best, metaphorical language functions phenomenologically, serving to convey the qualities of particular sensations: for instance, "the air buffets the cheek like the wing of a bird" (*MD* 158).[49] By contrast, Septimus's mind is never laid out in a metaphorical space; it is always aimed at *real* space, even if his psychosis tends to read into it signs and symbols of a conspiracy against him. This lack of metaphorical language is a logical conclusion to the character's materialist conception of mind: metaphorical language can only go so far in questioning dichotomies between mind and matter; a metaphorical paranarrative may narrow the divide between mental states and the world of physical things, but metaphor—as a mapping between distinct conceptual domains—still to some extent *presupposes* this divide. If one embraces the physicality of our brains, then metaphorical connections become unnecessary, because our brains are *materially* connected to our bodies, and causally shaped by the external world. In a sense, then, Woolf's *Mrs. Dalloway*, through its triangulation of characters, explores the tipping point of physicalist metaphors for mind: how metaphor may serve a heuristic function in probing and imagining the interconnectedness of mind and matter; but also how, once we've made this crucial step, we should dispense with metaphor and confront the materiality of our subjectivity in its own terms. This is not an easy truth to acknowledge, and Septimus will have to live—and die—with its consequences.

Conclusion

Metaphors for mental processes are part and parcel of folk psychology; they serve the crucial function of accounting for the elusive—and largely unconscious—workings of our minds. As we know from cognitive linguistics, metaphorical language has a built-in tendency to map the abstract and intangible onto the concrete and material: thus, the metaphors I have discussed in this chapter compare mind to scenarios or objects that can be experienced through direct perception and physical interaction. Building on previous accounts, I have developed a general typology of physicalist metaphors for mind. I have then applied this typology to three modernist novels, against the background of literary-historical claims about modernist fiction's engagement with mind.

I have argued that metaphorical language is key to the deeply embodied, physicalist conception of mental processes that informs my case studies, and modernist fiction more generally. By examining the metaphors and the larger paranarratives that they trace, as I have done here, we can see how literary language does not just passively mirror culturally circulating psychological views but is an important tool for extending such views and negotiating them in ethically charged contexts, such as those provided by Chopin's incipient feminism, Tozzi's portrait of rural Italy, or Woolf's exploration of mental illness. These authors show metaphors for mind at work in concrete narrative scenarios, revealing the subtle, but often significant, impact of conceptualizations of mind on social interactions. Further, these authors use metaphorical language to probe the ways in which the rejection of Cartesian dualism leads to a reassessment of the whole relation between (human) subjectivity and the nonhuman world of things and natural processes. A sense of deep entanglement emerges from my case studies, though it is at its most visible in Woolf's *Mrs. Dalloway*, where Septimus's radical materialism makes metaphor itself obsolete. Herein lies the relevance of the modernist engagement with mind to the contemporary world.

The past two decades have seen the rise of neuroscience, which places a strong emphasis on the neural underpinnings of our cognitive makeup and thus pursues a fundamentally materialist, anti-Cartesian project.[50] At the same time, embodiment has become one of the main research foci in the mind sciences, prompting a radical critique of mind-body dualism.[51] Despite the enormous differences in method, contemporary approaches to the mind have much in common with the empiricist psychologies that fed into literary Modernism. For today's readers, modernist fiction serves as an important precedent for envisioning the entanglement of our mental life and physical bodies; its influence is felt, for example, in Ian McEwan's *Saturday* or Richard Powers's *The Echo Maker*, two contemporary "neuronovels" that integrate—however partially and uneasily—the materialism outlined by Septimus in Woolf's *Mrs. Dalloway*.

But modernist fiction is also pertinent, in today's world, because it helps us reassess our position vis-à-vis the material and natural realities that surround us. As thinkers such as Timothy Morton have persuasively argued, the current ecological crisis prompts new questions about the interrelation between human history and the temporal and spatial scale of climatological or geological phenomena.[52] Clearly, the modernist works I've examined in these pages predate discussions of climate change and the impact of human activity on our planet. Yet they leverage creative metaphors to evoke a compelling vision of our species' interdependency with other kinds of realities—a vision that may leave a mark on their readers' imagination. This is what metaphor can do best: it brings together seemingly disparate things, exposing—and at the same time generating—a common ground between them. If modernist novels are so effective at yoking together the human and the nonhuman, it is because they do not depict the human-nonhuman enmeshment externally, as contemporary "Anthropocene fiction" tends to do[53]; on the contrary, modernist authors embed this enmeshment into the very workings of their characters' minds and brains. This, too, is a lesson for contemporary writers.

Notes

1 David Herman, "1880–1945: Re-Minding Modernism," in *The Emergence of Mind: Representations of Consciousness in Narrative Discourse in English*, ed. David Herman (Lincoln: University of Nebraska Press, 2011), 250–54.

2 Jesse Matz, "The Novel," in *A Companion to Modernist Literature and Culture*, ed. David Bradshaw and Kevin J. H. Dettmar (Oxford: Blackwell, 2006), 220.

3 Herman, "1880–1945: Re-Minding Modernism," 254.

4 Ibid., 255.

5. Howard Robinson, "Dualism," in *The Stanford Encyclopedia of Philosophy*, ed. Edward N. Zalta, available at https://plato.stanford.edu/archives/win2016/entries/dualism/, Section 1.2.
6. Paul M. Churchland, "Folk Psychology and the Explanation of Human Behavior," in *The Future of Folk Psychology: Intentionality and Cognitive Science*, ed. John D. Greenwood (Cambridge: Cambridge University Press, 1991), 51–69.
7. Alva Noë, *Action in Perception* (Cambridge, MA: MIT Press, 2004).
8. Jesse J. Prinz, *Gut Reactions: A Perceptual Theory of Emotion* (Oxford: Oxford University Press, 2004).
9. Judith Ryan, *The Vanishing Subject: Early Psychology and Literary Modernism* (Chicago: University of Chicago Press, 1991).
10. Ibid., 9.
11. Susan McCabe, "'Delight in Dislocation': The Cinematic Modernism of Stein, Chaplin, and Man Ray," *Modernism/Modernity* 8 (2001): 430.
12. Julie Taylor, *Djuna Barnes and Affective Modernism* (Edinburgh: Edinburgh University Press, 2012) and Kirsty Martin, *Modernism and the Rhythms of Sympathy: Vernon Lee, Virginia Woolf, D. H. Lawrence* (Oxford: Oxford University Press, 2013).
13. William James, "What Is an Emotion?" *Mind* 9 (1884): 188–205.
14. Antonio Damasio, *The Feeling of What Happens: Body and Emotion in the Making of Consciousness* (London: William Heinemann, 2000) and "William James and the Modern Neurobiology of Emotion," in *Emotion, Evolution, and Rationality*, ed. Dylan Evans and Pierre Cruse (Oxford: Oxford University Press, 2004), 3–14.
15. Stephen J. Burn, "Neuroscience and Modern Fiction," *Modern Fiction Studies* 61 (2015): 209–25.
16. Tim Rohrer, "Embodiment and Experientialism," in *The Oxford Handbook of Cognitive Linguistics*, ed. Dirk Geeraerts and Hubert Cuyckens (Oxford: Oxford University Press, 2007), 25–47.
17. George Lakoff and Mark Johnson, *Metaphors We Live By* (Chicago: University of Chicago Press, 1980).
18. Here, and throughout this chapter, I use the term "metaphor" in a loose way, including metaphors proper and similes—two linguistic devices that, from a cognitive-linguistic perspective, build on the same mechanism of "cross-domain mapping," the association between two semantic domains. See Israel Michael, Jennifer Riddle Harding, and Vera Tobin, "On Simile," in *Language, Culture, and Mind*, ed. Suzanne Kemmer and Michel Achard (Stanford, CA: CSLI Publications, 2005), 123–35.
19. Arthur S. Reber, "The Cognitive Unconscious: An Evolutionary Perspective," *Consciousness and Cognition* 1 (1992): 93–133.

20 Dedre Gentner and Jonathan Grudin, "The Evolution of Mental Metaphors in Psychology: A 90-Year Retrospective," *American Psychologist* 40.2 (1985): 181–92.
21 Ibid., 184.
22 John A. Barnden, "Consciousness and Common-Sense Metaphors of Mind," in *Two Sciences of Mind: Readings in Cognitive Science and Consciousness*, ed. Seán Ó Nualláin, Paul Mc Kevitt, and Eoghan Mac Aogáin (Amsterdam and Philadelphia: John Benjamins, 1997), 311–40.
23 These examples are drawn from Barnden, "Consciousness and Common-Sense Metaphors of Mind," 314.
24 Ibid., 325.
25 Michael S. Kearns, *Metaphors of Mind in Fiction and Psychology* (Lexington: University Press of Kentucky, 1987).
26 Barnden, "Consciousness and Common-Sense Metaphors of Mind," 328.
27 For more on this challenge, see Marco Caracciolo, "The Nonhuman in Mind: Narrative Challenges to Folk Psychology," in *The Edinburgh Companion to Contemporary Narrative Theories*, ed. Zara Dinnen and Robyn Warhol (Edinburgh: Edinburgh University Press, 2018), 30–42.
28 George Lakoff and Mark Turner, *More Than Cool Reason: A Field Guide to Poetic Metaphor* (Chicago: University of Chicago Press, 1989), 67–72.
29 Kearns, *Metaphors of Mind in Fiction and Psychology*.
30 Ibid., 37–38.
31 Ann Heilmann, "*The Awakening* and New Woman Fiction," in *The Cambridge Companion to Kate Chopin*, ed. Janet Beer (Cambridge: Cambridge University Press, 2008), 88–89.
32 Marianne DeKoven, "Modernism and Gender," in *The Cambridge Companion to Modernism*, ed. Michael Levenson (Cambridge: Cambridge University Press, 1999), 183.
33 Kate Chopin, *The Awakening and Other Stories*, ed. Pamela Knights (Oxford: Oxford University Press, 2000), 8. Hereafter cited in the text as *A*. My approach to mood in Chopin's novella is indebted to Marco Bernini's perceptive reading in "The Opacity of Fictional Minds: Transparency, Interpretive Cognition and the Exceptionality Thesis," in *The Cognitive Humanities: Embodied Mind in Literature and Culture*, ed. Peter Garratt (London: Palgrave Macmillan, 2016), 35–54.
34 Matthew Ratcliffe, *Feelings of Being: Phenomenology, Psychiatry and the Sense of Reality* (Oxford: Oxford University Press, 2008).
35 Benjamin Biebuyck and Gunther Martens, "Literary Metaphor between Cognition and Narration: The Sandman Revisited," in *Beyond Cognitive Metaphor Theory: Perspectives on Literary Metaphor*, ed. Monika Fludernik (London: Routledge, 2011), 58–76.

36 Giacomo Debenedetti, *Il Personaggio-Uomo* (Milan: Garzanti, 1998).
37 Eduardo Saccone, "Con Gli Occhi Chiusi," *Modern Language Notes* 110 (1995): 1–19.
38 Federigo Tozzi, *Eyes Shut*, trans. Kenneth Cox (Manchester: Carcanet, 1990), 26. Hereafter cited in the text as *ES*.
39 Marie-Laure Ryan, *Possible Worlds, Artificial Intelligence, and Narrative Theory* (Bloomington: Indiana University Press, 1991).
40 Federigo Tozzi, *Con Gli Occhi Chiusi*, ed. Ottavio Cecchi (Milan: Feltrinelli, 1994), 30.
41 Rolf A. Zwaan, "Experiential Traces and Mental Simulations in Language Comprehension," in *Symbols and Embodiment: Debates on Meaning and Cognition*, ed. Manuel de Vega, Arthur M. Glenberg, and Arthur C. Graesser (Oxford: Oxford University Press, 2008), 165–80.
42 Leonard Talmy, "Fictive Motion in Language and 'Ception,'" in *Language and Space*, ed. Paul Bloom, Mary A. Peterson, Lynn Nadel, and Merrill F. Garrett (Cambridge, MA: MIT Press, 1996), 211–76.
43 T. S. Eliot, "Hamlet and His Problems," in *The Sacred Wood and Major Early Essays* (New York: Dover, 1997), 55–59.
44 For more on the link between metaphor and mind style, see Elena Semino and Kate Swindlehurst, "Metaphor and Mind Style in Ken Kesey's *One Flew Over the Cuckoo's Nest*," *Style* 30 (1996): 143–66.
45 Martin, *Modernism and the Rhythms of Sympathy*, 102–5.
46 Virginia Woolf, *Mrs. Dalloway* (London: Penguin, 2000), 9–11. Hereafter cited in the text as *MD*.
47 As in the so-called extended mind hypothesis, see Richard Menary, ed., *The Extended Mind* (Cambridge, MA: MIT Press, 2010).
48 David J. Chalmers, "Facing Up to the Problem of Consciousness," *Journal of Consciousness Studies* 2.3 (2005): 200–19.
49 I discuss this phenomenological use of metaphor in "Phenomenological Metaphors in Readers' Engagement with Characters: The Case of Ian McEwan's *Saturday*," *Language and Literature* 22 (2013): 60–76.
50 Antonio Damasio, *Descartes' Error: Emotion, Reason, and the Human Brain* (London: Penguin, 2005).
51 Francisco J. Varela, Evan Thompson, and Eleanor Rosch, *The Embodied Mind: Cognitive Science and Human Experience* (Cambridge, MA: MIT Press, 1991).
52 Timothy J. Morton, *The Ecological Thought* (Cambridge, MA: Harvard University Press, 2010).
53 Adam Trexler, *Anthropocene Fictions: The Novel in a Time of Climate Change* (Charlottesville: University Press of Virginia, 2015).

4

Narratives of the Mind: Henry James's "The Private Life," Locke's Private Language, Wittgenstein's Public Privacy, and the Emergence of a Modernist Language of Mental Life

Garry L. Hagberg

The emergence of Modernism does not have one precise location. But one of a number of places where Modernism's distinctive attitude toward language—and particularly toward that part of language that describes and conveys a sense of mental life—comes into sharp focus is the later work of Henry James. But it was also Wittgenstein who said (correcting an entrenched dualistic misconception) that language itself is the vehicle of thought, and so a close look into some particularly telling passages of Wittgenstein's work in the philosophy of mind—where those passages and his broader work on this topic intertwine inseparably with his investigation of language—can cast light on the nature and philosophical significance of James's expansive literary investigation of linguistic consciousness. Thus, as I will suggest here, the approach to language and the mind taken by both James and Wittgenstein (although working entirely separately) converge in a striking and mutually illuminating way. However, it is important to see that it is not that James's literature functions, or can be made to function, as a mere literary example or illustration of separately identified observations about the mind and language as made by Wittgenstein (that would constitute a somewhat-shallow conception of the relation between their work, and it would miss what I am after here). Rather, the *kind* of investigation that James undertakes across, throughout, and within imaginative highly nuanced literary depictions of the mind's life can be better grasped, and particularly the modernist nature of his literary enterprise better understood, by considering Wittgenstein's version of what has been called the linguistic turn. Before that turn, language was broadly regarded as a transparent medium, or an inert sign-system, used to describe or convey cognitive content existing prior to and separable from that content's linguistic expression or articulate encapsulation; as we will see, Locke expresses this long-entrenched view with exacting clarity. But after Wittgenstein's version of the linguistic turn, language was seen very differently. The focus, indeed, was shifted *to the medium and its complexities itself*. And the special way in which this was done was, I will propose here, deeply consistent with the spirit of Modernism as it manifested itself in literature. By looking at some of James's writing alongside Wittgenstein on the mind (as it stands in contrast to Locke's premodernist conception), we will see how that profoundly original philosophical investigation into language and the mind was both deeply consistent with and revelatory of a newly emergent literary language of mental life.

In the first section I will consider the premodernist conception of language and its implications; in the second I will look into Wittgenstein both as a response to the premodernist conception and as a major step forward in understanding our relationship to language; in the third I will offer a reading of James in light of the issues brought up in the first two sections; and lastly, in the fourth, I will weave the strands together, summing up the themes that together constitute what I am suggesting is the emergent modernist approach to language.

I

"Cognitive content" is a phrase that can invite misunderstanding. And it does so through its quiet, but forceful, implementation of a philosophical picture, where that foundational picture dictates our subsequent thinking on the issue. That picture is one of objects in a room—the desk is here, the chair is there, the table between. And the room is itself a spatial container, a box with its objects placed within. And so the picture derived from modeling the inner on the outer? Consciousness makes a picture of itself as a room, a delimited space, with its objects—intentions, memories, hopes, fears, and the referents of all mental nouns—placed within. And this picture generates its corresponding models of introspection and self-knowledge: we turn our outward gaze inward and identify and inspect contents just as we would in an actual room. But on Wittgenstein's approach, the philosophy of mind and the philosophy of language are inseparably intertwined. And we see this intertwining here as a further correlated model of meaning: a word, we too easily think, means the object to which it refers. And so, with mind and language interweaving, "chair" means the object there in the room; "intention" means the object there in the mental space, the cognitive interior. On this model, language would be invariably secondary; that is, language would be a contingent matter of naming the things—the chairs, the desks, the intention, the fears—after the fact of their prior and separate existence. On this model, the meanings of words (because on this picture meaning is a function of a simple direct relation between word and referent) would always be beyond language itself; that is, it would be the things in the world, physical or mental, to which those words referred. According to this picture, physical things are prior to and separate from their names, just as then mental things would be prior to and separate from their names. The language of cognition would be secondary, it would be subservient, and the criterion of accurate usage would always be a simple matter of rightly attaching the correct name to the correct object. The meaning of "chair" is different from that of the word "desk" because of the different objects to which they are attached, and we determine which is which by looking, and we correct misuses accordingly. Thus, as the underlying picture and its corollaries would lead us to think, the meaning of the word "intention" is different from that of the word "hope" because they refer to different cognitive objects, and we correct mistakes or misuses by looking within.

There are good reasons for calling all of this a premodernist conception of language as it corresponds to a premodernist conception of the mind. John Locke, for example, in his great *An Essay Concerning Human Understanding*, Book III, sees words as first and foremost names. Observing that language could not function and would be far too vast if each individual object in the world had its own name, Locke explains that humanity hit upon the concept of a general term, a general name that has a class of objects as its referent. The class is, of course, an idea, not a particular physical entity, and so Locke sees that words as used meaningfully, or with what he calls signification, refer to ideas in the mind of the speaker. Thus to refer to the chair in the room, we refer to our present idea of the chair as given to us in empirical sensory experience, and properly speaking that is the thing to which the word refers—the mental thing that gives it meaning. This may seem different from, or even to challenge, the picture just described, but it does not do so. Rather, it preserves the picture by inserting the perception of the chair between the chair and the name of the chair—which, again, makes the referent in the first instance mental, not physical. That thus only reduces the distance between the outer model and the parallel inner model that it generates, and so the essential point remains: language is considered as an after-the-fact form of contingent naming. The room and its objects exist pre-linguistically, our perception of them follows, and our naming of them follows that. And so, with Locke, we think: the mental room, the cognitive chamber, exists with mental objects "furnishing" it, and our naming of those cognitive items follows. We could, according to this model, keep those thoughts within (and keep them in pre-linguistic form, an issue to which I will return later), but for reasons Locke identifies, we desire not to do so.

Locke writes,

1. God having designed Man for a sociable Creature, made him not only with an inclination, and under a necessity to have fellowship with those of his own kind; but furnished him also with Language, which was to be the great Instrument, and common Type of Society. *Man* therefore had by nature his organs so fashioned, as to be *fit to frame articulate Sounds*, which we call Words. But this was not enough to produce Language; for Parrots, and several other Birds, will be taught to make articulate Sounds distinct enough, which yet, by no means, are capable of language.

2. Besides articulate Sounds therefore, it was farther necessary, that he should *be able to use these Sounds, as Signs of internal Conceptions*; and to make them stand as marks for the *Ideas* within his own mind, whereby they might be made known to others, and the Thoughts of Men's Minds be conveyed from one to another.

3. But neither was this sufficient to make Words so useful as they ought to be. It is not enough for the perfection of Language, that Sounds can be made signs of *Ideas*, unless those *signs* can be so made use of, as *to comprehend several particular Things*: For the multiplication of Words would have perplexed their use, had every particular thing need of a distinct name to be signified by. To remedy this inconvenience, Language had yet a farther improvement in the use of general Terms, whereby one word was made to mark a multitude of particular existences: Which advantageous use of Sounds was obtain'd only by the difference of the *Ideas* they were made signs of. Those names becoming general, which are made to stand for general *Ideas*, and those remaining particular, where the *Ideas* they are used for are particular.[1]

Thus for Locke, words are sounds that function as signs of internal conceptions, where those signs make public something that is in the first instance private. Words make up an external sign system that conveys thoughts from one mind to another, where those thoughts can be particular or general. ("Please get that chair" vs. "Please get a chair"; "Good intentions pave the way . . ." vs. "That intention paves the way . . . .") And to clarify what comes first, what I have called previously pre-linguistic cognitive content, Locke writes,

> 1. Man, though he have great variety of Thoughts, and such, from which others, as well as himself, might receive Profit and Delight; yet they are all within his own Breast, invisible, and hidden from others, nor can of themselves be made to appear. The Comfort and Advantage of Society, not being to be had without Communication of Thoughts, it was necessary, that Man should find out some external sensible Signs, whereby those invisible *Ideas*, which his thoughts are made up of, might be made known to others. For this purpose, nothing was so fit, either for Plenty or Quickness, as those articulate sounds, which with so much Ease and Variety, he found himself able to make. Thus we may conceive how *Words*, which were by nature so well adapted to that purpose, come to be made use of by Men, as *the Signs of* their *Ideas*; not by any natural connection, that there is between particular articulate Sounds and certain *Ideas*, for then there would be but one Language amongst all Men; but by a voluntary Imposition, whereby such a Word is made arbitrarily the Mark of such an *Idea*. The use then of Words, is to be sensible Marks of *Ideas*; and the *Ideas* they stand for, are their proper and immediate Signification. (*EHU* 404–5)

That (a) our thoughts are made up of "invisible ideas," that (b) words are arbitrarily attached sounds, that (c) signs come after the fact of the real content, that (d) meaning is determined by a referent or a class of referents, that (e) the human mind is in the first instance metaphysically private or "within his own Breast"—these are the elements of a premodernist conception of language and of the mind that employs language. And these are the elements that Wittgenstein and James, in their respective ways, conceptually excavate, intricately scrutinize, and ultimately supplant.

Yet there is another element of Locke's thought about language and the mind that is essential to what I am describing as the premodern conception. It is this: (f) language invariably proceeds from (what one might call) the inside out—that is, where the cognitive content must be in place before any (what we think of as) externalization of that content can begin. This element both places the origin of meaning inside the mental room, the inner chamber, and assigns the words of language a representational, or proxy, function—they signify only by standing in place for their associated mental "furnishings." Thus Locke writes,

> *Words in their primary or immediate Signification, stand for nothing, but the* Ideas *in the Mind of him that uses them,* how imperfectly soever, or carelessly those *Ideas* are collected from the Things, which they are supposed to represent. When a Man speaks to another, it is, that he may be understood; and the end of Speech is, that those Sounds, as Marks, may make them known his *Ideas* to the Hearer. That then which Words are the Marks of, are the *Ideas* of the Speaker: nor can any one apply them, as Marks, immediately to any thing else, but the *Ideas*, that he himself hath: For this would be to make them Signs of his own Conceptions, and yet apply them to other *Ideas*; which would be to make them Signs, and not Signs of his *Ideas* at the same time; and so in effect, to have no Signification at all. (*EHU* 405–6)

The ideas, produced in the mind by the empirical sensory experience of the speaker, may be inaccurate or imperfect: I may misperceive the chair as brown rather than black; I may misperceive the distant hope as an immediate ambition. But the idea in the mind, however it does or does not match or reduplicate the actual properties of the particular sensory or mental object, is the signification of the word at that given moment of usage. The highest court of appeal concerning meaning is intended meaning of a kind that is internally contained and privately bounded. And so Locke adds:

> Words being voluntary Signs, they cannot be voluntary Signs imposed by him on Things he knows not. That would be to make the Signs of nothing, Sounds without Signification. A man cannot make his Words the Signs either of Qualities in Things, or of Conceptions in the Mind of another, whereof he has none in his own. Till he has some *Ideas* of his own, he cannot suppose them to correspond with the Conceptions of another Man; nor can he use any Signs for them. For thus they would be the Signs of he knows not what, which is in Truth to be the Signs of nothing. But when he represents to himself other Men's *Ideas*, by some of his own, if he consent to give them the same Names, that other Men do, 'tis still to his own *Ideas*; to *Ideas* that he has, and not to *Ideas* that he has not. (*EHU* 406)

And what if he or she uses words for ideas that he or she in truth lacks?

> Because Words are many of them learn'd, before the *Ideas* are known for which they stand: Therefore some, not only Children, but Men, speak several Words, no otherwise that Parrots do, only because they have learn'd them, and have been accustomed to those Sounds. But so far as Words are of Use and Signification, so far is there a constant connexion between the Sound and the *Idea*; and a Designation, that the one stand for the other: without which Application of them, they are nothing but so much insignificant Noise. (*EHU* 408)

So this piece of the fully developed picture is that pre-linguistic cognitive contents constitute ideas, ideas are associated with sounds, sounds function as signs for self and for others, and meaning is invariantly dependent on a kind of inner translation from idea to verbalization. Again, the modernist conception of mind and language ushered in by James and by Wittgenstein works its way free of the grip of this picture and its corollaries.

II

One could say that for Wittgenstein language does not work inside out; rather, it is much more the reverse—an outside-in model. But that would not only be too succinct, too telegraphic, to be comprehensible, worse, it would also make the mistake of presuming that his view is reducible to one briefly articulated position and then placing that position as an antithetical or polemical opponent to the Lockean position. Wittgenstein's view of language is not of that kind—and what he encompasses within that view is, one could say, of the length of a novel rather than of a proposition.

One might well think—and many do—that of the broadly Lockean theory of language, *but how else could it be?* That is, the picture seems not only right but in a sense also necessarily so. It is in *Philosophical Investigations* §115 that Wittgenstein writes the now-famous remark,

> A *picture* held us captive. And we couldn't get outside it, for it lay in our language, and language seemed only to repeat it to us inexorably.[2]

That is, when we focus on the philosophical question concerning what language is and how it essentially works, we turn our gaze to the use of a word or brief sentence, focus our attention on the psychological or cognitive content that stands (as, indeed, we spatially picture it) "behind" the utterance, and then think we have found precisely in that moment of word-usage within it what we have in truth only projected upon it given the preconceptions with which we are working. Following this remark, Wittgenstein continues in §116:

> When philosophers use a word—"knowledge," "being," "object," "I," "proposition/sentence," "name"—and try to grasp the *essence* of the thing, one must always ask oneself: is the word ever actually used in this way in the language in which it is at home?—

What *we* do is bring words back from their metaphysical to their everyday use.

The place where we see words as used by characters within expansive and humanly intricate contexts is literature; if we were to follow Wittgenstein's desideratum even at this early point we could turn to literature to see how mentally descriptive words function in changing contexts of discourse. On that view, the full collection of variegated usages that we assembled across the span of a novel or story, understood in detail within the contexts of their employment, would show us the meaning of the word or concept in question. That would indeed be a Wittgensteinian approach to word-meaning; it would be to see words as "brought back." But we have not seen enough to genuinely comprehend what these generic methodological pronouncements might mean. (Note: we naturally pursue a fuller understanding by looking into related things that Wittgenstein has written on this topic, and not by guessing about content hermetically sealed within his mind that only contingently finds public or social expression once inwardly translated into signs. So if we look to what we actually do to understand more, the grip of Locke's picture thereby lessens. I will return to this later.)

Wittgenstein captures the heart of what I am calling the premodern picture; in *Philosophical Investigations* §120, he writes,

> People say: it's not the word that counts, but its meaning, thinking of the meaning as a thing of the same kind as the word, even though different from the word. Here the word, there the meaning.

The picture leads us to think that the spoken word, as a sound, is physical—it is in the actual room. The meaning, the same kind of thing yet still different, is in the inner "room," the mental chamber. And the sign, as transducer, moves the one to the other. Somewhat later in the book, Wittgenstein, having considered a good number of the features of language as actually used that do not conform in any way to this picture (and indeed invariably work against it), writes that we make progress on these issues

> only if we make a radical break with the idea that language always functions in one way, always serves the same purpose: to convey thoughts—which may be about houses, pains, good and evil, or whatever. (*PI* 304)

If we think of language as a philosophical concept to be analyzed, we may well search for the essence, as Wittgenstein described this conceptual impulse earlier, of language—the element that makes language what it is and that appears in every case of language, every member of the class of things called "language." The premodernist conception believes itself to have found this single-defining uniform function, and that the Lockean picture (with variations on that theme across the centuries) captures it. But on this inside-out model, if we pause to reflect on the nature of the connection between the idea as Locke described it and the linguistic sign that is attached to it and then conveys it, the speaker would have to have a rule in place concerning that inward attachment and follow that rule inwardly. The prelinguistic cognitive content of a chair—the idea of a chair, would have to be attached (if very rapidly) to the word, the sign, "chair" (where that sign is formed by following the subordinate rule of composing that sign with the letters c, h, a, i, and r). Wittgenstein's much-discussed rule-following considerations are too lengthy and intricate to go into here, but for present purposes one aspect of these considerations points us toward an understanding of the modernist view that supplants Locke's model.

In considering cases such as following an instruction to copy a series of letters in a certain way or to continue a sequence of numbers ("Carry out 2, 4, 6, 8... to 100"), Wittgenstein shows that the criteria for understanding the rule and the criteria for correctness that emerge in each case will invariably break out of interiority. As in the more complex case of learning to play chess, he shows that such circumstantially emergent criteria for understanding and for correctness require for their intelligibility that they function outwardly. Or better, they function in a way that challenges the very dichotomy that is in play here, the metaphysical dichotomy separating the inner from the outer.

A practice, for Wittgenstein, is what we do, and not what we prismatically describe what we do under the influence of a philosophical picture. I mentioned earlier that a philosophical picture, once in place, can direct our subsequent thought on its issue; what in Wittgenstein's sense a close look at our actual practices gives (this was the fundamental imperative of ordinary-language philosophy) is a changed way of seeing, yielding a correction to a prismatic and philosophically misled description of those practices. It is for this reason that his reflections on rule-following are so often interlaced with examples (or sketches of examples for his readers to fill out), with cases that, once considered, possess the power to change our way of seeing the issue. An extremely brief, but also extremely powerful, observation captures what is relevant about the rule-following considerations for present purposes. In *Philosophical Investigations* §202, Wittgenstein writes,

> That's why "following a rule" is a practice. And to *think* one is following a rule is not to follow a rule. And that's why it's not possible to follow a rule "privately"; otherwise, thinking one was following a rule would be the same thing as following it.

In the private chamber of Locke's speaker, there would be no means by which to differentiate any case of correctly following the attachment rule from any case of thinking one was following the correct attachment rule. And (this point is not stated but is implicit—and implicit content itself is another function of language that is deeply inconsistent with the premodernist picture; I'll return to this later) because we can and do make (a) distinctions between thinking we are following a rule and actually following it, (b) distinctions between following the rule and following it wrongly, and (c) distinctions between levels or degrees of understanding and misunderstanding the rule in question, we do have and use criteria that move outside, indeed function outside, the hermetic bounds of the Lockean speaking mind. Or to put it another way: we could not make sense of the language we actually have, the language we actually use, while holding our reflections and our conceptual resources within those hermetic Lockean bounds. Were that the case, language, as both Wittgenstein and, as we will see, James, make clear, would not and could not be what it is. We could follow a rule privately—in the sense of resolving to follow it unto ourselves and telling no one about it. But that is of course not the "inner-chamber" philosophical sense of the word "private." For in this kind of case, the word is already brought back, already in established social or public use—already, if we are to stick with the dichotomy, a public use of "private."[3] The modernist view of language does not place its origins in a ghostly interior, and it does not hold that language is only contingently social, only contingently social. It is not contingently "brought out," because, indeed, it is not brought out at all. It is always already there.

So we are gaining some grasp of, and some insight into the motivating considerations for, the modernist conception. Another aspect of Wittgenstein's reflections can further shed light. If Locke's conception of the origin and content of language was accurate, then, as he says, each word would be learned individually, or to put it more precisely, cognitive content and its contingent signage would be atomistic in nature. Indeed, it would have to be, because the idea, the to-be-conveyed content of cognition, regardless of its accuracy or matching correspondence to the sense-impressions that generated it, would be whole unto itself by definition. And so language learning would be atomistic— learning would proceed one word at a time, as we learn to attach that word sign to an idea (again, according to an internally followed rule—without which we speak as parrots). This makes for neatness of theory, it makes the learning of language seem simple and uniform across all cases, and it preserves the hermetic autonomy of mind that as we have seen is part and parcel of Locke's dualistic picture of language. But it is grossly false to the evident facts of our practices. In *Philosophical Investigations* §224, Wittgenstein writes,

> The word "accord" and the word "rule" are related to one another; they are cousins. If I teach anyone the use of the one word, he learns the use of the other with it.

Verbal "relatives" of this kind are possible because the atomistic element of the Lockean picture is, as misled philosophy, indefensible once we turn from theory to (Wittgenstein's conception of a) practice.[4] Wittgenstein's question here could be stated as: How could one genuinely understand, genuinely comprehend, the concept "accord" or the phrase "in accordance with" without having in play the concept of a rule? The reverse question carries the same force. If we think of the meaning of the word "rule" as an atomistic, determinately bounded mental entity, a kind of entity that is both like the word (it is a bounded particular) and unlike the word (it is inner, not outer), we are thinking not of our actual uses, and our actual learning, of that concept, and we are not thinking of cases of instruction employing that concept, but rather we are thinking only in generic and schematic terms consistent with the original picture.[5] In short, we are thinking in the grips of a picture. And so Wittgenstein continues, in §225,

> The use of the word "rule" and the use of the word "same" are interwoven. (As are the use of "proposition" and the use of "true.")

It is important to note (and this is foundational to both Wittgenstein's and James's investigations into and presentations of language) that it is that the *words themselves* work together in these ways (and as James shows, it gets very much more complicated than what Wittgenstein captures in this remark here); it is not that the relations between them invariably take place first in the mind of the person using them. Or, one does not have to possess word-relational cognitive content in order for those relations both to exist and to mutually inflect. One can, of course, reflect on the relations between words and phrases and usages (James is one of the world masters at precisely this), but the existence of those relations, those interactions, and those creative chemical-like verbal or linguistic interactions is not dependent on any such prior determinate cognition for their existence. Again, as the modernist conception recognizes, they are already out there, *in* language, already in—as Wittgenstein called it—a form of life.⁶

As I mentioned earlier, if language were subservient, if it were merely a delivery system for pre-linguistic ideas and thus serving only as a secondary system of naming for the primary things named, the meaning of the word "pain" would obviously be determined by its referent. Wittgenstein never shies away from the difficult cases, and it would seem at a glance that a sensation and its name would require the Lockean model—seemingly unassailably, this would be pre-linguistic cognitive content arbitrarily associated with a sound that functions as its sign. And so he turns to precisely this case. In *Philosophical Investigations* 244, Wittgenstein writes,

> How do words *refer* to sensations?—There doesn't seem to be any problem here; don't we talk about sensations every day, and name them?

That indeed looks, straightforwardly, like the Lockean model in practice, in action, and unproblematically so. But he continues,

> But how is the connection between the name and the thing named set up? The question is the same as: How does a human being learn the meaning of names and sensations? For example, of the word "pain."

According to the dictates of the picture, we might too quickly say: it is set up simply—the introspective gaze is focused upon the sensation and the sound is attached to it, where a rule or association is born. This is central to what the modernist conception of language calls into question, and if a different account of the connection is possible, and if we recognize it—independently of the grip of the picture—as more familiar to life as lived than what that picture makes us think, then whatever else we say at this stage the essence of the relation between "the name and the thing named" has not been captured (the essence is supposed to be invariant across cases of word-meaning). And so Wittgenstein continues,

> Here is one possibility: words are connected with the primitive, natural, expressions of sensation and used in their place. A child has hurt himself and he cries; then adults talk to him and teach him exclamations and, later, sentences. They teach the child new pain-behaviour.
>
> "So you are saying that the word 'pain' really means crying?"—On the contrary: the verbal expression of pain replaces crying, it does not describe it.

This speaks of the connection between sensation and word (and so it uses the very terminology of the premodern picture), but as a philosophical Trojan Horse it enters in the guise of its opponent and then shows that what is considered the essential and irreplaceable connection is in truth neither. As Wittgenstein so often does, he voices a possible response from his imagined interlocutor ("So you are saying . . ."), but that attempted reduction to behaviorism is as quickly rebutted by saying that the word does not stand for, name, describe, or refer to, crying, but rather—instituting a completely different kind of relation between sensation and word—it replaces it, with the word in a sense growing organically from natural expression within the world of lived and embodied human practices.

But before moving forward, there remains one more element of Wittgenstein's thought that significantly enriches our understanding of what I am calling the modernist conception of language that James in part created and in part investigated with proto-Wittgensteinian subtlety.

The premodernist conception of language made a foundational assumption that blinded it to the social, public, shared, interactive, and, in the way we have begun to see, external character or nature of linguistic meaning. That assumption took form in the taking as granted concepts integrally involved in meaning-determination that should in truth be available only *after* the origin as the Lockean picture describes it, and not *as part of* that originating story as we saw Locke articulate it earlier. One could say that picture helped itself to too much too soon. This is not a simple matter, and it weaves throughout Wittgenstein's investigations into language in all its multifarious employments, but we can get a basic grasp of it from *Philosophical Investigations* §257. Wittgenstein's imagined interlocutor has just said, following his aforementioned remarks about the words replacing the behavior instead of serving as names for them, that if humans did not manifest pains in behavior by groaning, grimacing, and so forth, "then it would be impossible to teach a child the use of the word 'toothache.'" Wittgenstein could, but does not, reply, "But then you are not talking about *us*, and we are investigating *our* language here." And he could go on to say that, because of this imagined move into an alternative non-grimacing embodied species, therefore we could not genuinely comprehend the very idea of teaching a child. But he does not do so. Rather, more deeply, he writes,

> —Well, let's assume that the child is a genius and invents a name for the sensation by himself!—But then, of course, he couldn't make himself understood when he used the word.—So does he understand the name, without being able to explain its meaning to anyone?—But what does it mean to say that he has "named his pain"?—How has he managed this naming of pain? And whatever he did, what

was its purpose?—When one says "He gave a name to his sensation," one forgets that much must be prepared in the language for mere naming to make sense. And if we speak of someone's giving a name to pain, the grammar of the word "pain" is what has been prepared here; it indicates the post where the new word is stationed.

This passage, read in light of all that has preceded it, leaves the premodernist conception in unrecoverable shambles. It is not that language does not work like that. More powerfully, it could not. And, as the revolution in human understanding that Wittgenstein's philosophy is, it changes our understanding of our relation to language and our understanding of our life in it.

First, the very idea of inventing the concept of a name is problematic, precisely because the concept of a name functions within an already-existent language that in a sense surrounds it. One could say the same of the concept of a referent, which, as the sensation, is also in play here, also too early. Second, the child could not make himself or herself understood because only the child has the inner referent that allegedly secures the meaning of the name. (And so back to the preceding: is this following a rule or thinking one is following a rule?) Third, is his being able to explain its meaning a precondition of, or inextricably interwoven with, his ability to understand the name for himself? It would be difficult to answer this in the negative and still preserve any intelligible notion of understanding. Fourth, what has he done, in utter linguistic isolation and as an originary act, in "naming his pain"? (Naming takes place *in* language and not before it.) And what is this alleged act for? One might ask, what is the pragmatic underpinning of this semantic event? But fifth, and most powerfully, "one forgets," or, as I am suggesting, one easily presupposes far too much, far too soon. *Much must be prepared in the language for mere naming to make sense.* What Wittgenstein calls the "grammar," the entire background context of discourse within which such moves in circumscribed and sense-determining language-games can be made, is taken for granted here. If we desire an understanding of language, we need to look elsewhere—and with what Wittgenstein called a changed way of seeing. One needs to look at the full contexts in which words have their circumstantial homes, their resonances, their inflections, their undercurrents, their "chemical" interactions, their self-compositional power, their moral significance, their layered meanings, their shades of finely differentiated description, their uncountable non-subservient roles. One needs to look into the kinds of things that Henry James saw and used with such precision.

III

James knew he stood just at the pivot of some kind of cultural turning point—for him, a transition from the late Victorian aesthetic to the early modernist. But—appropriately for him—it was particularly the approach to language, and our relation to our words, that was changing under his pen. Of course, none of Wittgenstein's work was or could have been known to him; he missed the publication of the *Tractatus Logico-Philosophicus* by five years, and however strong the continuities across the span of Wittgenstein's work may be, the *Tractatus* is not the work of the much-later *Philosophical Investigations* that I have discussed earlier. But despite the historical miss, the affinity in approach to language for anyone who looks closely is remarkable. In Wittgenstein's extensive manuscripts, he often phrases, and then repeatedly rephrases, a thought in such a way that each variation slightly changes inflection, and slightly changes the light that some words cast on others. It is never simple, never—in its own way perhaps a bit like Kierkegaard—propositionally direct. One does not see everything he has to say, everything he has to mean, in one contained and thought-finishing sentence. Indeed, his writings show that such thought is not contained, not in a sense sealed, within the sentence, just as we have seen earlier that direct meaning is not contained within the word. The comparison of Locke's writing to Wittgenstein's is itself instructive: in Locke, we get directness and a sense of propositional containment. In Wittgenstein, we are thrown into a web of relations, resonances, and interacting words in such a way that one is always seeing one remark in the light of others, and one is thus always considering and reconsidering and seeing new and different light dawning right and left. Henry James wrote:

> The old dramatists ... had a simpler civilization to represent—societies in which the life of man was in action, in passion, in immediate violent experience. These things could be put upon the playhouse boards with comparatively little sacrifice of their completeness and their truth. Today we're so infinitely more reflective and complicated and diffuse.[7]

That for him is the difference between the premodernist and the modernist view of words and sentences and the nature of the narrative structures that they produce. In discussing this passage Terry Eagleton furthers the thought concerning the modernist difference; Eagleton observes, "because of this we need a narrative voice-over, which the novel can give us with less strain than the modern drama, which will help us unravel these subtleties."[8] James's employment of the narrator has of course, and for good reason, been the subject of much discussion. But what I want to suggest here is that the doubled structure of (a) the primary language of the characters describing and enacting on the level of word and deed within a literary work and (b) the narrator's voice, over the top of that, above and external to the scene of word and deed, is (because our language does not actually work in accordance with the simple inner-to-outer picture, the picture of directly expressed transparent cognitive content) the psychological structure of the modernist conception of language. It is like the experience of reading, and re-reading,[9] Wittgenstein rather than that of reading Locke. But how does James show this from inside literary narrative?

"The Private Life" is a tale with a readily discernible and sturdy narrative design: Clare Vawdrey, the greatest literary figure of the time, Blanche Adney, the greatest figure on the London stage at the time and her husband Vincent Adney, Lord and Lady Mellifont, as a pair the epitome of social perfection and grace, and the unnamed narrator, a figure who turns out to play the role of a kind of social detective, all meet in a Swiss inn for a holiday. From the start James positions his characters into a dense public web of relations. Wittgenstein employed the concept of the language-game and saw a deep analogy between language and chess; James initiates this tale by indicating that it was "a turn of the game"[10] that "pitched" them all together at the last of August. This is not to observe the mere fact that they both use game-analogies; rather, it is that they both see that persons, their interwoven words and deeds, are always already functioning in a public world and that their words and deeds would be incomprehensible without that contextual frame (what Wittgenstein called at one point "the whole hurly-burly"). The narrator reports, "We met, in London, with irregular frequency; we were more or less governed by the laws and the language, the traditions and the shibboleths of the same dense social state" (*PL* 192). Near the outset, James expands the conception of verbal communication to include things spoken, things unspoken, and things that cross over from the unsaid to the said: "We were frank about this, we talked about it" (*PL* 192). And James captures another feature deeply compatible with Wittgenstein's conception of language and not at all compatible with Locke's: he describes the sense or intimation one gets, drawn from words and deeds across time, that a person possesses ethical characteristics not yet brought to the surface of language, and even not yet inexactly verbally formulated in the imagination, but one that nonetheless has reason to believe, or again sense, are there in the person. Wittgenstein spoke of imponderable evidence at one point; this is of that kind. And this can be a kind of muted evidence about a person that, in sensing across an indeterminate span of time, will not be capturable within a word or phrase ("but that was too complicated to go into then") (*PL* 192)[11]; it is cognitive content concerning another's inner life that Locke's picture cannot accommodate and for which Wittgenstein's conception opens a space. (This opened space is another way of characterizing the modernist conception, but I will return to this.)

Clare Vawdrey, "a copious talker" (*PL* 193), as the narrator tells us, "used to be called 'subjective and introspective' in the weekly papers" but, the narrator tells us, in his experience "no distinguished man could in society have been less so" (*PL* 193). The words "subjective" and "introspective" speak of—or intimate in a web of associations—the inner chamber as the origin and locus of meaning; this character, for the narrator, is (despite journalistic reports on the tone of Vawdrey's writing) the opposite. James is mapping his character onto the inner-outer continuum, but here he is doing so in an interestingly doubled way: Vawdrey is at this early point in the story described as an embodiment of subjectivism (by his newspaper critics) and as its antithesis (by the narrator). Like Locke's chair, this places perception between the description and the thing described, but here in a way that intimates the possibility of both being true as (in Wittgenstein's phrase) different ways of seeing the same thing. Different sets of selected aspects justify, and make plausible and determine the context-specific meanings of, countervailing descriptions.

I mentioned earlier the phenomenon of the indirect communication of cognitive content; James is perhaps the literary master of this particular dimension of literary language (this aspect of language is also deeply important for Wittgenstein as well as for Kierkegaard before him).[12] And so we see it in this tale repeatedly: in one example, when Lady Mellifont asks the narrator "Do you know where they went?" the narrator replies "Do you mean Mrs Adney and Lord Mellifont?" and she replies quickly in turn, "Lord Mellifont and Mrs Adney." This is for her a social correction, but as the narrator grasps later, it is that and more than that. The narrator tells us, "Her ladyship's speech seemed—unconsciously indeed—to correct me, but it didn't occur to me that this might be an effect of jealousy" (*PL* 194). James is working in a complex and layered linguistic world: this seems initially a social correction from the most correct socialite—but she herself is then described as having made this correction unconsciously. James has her conveying cognitive content that she has not articulated to herself. And then the narrator, on hearing the correction, understands it as spoken at the time (he does not say "What do you mean?"), but then only later realizes that jealousy, unseen by both parties in the moment, could explain the motivation of the remark. What would be an unaccountable complexity to the premodernist picture, this is a commonplace of layered and semi-resolved verbal interaction for James. Wittgensteinian language-games are not mono-dimensional, not Lockean exchanges in which determinate ideas are transparently conveyed.

But in what is still the laying of the foundation for this curious story, James identifies a rarely discussed hidden by way of our linguistic practices. The narrator tells us of Vincent Adney that "it's difficult for a husband not on the stage, or at least in the theatre, to be graceful about a wife so conspicuous there; but Adney did more than carry it off, the awkwardness—he taught it ever so oddly to make *him* interesting" (PL 195). The details are intricate, but Adney *taught* this circumstance to bring him into a position of interest. What he did with the words and sentences of the persons surrounding him was to arrange them into a meaning-conveying network, beyond the reach of any single individual utterance, so that a special kind of light of interest was shed in his direction. What this means is that, as a minimal participant in the conversations of his life around him as they occurred primarily with Mrs. Adney as the focus, he functioned quietly on the sidelines as a conductor of an ensemble of sentences, bringing them to yield significance that none of them individually carried. As the result, he became "something rare and brave and misunderstood" (PL 196). Language can and does on occasion work like this, and it demonstrates yet another relation to language that an individual can have, and it puts on display another mode of meaning that not only was not, but also could not, have been dreamed of in Locke's philosophy of language.

And then there is the spirit of an utterance, of a conversation, of a verbal interaction. A non sequitur is an obvious form of discontinuity; there are far more subtle versions. When Lady Mellifont expresses her nervousness that Lord Mellifont has not yet returned from his walk near the glacier, the narrator offers her somewhat-empty reassurance: "Nothing can ever happen to a man so accomplished, so infallible, so armed on all points," and he adds to us, "I went on in the same spirit" (PL 196). By saying to us "in the same spirit," the narrator is showing us that he knows that his reassurances are empty: Lord Mellifont's social standing is irrelevant to his safety near the glacier. The narrator knows that he does not need to continue with any exact report or transcription of what he said, because he knows that we know—that speakers of our language will know—what the spirit of this kind of utterance is and that what it conveys is not what it expressly says. The spirit is both (a) recognizable (we—in Wittgenstein's sense of following a rule—know how to go on) and in terms of content (b) supplemental to its stated content. It is telling that we use the word "spirit" in this way: Wittgenstein's phrase was "a form of life." James sees all this and places us as readers within the conversational world of its enactment. It brings a broadening and deepening of the concept "language."

But there is more behind this exchange concerning a hint, an intimation of significance, the giving of a sense of something yet to be discovered (it is in these passages that the "detective" role of the narrator emerges and becomes clearer). Lady Mellifont says that she always becomes nervous when her husband is away from her for any time. The narrator asks, "Do you imagine something has happened to him?" And she replies, "Yes, always." Now, importantly in terms of this function of language, the narrator asks, "Do you mean his tumbling over precipices—that sort of thing?" and she replies—here the language intimates through imprecision and the ignorance of the referent on the part of the speaker—"I don't know exactly *what* I fear: it's the general sense that he'll never come back" (*PL* 196). The fear has its object and so is rationally intelligible, yet that object is at present unknown to the person who feels the fear. What James is showing here is that this case is not anticipatory to real language, not a proto-sentence awaiting its clear propositional expression, but rather that *this itself* is part of our language. The narrator will tell us later what it was that she sensed, but that does not negate this experience unto itself as it is here expressed with an unknown object of fear. Language, as Wittgenstein said earlier, does not always work in one way.[13]

James, of course, throughout his writing shows an exquisitely sophisticated awareness of the contribution that gesture, gait, stance, personal presentation, and particularly facial expression and nuances of gaze play in the determination of meaning, and we see much of that here: "The particular thing the eyes happened to say"; "What they [the eyes] usually said"; what they "at present added dimly, surreptitiously, and of course sweetly" (*PL* 199); and so on. But this becomes especially significant in the present context because this is the opposite of the view of language that would see purely cognitive, disembodied mental content as contingently conveyed by arbitrarily attached physical signs or sounds. That conception, as Wittgenstein knew, could never catch the inflections of content brought in by these embodied subtleties of delivery. But James actually shows that the point should be taken further to properly mimetically represent the reality of persons using language.[14] It is the very distinction between word and deed, broadly understood, that is in question here.

> The handsomest man of his period could never have looked better, and he sat among us like a bland conductor controlling by an harmonious play of arm an orchestra still a little rough. He directed the conversation by gestures as irresistible as they were vague; one felt as if without him it wouldn't have had anything to call a tone. This was essentially what he contributed to any occasion—what he contributed above all to English public life. He pervaded it, he coloured it, he embellished it, and without him it would have lacked, comparatively speaking, a vocabulary. Certainly it wouldn't have had a style, for a style was what it had in having Lord Mellifont. He *was* a style. (PL 199)

The familiar and easy point could be that part of his style was his mode of participation in conversation. James's further and much stronger point, both uniting word and deed and showing how pervasive a person's presence can be in setting a tone or in demarcating the boundaries of a linguistic style, is that the public conversation would not have had a style without *him*. His identity is present within and throughout the words. The image of language as an insensitive or somewhat-mechanical sign system is a reduction to caricature that Wittgenstein explicitly and James implicitly strongly reject, for precisely the reasons James is showing here.

Yet Mellifont's style is not perfect: even with all that the narrator has identified and praised here, he sees a possible revelatory flaw. The defect in Lord Mellifont's manner (this idea, he suggests to the reader, "only under his breath") was that he seems always to display more art, more artifice, more design in self-presentation, than even the most complex of circumstances could require. The verbal expression and the full articulation of a good thing can connote, if under one's breath, too much of a good thing, where that then awakens an association to (and thus conveys in this way too indirect cognitive content) some other unsaid issue or characteristic lurking in the unspoken subterrain (we will shortly learn what that is). And so again: any conception of language that misses this thereby reduces the accuracy and the focal acuity of that theoretical representation of language. Neither James nor Wittgenstein wants a blurred, over-general, imprecise picture, nor do they want to erase ambiguity from a fuller conception of language.

This, so far, is much about language for a short story, but James captures still more. His description, often beautiful, of Blanche Adney, marks the distance between achievement and aspiration and—importantly for understanding inflection in language—the way in which we can discern the quiet disappointment of unachieved aspiration in a person's words. Her higher ambitions, as yet unfulfilled even given her stardom, gave her mode of speech and interaction a very subtle yet still discernible "shade of tragic passion." She retained her "desire not to miss the great thing," and while years had passed, "none of the things she had done was the thing she had dreamed of" and this was "the ache beneath the smile." "It made her touching—made her melancholy more arch than her mirth." What the narrator finely spies just behind the thin veil of appearance is that despite all the success she "was haunted by the vision of a bigger chance" (*PL* 200) and had grown tired of her success with largely comedic roles that failed to fulfill her secret vision of the greater achievement. The narrator detected all this in the grain of her words, in the texture of her verbal style. In the face of such a case, the idea of separating this submerged but defining element of her persona from the words she used and the way they were inflected by this sensibility seems merely an anemic form of scientism: as Wittgenstein said and James showed, no genuine human understanding can come of that.

But it is the case of Vawdrey that takes us to the heart of the philosophical content of James's tale. Vawdrey is understood by all to be working assiduously on a new play. Yet inconsistencies arise concerning where he was at a given time, and on being asked about whether he was in his room writing in solitude or out with another party, the narrator detects "in his face a shade of confusion" (*PL* 201). This all leads to his saying to the group at dinner, "I don't think I really know when I do things," and not knowing what further to say, "he looked vaguely, without helping himself, at a dish just offered him." After dinner Vawdrey is invited, and expected, to read some passages of his new play, and Blanche offers to go to his room to retrieve the manuscript. He resists and as quickly insists that he will speak from memory, but in the moment "he had clean forgotten every word" and "his memory was a blank" (*PL* 202). Weaving together the growing significance of these sentences and their circumstances, later that evening the narrator goes up to retrieve Vawdrey's manuscript for a late-night perusal, and on entering the room sees that it is dark, but nevertheless sees that there is a man with the silhouette of Vawdrey hunched over a desk writing (he at first believes he has entered the wrong room). After a moment of disorientation, he calls out "Hullo, is that you, Vawdrey" (*PL* 207); the narrator will soon discover that the answer is both yes and no. He receives no response, and indeed no indication whatsoever that Vawdrey at the desk realizes he is there. He quietly leaves, unsettled and puzzled that Vawdrey seemed not to notice his presence at all and that he was writing in the complete dark. The narrator confides in us that his unsettled agitation increased with time rather than the reverse, precisely because "great anomalies are never so great at first as after we've reflected on them. It takes us time to use up explanations" (*PL* 208). The observation of James here is brief but profound: as we "use up explanations," we proceed through alternative explanations, deleting them as truth-candidates one by one—but usually in a way where the falsification of one inflects the plausibility of another. This is a matter of the interaction of sentences of a kind to which proponents of the coherence theory of truth have called attention: each small group of words assembled to form a declarative sentence does not carry their plausibility, their credibility, and ultimately their truth, in a manner wholly internal to them. As we saw in the discussion of Wittgenstein, words and sentences *themselves* interact. The tale could be read as a study in this aspect of language alone—the "detective" work of the narrator shows this interaction within his progress across the span of the story. But that is only one smaller part of a conceptually rich tale.

The narrator, having questioned various members of the group about where Vawdrey was at given times, makes his conclusion and states it boldly to Blanche Adney when she asks what he is driving at. He replies, "Simply to this, dear lady: that at the time your companion was occupied in the manner you describe he was also engaged in literary composition in his own room" (*PL* 211).

This connects back to the coherence theory issues: the narrator observes, in making his case about double identity to Blanche Adney, that the Vawdrey they see together, the person they know, does not display the genius the world sees in his writing. "Where is it in his talk?" (*PL* 212). His sentences in person do not stylistically fit with, interweave with, or unto themselves "converse" with, the sentences of his work, and in public, Vawdrey "disappoints every one who looks in him for the genius that created the pages they adore." Moreover, the person seated in deep concentration at the desk in the dark looked much more like the genius than does the Vawdrey they know. And so the narrator concludes: "There are two of them."

So for Vawdrey, "One goes out, the other stays at home" (*PL* 212). But James balances his narrative-philosophical structure by doubling the strangeness.

It emerges that Lord Mellifont "has the opposite complaint: he isn't even whole" (*PL* 214). That is, while there are two of Vawdrey, there is only one-half of Mellifont. He is only seen in public, and like Berkeley's claim that *esse est percipi*, he exists only in public and otherwise vanishes. His existence depends wholly on being perceived. Blanche Adney is beginning to puzzle this out, and in the conversation the narrator grasps the balanced form: Lord Mellifont "struck me as so essentially, so conspicuously and uniformly the public character that I read in a flash the answer to Blanche's riddle. He was all public and had no corresponding private life" (*PL* 215). James shows that, of course, Lady Mellifont could never learn this, precisely because when she was in his presence he always, by virtue of her perception of him, always existed (this is fundamentally a Kantian problem concerning the systematic inability to observe anything beyond the reach of our own perception and so to compare it to our perception—we are always there). Yet it made sense of her quiet suspicions of something amiss voiced earlier, and it now identifies the hidden object of her fear—that something would happen to him when away from her company. Indeed, the most extreme thing does happen to him when out of anyone's presence. (James prepares this with puzzles concerning his being there, then walking away and seeming not to be there, then startlingly reappearing when looked for and found.)

I will return to Mellifont later, but first let us consider how James deepens our understanding of Vawdrey's circumstance. Finally having had the experience of Vawdrey reading from "his" manuscript, Blanche Adney reports that it was "Magnificent, and he reads beautifully" (*PL* 218). And then the exchange, layered with significance, demands quoting in full:

"Almost as well as the other one writes!" I laughed.

This made her stop a moment, laying her hand on my arm. "You utter my very impression! I felt he was reading me the work of another."

"In a manner that was such a service to the other," I concurred.

"Such a totally different person," said Blanche. We talked of this difference as we went on, and of what a wealth it constituted, what a resource for life, such a duplication of character.

"It ought to make him live twice as long as other people," I made out.

"Ought to make which of them?"

"Well, both; for after all they're members of a firm, and one of them would never be able to carry on the business without the other. Moreover mere survival would be dreadful for either." (*PL* 218)

IV

This is the story of a mind bifurcated, a mind layered in linguistic complexity (the story literalizes the psychological spatial metaphors), divided between (a) the actor and speaker of words and deeds on the scene, and (b) an internal narrator working above or behind that scene. It is the modernist position described earlier, living and working *within* language in the way Wittgenstein sees it in all its dimensions, aspects, and—as he used the image of the complex village—with all its hidden alleys and byways. Let us consider the previous exchange in this light:

(1) "Almost as well as the other one writes": reading aloud in public, writing in private, and the ongoing process of comparison between the two; judging either one against the other; reconciling the competing demands of either against the other.

(2) "In a manner that was such a service to the other": drawing resources from one to the other; recognizing that these two voices collaborate; listening to the advice the inward writer whispers to the outward speaker.

(3) "Such a totally different person": recognizing and acknowledging difference within oneself; understanding it as a source of personal "wealth" and drawing on it; finding and inner resourcefulness through it.

(4) "Live twice as long": seeing that an enriched consciousness in this sense doubles; comprehending the two as members of a single "firm"; recognizing inwardly the enriching interdependence.

This is certainly not the Lockean mind, but it is the Wittgensteinian (who said that most of his philosophical writings are conversations with himself tete-a-tete) and it is, of course, the Jamesian. All of this, taken together, gives content to the contrast between the premodernist and the modernist conceptions of the mind's self-negotiating narrative.

But what then of this line?

(5) "mere survival would be dreadful."

This phrase takes us back to Mellifont. At one moment, Mellifont believes that his walking companion, Blanche Adney, is gone, and he disappears. Just as quickly he reappears when in company. Living a gap-inclusive existence, Mellifont is there, and then "utterly gone, as gone as a candle blown out," and then again, as Adney reports, "as soon as my voice rang out—I uttered his name—he rose before me like the rising sun." In response to the narrator's question, "And where did the sun rise?" she answers, "Just where it ought to—just where he would have been and where I should have seen him had he been like other people" (*PL* 222). This is the polemical extreme of lacking the inner resources described earlier; it is a mind utterly absent the internal narrator. And although, of course, there are no such actual people, James has demarcated the polemical extremes marking a continuum along which we all are placed. And being complex creatures of the kind James is portraying, we are placed at different positions along that continuum at different times—at different stages of life, at different times of year, month, day, or hour. (A close reading of James's final three great novels with this single theme highlighted could show this handily.)[15]

At the close of this tale there are still more cases where language is presented as far more intricate, and as we saw above layered, than any premodernist Lockean account could accommodate: the narrator, almost ready to act on the impulse to open Lord Mellifont's room door suddenly and without making a sound to "see what he will see" (*PL* 226) (i.e., an empty room until the moment he makes his presence audible) he finds Lady Mellifont just next to him. "Her lips formed the almost soundless entreaty: 'Don't!'" But discerning countervailing meaning beneath this, the narrator says, "Yet I thought I caught from her frightened face a still deeper betrayal—a possibility of disappointment if I should give way. It was as if she had said: 'I'll let you do it if you take the responsibility'" (*PL* 226–27). He does not go in, and later in bidding him farewell she said goodbye but in a way that what "she really conveyed" was thanks for what he might have done but that "it's better as it is" (*PL* 228).

Direct statement, indirect statement, allusion, direct or subtle implication, half-hidden reference, mid-sentence reconsideration, measures of one sentence against a possible or imagined better or subtlety different sentence, variations in the force of an utterance, meaning-shading variations in the tone of an utterance, the inextricably interwoven nature of sentence-meaning, ethical sensitivity shown in a withheld or paused or reframed sentence, and so many more fine linguistic nuances are presented and investigated by James just in his philosophical story. He presents language as we actually use it and have long cultivated it—precisely Wittgenstein's fundamental philosophical aspiration against the dehumanizing scientistic picture of an ideal language "purified" of everything that makes it *ours*.

It is for all these reasons that James's work can fall under the generic heading "realism" and that his work can be regarded as philosophical literature.

(Wittgenstein also mentions the difficulty of maintaining realism in philosophy but without reducing this to empiricism.) But in closing, let us sum up the reasons James can be regarded (as I mentioned at the outset) as standing near the front of an emerging distinctively modernist narrative sensibility.[16] James's entire approach to language is fundamentally incompatible with the Lockean picture and deeply consistent with the modernist elements in Wittgenstein's approach; Wittgenstein's considerations of word-meaning, extending into sensation-naming, idea-association, the nature and expression of cognitive content (with a reconsideration of the inner-chamber model that can be implied by "content"), the concept of mental privacy, the notion of rule-following, the "bringing back" of words, the very idea of an originary act of naming, the grip of a "picture," the dubiousness of the distinction between word and deed, and the encompassing idea of language as a form of life are all of a piece with James's narrative language. Just as words and sentences interweave and inflect each other, so on a larger scale do Wittgenstein's philosophy and James's writing. And within James's story we saw (a) webs of relations within which words *work*; (b) words spoken and unspoken and the meaning-determining space between; (c) the intimation of content not yet articulated; (d) steps into the realm of indirect communication; (e) unconscious motivations or linguistic meaning only discerned later; (f) the "conducting" of an "orchestra" of sentences that deliver a meaning that they individually do not express; (g) the idea of the spirit of an utterance and knowing how to go on within a given spirit (and a connection between such "spirit" and Wittgenstein's phrase "a form of life"); (h) an emotion (in this case, fear) that has an object one senses but cannot yet either articulate or face squarely (so this is a variety of meaning that is in a sense in language but not in the words of that language); (i) the nuanced relations between human gestures and expressions and their force in determining precise meaning; (j) again, the questioning of the distinction between word and deed, but here as shown in literature; (k) the idea of a *style* in speech, what language as a sign system could not capture, and the possibility of hidden revelatory aspects of a verbal or expressive style; (l) how we can hear unspoken aspects of a person's life within the fabric or grain of a person's words (e.g., unfulfilled aspirations, quiet disappointment, "a shade of tragic passion"); (m) how evidence mounts by sentences working together (and all that this implies for the problems of atomism in linguistic analysis); (n) the way we "use up" explanations in driving toward truth and the interactions between words and sentences themselves independently of our intentional content; and (o) the idea of a stylist fit between speech and text and our ability to judge this beyond the scope of any single statement or utterance.

As we saw, James wrote of how complex we are now, and how much more difficult that psychic and thus linguistic complexity is to present, to capture, on the boards of a theater stage. On the premodernist Lockean picture, we could present mental life and its workings with, in James's words, "comparatively little sacrifice of their completeness and their truth." If such a model were accurate, there would be little to sacrifice. In the case of Lord Mellifont, the extreme case, there is nothing to sacrifice. But with Clare Vawdrey in there, always writing with a world of linguistic consideration and reconsideration interminably swirling around him as he composes the multiple and layered words of his life, there would be so much potential loss of completeness and truth that we would need a Ludwig Wittgenstein and a Henry James to begin to accommodate the intricacy. "Today we're so infinitely more reflective and complicated and diffuse."

Notes

1 John Locke, *An Essay Concerning Human Understanding*, ed. Peter H. Nidditch (Oxford: Oxford University Press, 1979), 402. Hereafter cited in the text as *EHU*.

2 Ludwig Wittgenstein, *Philosophical Investigations*, 4th ed. revised, ed. P. M. S. Hacker and Joachim Schulte, trans. G. E. M. Anscombre, P. M. S. Hacker, and Joachim Schulte (Malden, MA: Wiley-Blackwell, 2009), §15. Hereafter cited in the text as *PI*.

3 Robert B. Pippin captures this point exceptionally well in his writing on James; his observation is acute. He writes: "Here [*What Maisie Knew*] and in other novels and stories, James seems to suggest a link between a *resistance to the exercise of power over one* and the *achievement of an inner realm of one's own* as well as a link between a *first-personal avowal* or expression or assertion of such a view of one's own and *a stand taken* in the social world that affects what others would otherwise be able to do, often against what they propose to do, and in a way that can function as a sort of test of the genuineness of the avowal. He treats these two dimensions, private and social, as virtually co-constitutive; it is by resisting the 'incursions' of others that such a realm is achieved. . . . This is contrary to views of some *prior* private, inner realm." Robert Pippin, "On Maisie Knowing Her Own Mind," in *A Companion to Henry James*, ed. Greg W. Zacharias (Malden, MA: Blackwell, 2008), 127–28. Pippin sees that James is showing, and investigating the intricacies of, the co-constitutive nature of the private and the public. The private, if an intelligible concept, is in this sense inextricably housed within the public.

4 See Garry Hagberg, "Word and Object: Museums and the Matter of Meaning," in *Philosophy and Museums: Essays on the Philosophy of Museums*, ed. Victoria Harrison, Anna Bergqvist and Gary Kemp (Cambridge: Cambridge University Press, 2016), 261–93.
5 In a remarkable passage in James's *Prefaces to the New York Edition*, he writes as if having just read Wittgenstein on the foundational importance of particularity in investigating meaning in language. James writes, "They [a group of stories he has assembled] testify indeed, as they thus stand together, to no general intention—they minister only, I think, to an emphasized effect. The particular case, in respect to each situation depicted, appealed to me but on its merits." Henry James, *The Figure in the Carpet and Other Stories*, ed. Frank Kermode (London: Penguin, 1986), 37.
6 I offer a discussion of this phrase and its significance for aesthetic understanding in Garry L. Harberg, *Meaning and Interpretation: Wittgenstein, Henry James, and Literary Knowledge* (Ithaca, NY: Cornell University Press, 1994), 45–83; central to the topic is Wittgenstein, *Philosophical Investigations* §241.
7 Cited in Terry Eagleton, *Sweet Violence: The Idea of the Tragic* (Oxford: Blackwell, 2003), 191.
8 Ibid., 191.
9 I discuss reading and re-reading from a Wittgensteinian point of view in Garry L. Hagberg, "Wittgenstein Re-Reading," in *Wittgenstein Reading*, ed. Sascha Bru, Wolfgang Huemer, and Daniel Steuer (Berlin: Walter de Gruyter, 2012), 243–62.
10 Henry James, "The Private Life," in *The Figure in the Carpet and Other Stories*, ed. Kermode, 191. Hereafter cited in the text as *PL*.
11 James, in his prefaces for *The New York Edition*, describes precisely this experience with language (sensing a rich range of connections and associated cognitive content but not being able to presently articulate them without further investigation); he writes of his initial idea for "The Private Life" that the "piece . . . rests for me on such a handful of acute impressions as I may not here tell over at once." Capturing this in a beautiful phrase, of the growing idea in his mind for the story he writes that, as he contemplated it, "the whole possibility was made to glow." Such ideas "glow" precisely because of the detection of meaning-associations in a sense present yet still beyond what one can presently in that moment see or name. James, of course, understands how this phenomenon in language directly interconnects to person-perception; of his initial thinking about the story, he refers to an actual person (a model for Vawdrey) whose "rich implications and rare associations" and "the genius to which he owed his position and his renown" were not in evidence in personal contact. Sensing content beyond what one empirically sees is Wittgenstein's "imponderable evidence" but in the attributes and qualities of

persons rather than exclusively in language (not to suggest that these are ultimately separable categories). James, *The Figure in the Carpet and Other Stories*, 50–52.

12 James was especially sensitive to the issue of implied or connoted content that enriched the words on the page, and one important aspect of his art was to manage this dimension of linguistic content with extreme care. In many places, in life as in literature, what one wants to preserve is the sense of further content not articulated; one can say too much and, in making too much explicit, ruin the expression. (The space of implication, the space between what is directed, stated, and the further reach of those stated words beyond the explicit, is the "opened space" of the modernist approach or focus on this aspect of language that I mentioned earlier.) In James's book *Hawthorne*, having just quoted a long passage from *The Scarlet Letter*, James writes, "That is imaginative, impressive, poetic; but when, almost immediately afterwards, the author goes on to say that 'the minister looking upward to the zenith, beheld there the appearance of an immense letter—the letter A—marked out in lines of dull red light,' we feel that he goes too far, and is in danger of crossing the line that separates the sublime from its intimate neighbour. We are tempted to say that this is not moral tragedy, but physical comedy. In the same way, too much is made of the intimation that Hester's badge had a scorching property, and that if one touched it one would immediately withdraw one's hand. Hawthorne is perpetually looking for images which shall place themselves in picturesque correspondence with spiritual facts with which he is concerned, and of course the search is of the very essence of poetry. But in such a process discretion is everything, and when the image becomes importunate it is in danger of seeming to stand for nothing more serious than itself." Henry James, *Hawthorne,* forward by Dan McCall (Ithaca, NY: Cornell University Press, 1997), 94. To put the matter in Wittgensteinian terms, one could say that moral tragedy shows more than it says.

13 Clifton Fadiman captured the way that James works inside of language, free of any direct-expression picture of language, well. He wrote, "To James, writing is not an opportunity for self-expression, or at least not merely for self-expression. It is first a problem, not first a solution. He thought about writing as Mozart must have thought about music. . . . That writing must express something goes without saying, but everything, for James, lies in the manner, the method of the expression. What is to be expressed must first be grasped in all possible relations (the opposite of impressionism); then a form must be discovered to enclose all these relations in the best conceivable way." Clifton Fadiman, Introduction to *The Short Stories of Henry James*, ed. Fadiman (New York: Random House, 1945), xvii. Fadiman's remark about impressionism is particularly insightful: impressionism is the direct artistic analogue of Lockean empiricism. A way of characterizing Wittgenstein's starting point in his philosophy is that we should see word-meaning not in terms of

a one-to-one match between sign and referent but rather in terms of a network of relations within which the word has resonance and function.

14 Garry L. Hagberg, "A Person's Words: Literary Characters and Autobiographical Understanding," in *Philosophy and Autobiography*, ed. Christopher Cowley (Chicago: University of Chicago Press, 2015), 39–71.

15 There is also a sense in which James's own work in preparing *The New York Edition* itself represents the kind of modernist doubled narrative mind or intellectual sensibility that I am discussing here. The many hundreds of revisions of *The American* for that late uniform edition show a mind rewriting, or in its way providing a voice-over for, its prior depiction of a mind in action and in reflection. It is a reading of the original 1877 version with James's own handwritten emendations of 1907 that shows this unmistakably. See Henry James, *The American: The Version of 1877 Revised in Autograph and Typescript for the New York Edition of 1907*, Houghton Library Manuscript Facsimiles I (London: Scolar Press, 1976). For example, in 1877: "Presently she returned, rubbing her hands." In 1907: "Presently she returned, clasping her hands together and shaking them at him" (46). Every page has dense changes; some have supplemental inserts of four pages, some have handwritten inserts of six or more. One could claim that a study of all the changes shows on the level of fine linguistic detail the transition from a late Victorian to an early modernist sensibility, and that would be right. But my point at present is a different one: the very fact that there are so many exceedingly intricate changes itself shows the modernist sensibility of James's mind; like Vawdrey, he is forever in a world of formulation with selected and rejected reformulations "hovering" around the words on the page. Again, he is working inside the world of words, and not seeing them as mere transducers for independent and prior cognition. One could say the massive undertaking represented in *The New York Edition* is itself a large-scale depiction and enactment of the modernist mind-in-language.

16 Before closing I should mention that it would be easy (as indeed I may have suggested here) to draw the contrast too sharply between what I am identifying as the premodernist and the modernist intellectual sensibility and approach to language. There are anticipations of this position in numerous periods, but one striking case is in one of the first philosophical autobiographies. Of Augustine's *Confessions*, Frank Kermode writes, "Augustine's meeting of himself reminds us once more that in a sense all autobiographers take on the properties of doubles, acquiring a sort of personal ambiguity." See Frank Kermode, *Pieces of My Mind: Essays and Criticism, 1958–2002* (New York: Farrar, Straus and Giroux, 2003), 291, which he goes on to discuss in terms of competing and ever-reformulating self-descriptions, among other aspects of doubleness. But then one could also draw the contrast too weakly: historical anticipations are cases specifically of

autobiography, and it may be true that the modernist approach brings out fully, continuously, and in high relief what was before only the special-case exception. It was Virginia Woolf, also standing at the pivot between late Victorian and early modernist, who famously claimed that on or about December 1910, human character changed. Of course, this is too suggestive, too vague, and too strong all at once to be genuinely compelling (however enticingly suggestive it may be), but if one looks into her writing one sees that she meant by "character" human psychology and even, perhaps, our approach to language and the nature of our relation to it. The fact that there is too much in her unwieldy claim does not mean that there is nothing in it. And to be fair, she herself noted the arbitrariness of this dating, and she said that the change she sensed was not immediate but rather gradual across a number of years around that time. One imagines a Jamesian asking her: "You mean we are all now Vawdreyesque?" I offer a discussion of Augustine in connection with these themes in "Wittgenstein, Augustine, and the Content of Memory," in *Augustine and Wittgenstein*, ed. Kim Paffenroth (Totowa, NJ: Rowman and Littlefield, forthcoming).

5

Henry James and the Crypto-Psychological Novel: Remarks on the Mindfulness of *The Awkward Age*

José Antonio Álvarez-Amorós

It is part of the critical convention to argue that Henry James's post-dramatic evolution toward modernist forms of fiction in the late 1890s was enlivened by the occurrence of a narrative oddity such as *The Awkward Age* (1898–99). If there is a work in his canon that flies in the face of expectation and merits description in broadly synonymous terms such as "objective," "dramatic," or even "behaviorist" in view of its scenic quality and sustained dialogic makeup, it is no doubt the story of Nanda Brookenham and her smart associates in fin-de-siècle, well-to-do London society. The implications of this uninspiring truism, however, have been too often extended to the presentation of mental functioning in this novel with the net result that, barring some local exceptions, the whole narrative is persistently viewed as mind*less*—in other words, as a vast surface where only occasional and unintended chinks allow brief glimpses of mental states and dispositions that generally count as so many slips in James's modus operandi rather than as deliberate compositional moves. This is simply not true, or, at best, it is just a partial account of how fictional minds are constructed and represented in *The Awkward Age*. It can be argued, I think, that this novel contains no less information about the interiority of characters than other, more overtly "psychological," Jamesian narratives, and so, from this particular angle, it should not be viewed as a glaring anomaly. In the ultimate analysis, it turns out to be a novel that displays a high density of mind—at least higher than most commentators have so far acknowledged, harnessed as they are to the so-called internalist paradigm within which mental life is conceived of as something hidden, unfathomable, opaque, and ruminative that can be exposed only by unnatural means such as narrative omniscience or dramatic soliloquy.[1]

The alleged absence from *The Awkward Age* of conventional, propositional methods to probe minds and describe their contents, coupled with the overwhelming presence of dialogue, has led critics to view this novel as a curious deviation from James's compositional norm. But if we read it within the limits of the externalist paradigm, which contemplates mental life as a public, social phenomenon fully geared to external action and behavior, and dialogically operative *between* individuals rather than *in* them, it seems indisputable that James retains in this novel the title of "historian of fine consciences" that was bestowed on him by his friend and fellow-novelist Joseph Conrad early in the twentieth century.[2]

Following this line of thought, I would like to suggest that the undeniable formal peculiarities of *The Awkward Age* only marginally affect its psychological thrust or impair its capacity to conjure up mental life for the reader. All that is required is a modest shift of paradigm, some adjustment of the critical gaze, to bring the whole gamut of indices of mental functioning into view and contribute to turning a seemingly mind*less* novel into a genuinely mind*ful* one. To achieve this purpose, I shall draw on the theoretical and critical insights developed by cognitive narratology, and especially on three basic principles that I will briefly outline later to contextualize my discussion—that is, the emphasis laid on the functional identity of real-life minds and fictional minds; the inborn compulsion of human beings to see minds behind all external actions; and, finally, the conviction that the verbal functioning of consciousness is *only* a part of a much larger phenomenon. These three principles and their subsequent ramifications will inform my attempt to lay bare the remarkable saturation of mind hidden away by the narrator beneath the seemingly behaviorist surface of this perplexing novel.

Some Context: *The Awkward Age* and James's "Years . . . within the Black Abyss"

Leon Edel, James's influential biographer, editor, and critic, always showed a special knack for coining lapidary phrases to describe Jamesian circumstances and achievements. The six-year period that intervened between the notorious failure of his play *Guy Domville* early in 1895 and the turn of the century, for instance, is best known as his "treacherous years," after the title of one of Edel's sections of his biography of James.[3] Not so popular, but equally descriptive and accurate, is his reference to James's post-dramatic period as his "years . . . within the black abyss."[4] Both coinages are, to my mind, essentially apt. The catastrophic end of his career as a playwright dealt a harsh blow to his self-esteem and deeply affected his personality and mental disposition, as well as his professional and artistic outlook. During these abyssal years of dejection and insecurity, James published four novels, *The Spoils of Poynton* (1896), *The Other House* (1896), *What Maisie Knew* (1897), and *The Awkward Age*; three novellas, "The Turn of the Screw" (1898), *In the Cage* (1898), and, somewhat later, *The Sacred Fount* (1901); and a number of tales, of which "Covering End" (1898) is directly relevant to my discussion. If one sets *The Awkward Age* against this background, a kind of nuanced uniqueness seems to emerge. In questions of form, it shares the supremacy of dialogue with *The Other House* and "Covering End," but not with the others, which rather adhere to the conventional Jamesian alternation of narrative, thought report, and conversational snatches. Only the latter parts of *What Maisie Knew* tend to show a predominance of dialogue, as if forming a transition to James's compositional choice in *The Awkward Age* one year later. The overwhelming weight of dialogue in *The Other House* and "Covering End" stems from the fact that both were initially scripted for the stage and assumed a narrative mold only when they failed to interest theater managers. But this is not the case with *The Awkward Age*, for there is no evidence that James ever thought of it as a prospective play. If we adopt quality as the yardstick, *The Awkward Age* stands quite clear of the other two dialogue pieces. While James disparages the latter in his private correspondence as hack work for the benefit of his pocket, he goes out of his way to praise *The Awkward Age* as "a fable of superior quality,"[5] calls it a "treasure,"[6] and, on re-reading it a decade later, confesses to being "positively struck by the quantity of meaning and the number of intentions."[7] Finally, discrepancies also accrue when one considers how James treats his *données* in his notebooks, and the finished works in the much-later prefaces to *The New York Edition*. While *The Awkward Age* was never envisaged in dramatic terms in the notebook stage, *The Spoils of Poynton*, *The Other House*, and *What Maisie Knew* enjoyed this privilege more or less extensively. However, the dramatic qualities of *The Awkward Age* do focus most of James's attention in the 1908 preface to this novel, whereas the other works—save for *The Other House*, which was excluded from *The New York Edition*—are never discussed as plays in their respective prefaces, or in any terms that may hint at James's visualization of them as such.

The Awkward Age is customarily viewed as crowning James's post-dramatic years—his years within the black abyss—with a remarkable feat of creative strength. Not only did he produce a "monstruous" volume when a small, simple story was initially intended (*AN* 99), but daringly opted for a sustained dialogic form that had proved inadequate in his hands to convey complex subjects a few years earlier, when he temporarily dropped the novel for the stage. No serious critic has denied *The Awkward Age* its condition as "a fable of superior quality," though many have noted James's skill in presenting both character and situation with little or no degree of mental display. As suggested earlier, critical judgments of this type need qualification, and this is best provided, in my view, within the externalist approach to the fictional mind.

Dialogue, Narrative Objectivity, and the Poetics of (Not) "Going Behind"

Ever since its earliest reviews, most of the critical attention received by *The Awkward Age* has focused around thematic, ethical, and reader-response issues rather than on the singularity of its compositional form. It was James himself who first subscribed to this critical line in the privacy of his notebooks when he sketched the basic situation for this novel without the slightest hint at the consistent dialogic technique that he adopted later, probably as a felicitous afterthought.[8] A cursory look at the reviews of 1899 will throw up a set of recurrent features that sensitized contemporary readers, such as immorality, the novel being "to some extent a study of degeneration"[9]; lethal, satiric depiction of smart London society in "microscopic detail"[10]; boundless subtlety that impairs comprehension and makes the novel enigmatic, "the very quintessence of riddle"[11]; the coolness and bloodlessness of characters, their "intellectual remoteness from the flesh" and "lack of virility"[12]; and, of course, James's craftsmanship and attention to technical minutiae that are mostly seen as compensation for an otherwise-thematically unpleasant novel. Yet the unusual persistence of dialogue in *The Awkward Age* scores fairly low in the reviewers' scale of interest. One can hardly find a few passing references to it, often thrown in simply as evidence of its insufferable emptiness. "Nine-tenths of the book are conversation," reads the *Saturday Review*, "and consist of tedious vain repetition,"[13] while the *Indianapolis News* follows suit and tells its readership that the novel "is made up almost entirely of dialogue, or chatter, which is . . . vacuous and inane."[14] Further allusions exist, but they are just brief, factual descriptions that do not even relate the dialogic consistency of *The Awkward Age* to James's recent theatrical experience.[15]

Such general indifference to the pervasiveness of dialogue in this novel and its many implications was not to last long. In his 1908 preface, James amply amended his omission of the dialogic issue from his notebook entries and, in a belated though predictable move, discussed at length not only his choice and the reasons for it but also the dramatic impulse behind the composition of this novel. In a mood of elation, he recollects how he composed *The Awkward Age* as if he were "in fact constructing a play," records his present anxiety "to keep the philosophy of the dramatist's course before [him]," and insists that Nanda's situation "presents itself on absolutely scenic lines, and . . . abides without a moment's deflection by the principle of the stage play" (*AN* 113, 115). This seems to have thrown critics onto the right scent. Just after James's death, Beach summarizes the features that bespeak the play behind the novel, namely the almost-total restriction "to what is said," the wealth of paralinguistic indicators of how "remarks are delivered or received," and the minute attention to "the position of his actors on the stage," their exits and entrances.[16] In 1921, Lubbock insisted that this work "might indeed be printed as a play," since "whatever is not dialogue is simply a kind of amplified stage direction";[17] and later critics, such as Geismar, Isle, Perosa,[18] and many others, whether devotees or not of this kind of play-novel, are also categorical in this respect.

But formal continuity between James's dramatic and post-dramatic years is not the only reason for the centrality of dialogue in *The Awkward Age*. The novelist himself gave a sound, straightforward explanation in his preface, which successive generations of critics have chosen to ignore and replace with increasingly strained ones. Both in the notebook entry of April 19, 1894, in his letter to Henrietta Reubell of November 12, 1899, and in the said preface, James describes the theme of his work as "belonging essentially to the ironic, to the order of fine comedy,"[19] as lending itself "to an ironic—lightly and simply ironic!—treatment,"[20] and as being only properly addressed "with light irony," since "it would be light and ironical or it would be nothing" (*AN* 106). Leaving aside his puzzling insistence on irony and levity in a rather dismal work like *The Awkward Age*, James is quite definite that the tone envisaged for this novel made him choose what he calls "the least solemn form to give it" (*AN* 106)—in other words, the dialogue-based narrative. However, James is not explicitly referring to dialogue here, for he only establishes this equation in a roundabout way by linking his "least solemn form" to that practiced by Gyp, the pseudonym of a contemporary French female writer of dialogue romances intended to be read rather than enacted. Though critics like Tintner have argued that her influence on James was both formal *and* thematic,[21] he only acknowledged having borrowed from her the dialogic technique, albeit with a fundamental difference—instead of placing the characters' names before their lines, as happens in dramatic scripts, he resorted to the more novelistic expedient of transferring the identification of speakers to attributive tags such as "Mr Mitchett replied" or "said his lordship."[22] James's experience of having unsuccessfully published playbooks like his two series of *Theatricals* (1894) convinced him that the British public would not read printed plays unless paraphrased as novels. Hence his epistolary confessions that old, unacted plays had better be disguised as narratives before bringing them out,[23] or his intimations in the preface that he had to dissimulate "the Gyp taint" and "the baleful association" by "the covering of [his] tracks," in which he feels he was completely successful (*AN* 108). So James's plan to match light irony and comedy with "the least solemn form" is internally coherent, though one may doubt if *The Awkward Age* merits this description or even wonder why dialogue should intrinsically be a lowly literary form.

To conceive of *The Awkward Age* as a play-novel, that is to say, as an uncanny artifact placed astride two genres, brings in a number of issues related to the location and functioning in it of fictional minds, since dialogue is often viewed as inducing an acute mindlessness in this work.[24] This unexpected condition in a medium so congenial to psychological analysis as James's narrative can best be defined by the interplay of three notions—exteriority, objectivity, and (absence of) "going behind." This last is a Jamesian coinage whose meaning should be explored beyond the obvious, while the others are fairly current ideas in elementary narrative theory. Though not exactly coextensional, all three have been rendered almost interchangeable by casual critical usage.

By exteriority we understand a text's resistance to the construction and representation of minds. In the case of *The Awkward Age*, such resistance seems to enjoy wide critical endorsement, for I have only found three cursory references to James's "psychological" management of character and situation in contemporary reviews, and only one of them about the display of "mental states . . . in 'The Awkward Age'" through "the evolutions and intricacies of expression"[25] is specific to this novel and actually encodes an accurate perception of how minds can underlie external action. That only one of these allusions to the mentalist nature of *The Awkward Age* is actually convincing should not conceal the fact that early newspaper commentary often differs from later, more reflective criticism, as when the former remained insensitive to the uncommon weight of dialogue in this novel, while the latter made much of it.

Professions of exteriority in *The Awkward Age* are the critical norm rather than the exception and tend to come in two flavors—direct and indirect. When Lubbock states that "there is no insight into anybody's mind" in this novel;[26] when, seventy years later, Tintner opposes Gyp to James in that one "recorded the thoughts of Paulette," while the other "kept such material out of his novel";[27] or when Kurnick, in a different key, ascribes to this work a "cultivated disinterest in questions of psychological depth" and an "active disinterest in questions of psychological truth,"[28] they are all making direct commitments to the formal mindlessness of *The Awkward Age*. Equally frequent are those professions of exteriority that, instead of plainly advocating a mental void for this novel, make its existence contingent on the meaning attached to other terms such as "objectivity" or (absence of) "going behind." For instance, Perosa's "objectivity of presentation" and "total avoidance of 'going behind,'" Teahan's "deliberate renunciation of 'going behind,'" and Stevenson's statement that "James 'goes behind' none of the characters" entirely depend on how we construe these two terms.[29]

"Going behind," or its absence, is a Jamesian expression that has gained some currency among critics working on his post-dramatic narrative. It is based on a spatial analogy that embodies a nonspatial domain, and it is this domain that is not easy to pin down. James does not think of a horizontal surface, for, in this case, he would have probably said "go beneath"; nor does he imagine an enclosed cavity, like the usual spatial projection of consciousness, for he would have resorted to terms like "enter" or "penetrate," quite popular with theorists and critics when they wish to present minds as internal phenomena. He rather says "go behind," and the precise movement denoted by this phrase conjures up a kind of vertical surface that can be readily associated with the theater backdrop and the bustling, unsavory world that exists behind it. The familiar idiom "(to go) behind the scenes," for instance, is based on this same idea of disclosing to the uninitiated a private space beyond that which meets the naked eye.

Four Jamesian passages containing this expression bear directly on my discussion, two excerpted from his correspondence and two from his prefaces.

In a celebrated letter to Mrs. Humphry Ward of July 26, 1899, in which he vehemently puts her right about his compositional assumptions, James admits that "there are as many magnificent and imperative cases as you like of presenting a thing by 'going behind' as many forms of consciousness as you like," and goes on to say:

> I "go behind" right and left in "The Princess Casamassima," "The Bostonians," "The Tragic Muse," just as I do the same singly in "The American" and "Maisie," and just as I do it consistently *never* at all (save for a false and limited *appearance*, here and there, of doing it a *little*, which I haven't time to explain) in "The Awkward Age."[30]

In another letter to Henrietta Reubell of November 12, 1899, while discussing *The Awkward Age* in quasi-behaviorist terms, he speaks of "no going behind, no *telling about* the figures save by their own appearance and action and with explanations reduced to the explanation of everything by all the other things *in* the picture."[31] Almost one decade later, the prefaces provide two additional instances of this expression, one in reference to *The Tragic Muse* (1890) and another—a crucial one—to *The Awkward Age*. "I never 'go behind' Miriam," he says, talking of his leading characters in *The Tragic Muse*, "only poor Sherringham goes, a great deal, and Nick Dormer goes a little, and the author . . . goes behind *them*" (*AN* 91). But given the extremity of form employed by James in *The Awkward Age*, it is this passage that has gained most critical prominence:

> This objectivity, in turn, when achieving its ideal, came from the imposed absence of that "going behind," to compass explanations and amplifications, to drag out odds and ends from the "mere" storyteller's great property-shop of aids to illusion: a resource under denial of which it was equally perplexing and delightful, for a change, to proceed. (*AN* 111)

Even a brief glance at these fragments will reveal that James uses his phrase in two closely related, though dissimilar, meanings. One of these is specific, exclusive, or "strong"; the other is less so in all respects and encompasses a wide range of compositional attitudes that describe what we could loosely call objective or behaviorist narrative. The only case in which James expressly links the notion of "going behind" to mental reporting is in his Mrs. Humphry Ward letter. He does so in two ways—overtly, by associating the term in question with the idea of consciousness; and covertly, by listing some of his novels and indicating *precisely* the kind of mental presentation he carries out in each, "right and left" meaning indiscriminate sounding of the minds of several characters, "singly" that of only one character per novel, whether Christopher Newman or Maisie Farange, and "consistently *never* at all" renouncing this privilege altogether. James, however, knows very well what he is on about, and enigmatically acknowledges some exceptions in *The Awkward Age*. As will be shown later, within the mass of evidence that supports the mindfulness of this novel, one can find a large number of authoritative, unambiguous statements of mental life in characters. Yet James's insistence on the *falsity* and *appearance* of his exceptions does not seem to point to this sort of statement, but rather to the wealth of inferential reports of mind introduced in this novel by operators like "evidently," "as if," or "it seemed," known to theorists as words of estrangement and instrumental in identifying conjectural access to interiority.[32]

In the other three cases, the gesture of "going behind" has a "weaker," more inclusive meaning. One can gather that mental reporting forms part of it, but such reporting is clearly diluted among a wider set of features whose absence characterizes narrative objectivity. In the Henrietta Reubell letter, abstention from "going behind" means "no[t] *telling about* figures save by their own appearance and action" and giving no explanations that do not follow from "all the other things *in* the picture"—in short, a commitment to objective reporting, to a kind of camera-mode narrative, in which there seems to be little room for mental construction and representation, if we stick to a conventional, internalist view of mind. The passage taken from *The Tragic Muse* preface is also ambiguous and a bit puzzling, for it implies that characters can "go behind" each other in varying degrees. In realistic narrative, and within the postulates of internalism, characters cannot sound each other's minds authoritatively as if they were omniscient narrators, but they can certainly discuss antecedents, give explanations, and form hypotheses about motives and mental states, which is, to my mind, what James is intimating here. The last passage is fairly equivalent to that in the Reubell letter, except for its rhetorical flair. In both, "explanations" are opposed to the idea of not "going behind," a movement toward narrative objectivity that this fragment explicitly underlines. But in none of them is "going behind" expressly associated with the process of mental reporting. For James, objectivity consists in withdrawing all explanations and amplifications of sense that cannot be observed by a keen onlooker, and this surely excludes strategies—"odds and ends"—such as authorial commentary and characterization, furnishing antecedents, and sliding up and down the temporal sequence, but also, implicitly, providing conventional access to minds. What James does in the last passage is to give a figurative, brief account of his usual pre-dramatic methods of the late 1870s and 1880s in order to show how he rejected them, for a change, in the composition of *The Awkward Age*.

Critics have mostly interpreted the gesture of "going behind" in what I have called its "strong," exclusive meaning of authoritative mental access, even if this usage is barely supported by the literality of James's own comments. Owen's view, for instance, is that dialogue stripped James of "one of his most powerful resources, the 'going behind' into the thoughts of his personages."[33] Both Isle and Brooks similarly concur. "No 'going behind'" equates to "no attempt to explore the psychology of the characters," says Isle, while Brooks outdoes James himself as he argues that "'going behind' is James's term for entering the mind of a character . . . and informing the reader of the processes at work in that consciousness."[34] Others, however, subscribe to a more comprehensive, if weaker, sense of not "going behind" and read James's refusal as "the omission of the novelist's traditional use of exposition to define his subject."[35] What eventually results from this brief analysis is the odd feeling that commentators have been using James's expression for decades without a definite sense of what it meant to him and how it affected their critical discussions. My own view is that the novelist employed it both with a general and a particular meaning, the latter being a kind of subset of the former. Narrative objectivity thus entails a number of compositional attitudes and procedures that could very well fit under the general rubric of not "going behind," but one of these procedures—want of mental reporting—outgrows its condition as a part of, and often becomes identified with, the whole.

Looking at a dialogue narrative like *The Awkward Age* in light of the triad composed by exteriority, objectivity, and (absence of) "going behind" yields some clear facts. With a few exceptions to be found in contemporary reviews, the critical stereotype for almost a century has been to conceive of this novel as mindless, that is, as if its dialogic format had inhibited the construction and reporting of characters' interiority. This stereotype has come down to us either in direct or indirect fashion, that is, either by categorically denying the existence of any mental insight or by defaulting to terms that have been unilaterally read as opposing such existence. Either way, Nanda's story has suffered a severe mental depletion—a lobotomy of sorts—administered by internalist critical practice, which, to me, does not seem irreversible.

Visible Minds in *The Awkward Age*: Theory and Practice

That objects and notions take on significance when considered within a specific intellectual paradigm has nothing startling about it. Likewise, to say that a shift of paradigm in the loosely Kühnian sense of the term will illuminate and make visible phenomena that would otherwise remain in the dark is not surprising either. As suggested at the outset, this is precisely the case with *The Awkward Age*, for we tend to see in it two different types of novels according to the conception of mind we adhere to. Generally speaking, classical narratology adopted the internalist perspective, from which the fictional mind is an entirely private, internal affair, whose presentation was just embarrassing because bringing it to the surface called for complicated, unnatural methods. Curiously enough, this position is shared by scholars who differ vastly in many other respects. For a mainstream Jamesian critic like Davidson, the mind is an enigmatic core, since "no outward signs can absolutely betray the precise content of complex and explicit thought"; whereas theorists like Margolin and Culpeper compatibly argue that "mental activity is essentially and inalienably individual" and that "we have no access to a person's mind."[36] For its part, and rather than banishing the internalist paradigm altogether, postclassical narratology focused on the tensions between the internal and the external views of mind. The externalist perspective conceives of the mind as a public, intersubjective phenomenon, not sited in the innermost recesses of the self, but on the surface, in the interstices between the individual nodes of the social tissue. It is thus reflected on our faces, actions, and general behavior, not requiring introspection or highly obtrusive methods to represent it. Once this externalist outlook has been absorbed by critical practice, indexes of mental functioning perceptibly begin to emerge and multiply.

In consequence, if set against a background of internalism, *The Awkward Age* is a mindless, almost behaviorist novel, in which mental reporting is infrequent and probably the result of a lapse of consistency on James's part. On finding little or even no propositional evidence of such reporting, this novel is pronounced an oddity—with James himself acquiescing to this view in his preface. The externalist paradigm, however, provides the theoretical foundation to apprehend *The Awkward Age* as a psychological narrative, for much information that could hardly be connected to mental functioning can now be decoded as clear signs thereof. Within the externalist paradigm, no novel can fail to construct and represent minds, except under strict experimental conditions.[37] In absolute terms, therefore, behaviorist novels are just mythical creatures, and it would be more accurate to rename them crypto-psychological, for that is precisely what they are.

Among the set of principles that substantiate the idea of a cognitive narratology, three are especially apposite to the kind of argument developed in this chapter. First, there is the conviction that fictional minds are not functionally different from their real-life counterparts,[38] a conviction that is often extended synechdotically to the whole of the literary character and its construction out of a mere string of words on the page. Ontologically, they are dissimilar phenomena, of course, but from a functional perspective—that is, what they can do or what effect they can make, rather than what they are—obstacles to assimilate both do not seem so formidable. One substantial difference between fictional and real minds persists, however, and it is that in appropriate circumstances of genre and cultural context one can have total authoritative access to the former, but hardly to the latter.

This functional identity underpins the second principle of cognitive narratology to be invoked here, namely the propensity among readers, narrators, and characters to posit minds behind observable behavior to make sense of it. Collectively known by the suggestive name of mind-reading or, more technically, as the Theory of Mind Mechanism (ToMM), a whole set of phenomena clustering around the indissoluble unity of thought and action—its visible terminal—lie behind this formulation. The automatic, biologically compulsive operation of ToMM counters mindlessness and opacity, thereby inhibiting the existence of totally behaviorist narratives, as indicated earlier. Only dichotomic from an internalist perspective, thought and action are two manifestations of the *same* phenomenon. Lubbock, a notable internalist, insists, for one, that *The Awkward Age* shows "action essentially, not the picture of a character or a state of mind."[39] From an externalist perspective, however, most of the information given in novels "inhabit[s] the large gray area" between mind report and external description of action.[40] In the fabricated sentence, "Nancy grimaced when her ex-husband entered the room," who can positively say if "grimaced" denotes a state of mind or an observable action? In such cases, any attempt at discriminating between both reveals a wishful, rather than analytic, attitude.

It is obvious, however, that mind-reading or decoding action as thought comes at the expense of a fairly low resolution in the presentation of interiority. This fact introduces a third principle of cognitive narratology—that is, that the verbal component of thought, often known as "inner speech," is but a small section of the whole mind, despite its privileged magnification by modernist stream-of-consciousness literature and classical, internalist narratology. Mind theorists focus on the whole mind as a composite of inner speech and, above all, nonverbal states of mind.[41] So, for them, it is seriously reductive to present characters' interiority by means of more or less mimetic categories such as direct, indirect, or free indirect thought that were originally developed for the reporting of speech;[42] they rather tend to prefer heavily diegetic modes, such as thought report, that, having no claim to literality, are best prepared to represent the blend of mind and action that characterizes this approach. The term "grimaced" in the preceding example is an extreme case of thought report, in which mental disposition and physical gesture are difficult to tell apart.

In a casual comparison carried out by Palmer between Dickens and James, the latter is labeled "the more internalist Henry James."[43] This is true in a sense, for, broadly speaking, James chose to follow in the 1890s an innovative path that eventually led to the typical modernist novel of consciousness. But it is also true that Dickens never attempted to write novels like *The Other House*, *The Awkward Age*, and *The Outcry* (1911), or tales like "Covering End," in which the mind leaves the depths of the self and occupies the social space between individuals owing to the dialogic form predominantly adopted. One should not forget that characters are *rarely* alone in *The Awkward Age*, and so the social aspects of mental functioning override introspection. Their minds are constantly engaged in controlling and negotiating interpersonal exchanges, the textual sections in which they are alone being comparatively negligible. Even when this happens, their minds are set on the upcoming social occasion, anticipating interaction, or reviewing previous encounters and their outcome, as when Vanderbank, left by himself in an empty room at the beginning of Book 8, fidgets around for a while and keeps looking at his watch in a state of expectancy coupled with mild impatience (*Age* 383–84). In rough numbers, conversation makes up 54 percent of the text of *The Awkward Age*, while in another contemporary dialogue narrative such as *The Other House* it only totals 47.5 percent. This is a high proportion indeed, though, judging by impression, one would expect an even higher one. It is just possible that the effect on the reader is enhanced, beyond the objectivity of figures, by an unconscious comparison with other Jamesian narratives and even with the prevailing *fin-de-siècle* realistic norm. In any case, the narrator still has 46 percent of the text available to build a solid density of mind in this novel, which he certainly does.

A close reading of *The Awkward Age* reveals several ways in which such construction and representation are effected. Two of them are basic and universal, unless deliberately avoided for experimental reasons, while the others branch off from these and show features that make them more specific to this novel. The two basic methods are authoritative direct access, and inferential or conjectural access. In its most overt, propositional form, direct access has been generally favored by classical, internalist narratology, and, held to be unusual in *The Awkward Age*, has originated the myth of mindlessness. Inferential access, for its part, builds on the principle that we are genetically primed to see minds behind external actions or gestures thanks to our inborn mind-reading skills, whereby we make sense of what we and others do. As noted earlier, it requires a shift of paradigm, but, once this has been achieved, the outcome is quite rewarding.

How are these two approaches textually implemented in *The Awkward Age*? In other words, how does the reader experience minds in this novel? What I have called authoritative direct access occurs when the narrator uses the world-constructing powers accorded to him by convention and creates a consciousness just by talking of it—a genuine performative act. This is the traditional omniscient narrator that Culler renames "telepathic" on account of how the task seems to be carried out.[44] Three aspects of this type of access merit discussion, namely modes, markers, and extent. Modes are the structures that channel mental activity in texts; markers are the words or expressions that denote such mental activity and may even articulate it syntactically; and extent is the physical magnitude of an instance of direct access, that is, whether it is an isolated term descriptive of a mental state ("anxious," e.g., *Age* 119, 229, 233) or a full propositional expression that can take up a significant textual fragment ("Vanderbank was more and more aware that kind of amusement he excited would never in the least be a bar to affection," *Age* 7). A few interconnected remarks on these three aspects may show *The Awkward Age* in a fresh light.

Many classifications of modes for representing consciousness were proposed in the 1970s and 1980s, the heyday of classical narratology.[45] They often adapt to inner speech the modes identified for the reporting of external speech, and, in this regard, the Leech-Short taxonomy is paradigmatic. The usual correlation between the verbal and the nonverbal mind and these reporting modes tends to associate inner speech with presumedly mimetic structures such as direct, free indirect, and indirect thought,[46] while an essentially diegetic mode like thought report can render the whole spectrum of mind and is thus privileged by cognitive narratologists for its "indispensable and pivotal role . . . in linking individual mental functioning to the social context."⁴⁷ In *The Awkward Age*, there are some instances of free indirect thought that may report snatches of inner speech. When Mitchy is left alone with Mr. Longdon we have a peep at his articulate mental reaction that bears the discursive hallmark of free indirect thought, "What was it? the fellow Vanderbank had made it a matter of such importance he should 'really know.' But were they simply to have tea together? No" (*Age* 119). Two other fragments may be equally interpreted, "Wouldn't that be a better finish of the evening than just separating in the wet?" (*Age* 4) and "Did this specimen of his class pull the tradition down or did he just take it where he found it . . . ?" (*Age* 242). Both are doubtful, however. The context does not clarify whether the former case represents internal or external speech; as for the latter, it could be either free indirect thought or a question rhetorically put by the narrator. Yet the immediate reference to Mr. Longdon wishing to avoid "a mental dilemma" rather upholds the first option.

Given its capacity to diegetically render all kinds of mental processes and states, it is thought report that carries the burden of direct access to mind in *The Awkward Age*. As noted earlier, it can take full propositional form, as for instance, "he therefore recognised . . . a congruity between the weather and the 'four-wheeler'" (*Age* 3), "he liked his new acquaintance, who struck him as in a manner clinging to him" (*Age* 4), "he . . . enjoyed . . . the sense of making a night of it" (*Age* 4), "Vanderbank wondered a moment what things in particular these might be" (*Age* 8), "Mrs Brookenham knew perfectly the meaning of this glance" (*Age* 48), "she . . . [was] pleased again to see no one else appear" (*Age* 204), "Both girls struck him as lambs with the great shambles of life in their future" (*Age* 239), "they recognized in silence that they were trying each other" (*Age* 265), and so on. Quite often, thought report shrinks to a finite verbal phrase indicating mental activity, but not elaborating on the content of such activity. These cases occur almost on every page—for example, "Vanderbank thought" (*Age* 15), "Mr Longdon pondered" (*Age* 13), "Again he meditated" (*Age* 70)— and a great many could be readily identified. Furthermore, there are also a large number of phrases or even single words semantically related to mental states and processes that contribute to direct description—for example, "flushed with recognition" (*Age* 127), "ignorance" (*Age* 239), "anxiety" (*Age* 262), "angry" (*Age* 297), "responsibly" (*Age* 347)—and should be considered micro-samples of thought report in their own right. In such cases, however, we come close to the boundary between direct and inferential access, for it is hard to say whether a term such as "amused" in "The friendly Mitchy was also much amused" (*Age* 81) exclusively depicts a mental state or also a visible complex of external action and body language.

Reference to these phrases and words and their semantic properties raises the issue of markers. Any reporting mode that is not "free," that is, syntactically independent of the linguistic context, has at its core a marker, an operator, either a *verbum cogitandi* or *sentiendi*. Canonically, they are verbs of consciousness that can attribute mental activity to characters and mark it as such, as is the case with most instances of propositional thought report quoted earlier. Words of this class, however, should not be restricted to those verbs semantically and syntactically framed to introduce mental content either as subordinate clauses ("Mrs Brookenham . . . hoped that Edward would accept the protest," *Age* 65) or as complements ("Mitchy thought of it," *Age* 473), but rather include *all* terms semantically equipped for mental description that just by themselves—for example, "emotion" (*Age* 97)—or in combination with others—for example, "not heedful of it" (*Age* 142), "the little worry of his contradiction . . . continued to fill his consciousness" (*Age* 154)—provide authoritative access to the minds of characters. This obviously connects to what I have called "extent," and, on another level, to the persistent critical claim of mindlessness in this novel. Such a claim is based, I think, not on the absence of mind reporting from *The Awkward Age*, but rather on the failure to recognize it unless it squares with our preconceptions. Unless, that is, it appears in full propositional terms over substantial textual stretches, since isolated words and phrases will seemingly not do. Traditionally identifiable mind reporting is not a rarity in *The Awkward Age*, as has been summarily shown, but it is also true that James's decision to dialogize this work did not form the best environment for it to thrive.

Inferential access, on the contrary, is ubiquitous and only by ignoring it altogether can one attribute any mindlessness to *The Awkward Age*. By no means reluctant to establish, for instance, that Nanda "felt herself at last to have found the right tone" (*Age* 503) or drop countless mind-determining words or phrases, the narrator often becomes squeamish within lines of having wielded his authority. In a paraliptic exercise,[48] he renounces his powers and resorts to conjecturing characters' interiors or silently passes the burden of mind-reading to the reader. It is the narrator himself who explains this modus operandi by willingly equating his cognitive capacity to that of his characters when he says, "As Mr Van himself couldn't have expressed . . . the particular effect upon him of the tone of these words, his chronicler takes advantage of the fact not to pretend to a greater intelligence" (*Age* 211–12), and so limits himself to behaviorist observation. Inferential access is ontologically non-authoritative, though functionally "description of surface behaviour can be as informative as the most direct inside view."⁴⁹ It requires the reader to become involved in second-degree gap-filling, mind-negotiating processes, for even the mental snapshots that allow him or her to construct a continuing consciousness frame are integral to action and have to be decoded from it.

The key question is, of course, how mental states are inferentially ascribed in *The Awkwrad Age*, or, in other words, *whose* mind-reading mechanism is activated at a given moment and how it is seen to operate in the text. My proposal is that there are two ways in which authoritative access is foregone in this novel and characters' minds are revealed and reflected in action. On the strength of the functional identity of real and fictional minds mentioned earlier, two figures engage in inferential attribution on the intratextual and extratextual planes—the narrator and the reader.⁵⁰ Intratextual decoding of action into thought is operated by the narrator in *The Awkward Age* and can be easily identified because it leaves two types of traces, namely the frequent use of words of estrangement,⁵¹ and the deployment by the narrator of an invented spectator or observer in order to deflect responsibility for mind-reading, a phenomenon that has been discussed by Herman under the rubric of hypothetical focalization.⁵² In both cases, the narrator disclaims authoritative reporting of mind and marks such reporting, in one way or another, as the inferential outcome of translating visible behavior into thought.

Words of estrangement are modal operators that facilitate mental description from an external perspective or, put differently, that highlight the explicit use of visible action as a key to interiority. If the narrator just says, "the taste of it all came back to him with a faint sweetness" (*Age* 32), he is authoritatively portraying a mental experience; but if he says, "he sighed out *as if* the taste of it all came back to him with a faint sweetness" (*Age* 32, my italics), he is inferentially decoding a physical gesture into mind, probably as a result of having adopted temporary anthropomorphic limitations. Words of estrangement can be viewed either as structural markers of perspective, whose occurrence does not affect the certainty of the reported thought,⁵³ or, closer to my conception, as indicators that may interfere with the ontological status of inner experience.⁵⁴ To say "He seemed disappointed at his wife's want of resources" (*Age* 72) is not the same, in my view, as saying "He was disappointed at his wife's want of resources." It is true that "seemed" allows the report of a mental state from an external angle, but it casts some doubt on such a state and underlines the inferential procedure whereby the narrator has come by it.

The scenic nature that James wanted for *The Awkward Age*, coupled with his inveterate taste for mental analysis, results in the use of many words of estrangement to hypothesize what the scenic method cannot, in principle, directly yield. Just by way of example, the narrator employs 196 instances of "as if," 106 of "appeared," 98 of "seemed," 41 of "perhaps," 25 of "visibly," 24 of "evidently," and other less frequent phrases such as "with an air of," "in all probability," "there might have been," and so on—all of them to modalize the representation of interiority. Thought report is the rendering mode generally associated with these words, but others are also possible, as is this rare instance of inner speech presented in direct thought and qualified by "perhaps": "Her companion for an instant perhaps meditated. 'It is probably not in my interest to say that . . . '" (*Age* 247). Given the abundance of dialogue in this novel, it is in the speech tags where these indicators tend to accumulate and make their effect.

The relative incompatibility of scenic makeup and mental reporting leads James to the ruse of frequently positing a spectator or observer and projecting on him the responsibility for inferring mental states out of externals. Save for this projection, I think, the method would be wholly analogous to the use of words of estrangement. This is a typical instance:

> A supposititious spectator would certainly on this have imagined in the girl's face the delicate dawn of a sense that her mother had suddenly become vulgar, together with a general consciousness that the way to meet vulgarity was always to be frank and simple and above all to ignore. (*Age* 323)

The narrator might have conjectured Nanda's feelings about vulgarity by linking gesture to mental state via words of estrangement, as he constantly does elsewhere, but in this passage he doubly disclaims the nature of her feelings, first because he does not state them authoritatively—for example, "Nanda sensed that her mother had become vulgar"—and second because he even refuses to take direct responsibility for inferring a mind behind the girl's countenance—for example, "Nanda's face seemed to show her sense that her mother had become vulgar." The positing of such a spectator or observer is not as pervasive as the occurrence of words of estrangement, and yet it forms a fairly obtrusive pattern. In this role, the word "spectator" appears sixteen times, "observer" fifteen, "auditor" three, and "analyst" once. In the case of "auditor," it is the quality of Van's laughter, for instance, which links to his state of uneasiness (*Age* 262). At times, moreover, a question can function as though an observer were invoked, as in "who can say whether or no [sic] she acutely guessed from his expression that he recognised this particular juncture . . . ?" (*Age* 234). Other contemporary dialogue narratives like *The Other House* or "Covering End" are also noted for constantly featuring invented spectators and observers who deputize for the narrator in questions of inferential attribution of minds.[55]

While it is the narrator's prerogative to leave explicit traces of mental access in a novel, the extratextual agent who performs mind-reading—the reader—is unable to do likewise in a peculiar, though, after all, conventional narrative like *The Awkward Age*, in which ontological boundaries remain intact and metalepses are unthinkable. Within the externalist paradigm and its insistence on the visibility of thought in action, readers may read Hemingway's "The Killers" (1927) as if they were reading *Madame Bovary* (1856), only with a larger demand on their ToMM, which intuitively strains to make mental sense of the behavioral data at its disposal. All actions have minds behind themselves, but this does not mean that all actions are equally transparent. In fact, one could place them along an axis of transparency. At one extreme, we have mentally loaded actions denoted, even in the isolation of dictionaries, by words whose definitions show a strong mental component—for example, "grimace," "fidget," or "wince"; at the other, we have more neutral ones that are harder to interpret as representing minds, or, more precisely, that can report mental content at a much lower resolution. Being a continuous axis, however, it is difficult to establish transitional boundaries between degrees of transparency, and so the mental weight of a particular action often depends on pragmatic issues, such as the reader's gap-filling ability.

Both in the narrative frame and omnipresent speech tags of *The Awkward Age*, description of significant action—that is, action that *begs* to be mentally decoded[56]—has an overwhelming presence. Take, for instance, the fact that "Mrs Brooks just hesitated" (*Age* 81) and try to determine how much of "hesitated" is external, visible gesture, and how much a mental condition. The perception that both do overlap recurs throughout the novel in a host of equivalent cases and contributes to its mindfulness. For instance, can one separate mind from physical gesture in the attribution of "deliberation" (*Age* 141) and "solicitude" (*Age* 231) to Nanda's movements and gaze, respectively, "diffidence" (*Age* 159) to Harold's demeanor, "irritation" to Van's questioning, "awkward[ness]" (*Age* 487) to Mitchy's reception of Mr Longdon's interruption, "sad[ness] and sharp[ness]" (*Age* 488) to the latter's headshake, and so on? Similarly, to give someone "a hard look" (*Age* 445) or an "infantine stare" (*Age* 466), to say that Nanda's "voice ... trembled" (*Age* 523), that she sat "sombre" (*Age* 539) at the window, or that Mitchy was "apologetic" (*Age* 487)—can these instances fail to present a complex of behavioral data and consciousness? Even if we resort to less mentally loaded descriptions of action, such as "He [Van] looked at his watch ... then turned to speak again to the servant, who had ... already closed him in" (*Age* 383), it is impossible for the reader not to ascribe to Van the concurrent mental states of surprise and impatience at being left alone in a salon at Mrs. Grendon's house. Not to mention the fact that it is signally difficult to identify in *The Awkward Age* a description of an action that is not mentally significant in itself or thanks to the adverbial information associated with it.

Among the many insightful claims made by Sharon Cameron in her 1989 book *Thinking in Henry James*, one is particularly relevant to the foregoing discussion. For her, even if James's novels picture consciousness as a social phenomenon extending beyond the limits of the self, his own prefaces tend to undermine this notion by upholding the idea that consciousness is individual, autonomous, and coextensional with the self.[57] Cameron specifically explores this discrepancy in *Roderick Hudson* (1875), *The Portrait of a Lady* (1881), and *What Maisie Knew*, three of James's undisputed novels of consciousness. Another version of it, however, can be seen to operate in a crypto-psychological novel like *The Awkward Age*. For almost a century, and with James's own cooperation in the preface, a strong critical case has been built for the mindlessness of this novel. The image of James usually associated with it is that of a psychological novelist who, for reasons primarily related to his nostalgic fixation with theater, wished to write a behaviorist, dialogic text, in which "going behind" characters' minds would be forbidden territory. And yet the novel itself belies this purpose. Apart from inferential access via intratextual and extratextual mind attribution on the principle that action and consciousness are heads and tails of the same coin, there are countless robust cases of direct, authoritative access of the most conventional type. Even if critics outside the externalist paradigm by epoch (Lubbock) or intellectual outlook (Tintner) fail to perceive the density of mind packed away behind most descriptions of action, we are still left with many unmistakable cases of authoritative thought report, which ostensibly contradict the absence of mental insights from this novel. I would not like to conclude on a rather trivial note, but probably all this boils down to an issue of thwarted expectations. Placed between *What Maisie Knew* and *The Wings of the Dove* (1902), and mostly cast in dialogue, the relative impression made by *The Awkward Age* is one of utter exteriority, especially if the novel is made to fit in the frame set up by its preface. The constraint imposed by dialogue on the physical space available for lengthy stretches of contextual thought report and the reluctance to see minds in action, and, above all, *realize* that you are seeing them, have probably consigned *The Awkward Age* to an odd limbo of undeserved mindlessness.

Notes

1 Alan Palmer, *Fictional Minds* (Lincoln and London: University of Nebraska Press, 2004), 130–31; Alan Palmer, *Social Minds in the Novel* (Columbus: Ohio State University Press, 2010), 39–41.
2 Joseph Conrad, "Henry James: An Appreciation" (1905), in *Henry James: Critical Assessments*, 4 vols., ed. Graham Clarke (Robertsbridge: Helm Information, 1991), 2:364.
3 Leon Edel, *The Life of Henry James*, 2 vols. (Harmondsworth: Penguin, 1977), 2:153–365.
4 Ibid., 2:291.
5 Henry James, *Letters*, 4 vols., ed. Leon Edel (London: Macmillan; Cambridge: Belknap Press, 1974–84), 4:89.
6 Ibid.
7 Henry James, *The Art of the Novel*, ed. Richard P. Blackmur (1934; rpt. Boston: Northeastern University Press, 1984), 116. Hereafter cited in the text as *AN*.
8 Henry James, *The Complete Notebooks*, ed. Leon Edel and Lyall H. Powers (Oxford: Oxford University Press, 1987), 117–18.
9 Kevin J. Hayes, ed., *Henry James: The Contemporary Reviews* (Cambridge: Cambridge University Press, 2010), 330.
10 Ibid., 329.
11 Ibid., 317.
12 Roger Gard, ed., *Henry James: The Critical Heritage* (London: Routledge and Kegan Paul, 1986), 298, 346.
13 Hayes, *Henry James*, 322.
14 Ibid., 323.
15 For instance, ibid., 318, 320, 326.
16 Joseph Warren Beach, *The Method of Henry James* (1918; rpt. Philadelphia: Saifer, 1954), 244–45.
17 Percy Lubbock, *The Craft of Fiction* (London: Cape, 1921), 190.
18 Maxwell Geismar, *Henry James and the Jacobites* (Boston: Houghton Mifflin, 1963), 179; Walter Isle, *Experiments in Form: Henry James's Novels, 1896–1901*

(Cambridge, MA: Harvard University Press, 1968), 185, 203; Sergio Perosa, *Henry James and the Experimental Novel* (New York: New York University Press, 1983), 7.
19 James, *Complete Notebooks*, 91.
20 Henry James, *The Letters of Henry James*, 2 vols., ed. Percy Lubbock (New York: Scribner, 1920), 2:341.
21 Adeline R. Tintner, *The Cosmopolitan World of Henry James: An Intertextual Study* (Baton Rouge and London: Louisiana State University Press, 1991), 143–46.
22 Henry James, *The Awkward Age*, vol. 9 of *The Novels and Tales of Henry James*, 26 vols. (New York: Scribner, 1936), 94, 95; hereafter cited parenthetically as *Age*.
23 James, *Letters*, 4:86.
24 For instance, Elizabeth Owen, "*The Awkward Age* and the Contemporary English Scene," *Victorian Studies* 11.1 (1967): 65; David Kurnick, "'Horrible Impossible': Henry James's Awkward Stage," *The Henry James Review* 26 (2005): 110, 116.
25 Hayes, *Henry James*, 227–28; see also Gard, *Henry James*, 283; and Hayes, *Henry James*, 333.
26 Lubbock, *The Craft of Fiction*, 190.
27 Tintner, *The Cosmopolitan World of Henry James*, 144.
28 Kurnick, "Horrible Impossible," 110, 116.
29 Perosa, *Henry James and the Experimental Novel*, 69, 71; Sheila Teahan, "Representational Awkwardness in *The Awkward Age*," in *The Rhetorical Logic of Henry James* (Baton Rouge: Louisiana State University Press, 1995), 144; Elizabeth Stevenson, *Henry James: The Crooked Corridor* (1949; rpt. New Brunswick: Transaction, 2000), 150–51.
30 James, *Letters*, 4:110.
31 James, *Letters of Henry James*, 2:341.
32 Boris Uspensky, *A Poetics of Composition* (Berkeley: University of California Press, 1973), 84–87.
33 Owen, "*The Awkward Age* and the Contemporary English Scene," 65.
34 Isle, *Experiments in Form*, 167; Peter Brooks, *Henry James Goes to Paris* (Princeton, NJ: Princeton University Press, 2007), 94.
35 Geismar, *Henry James and the Jacobites*, 169.
36 Arnold E. Davidson, "James's Dramatic Method in *The Awkward Age*," *Nineteenth-Century Fiction* 29 (1974): 325; Uri Margolin, "Telling in the Plural: From Grammar to Ideology," *Poetics Today* 21 (2000): 604; Jonathan Culpeper, "Inferring Character from Texts: Attribution Theory and Foregrounding Theory," *Poetics* 23 (1996): 339.
37 See Lisa Zunshine, "Style Brings in Mental States," *Style* 45 (2011): 349–56.
38 See, for instance, Lucy Pollard-Gott, "Attribution Theory and the Novel," *Poetics* 21 (1991): 505; Palmer, *Fictional Minds*, 198–200; Palmer, *Social Minds*, 19, 56;

Culpeper, "Inferring Character from Texts," 336; Marie-Laure Ryan, "Narratology and Cognitive Science: A Problematic Relation," *Style* 44 (2010): 477; Lisa Zunshine, "Cognitive Alternatives to Interiority," in *The Cambridge History of the English Novel*, ed. Robert L. Caserio and Clement Hawes (Cambridge: Cambridge University Press, 2011), 150.
39 Lubbock, *The Craft of Fiction*, 192.
40 Palmer, *Fictional Minds*, 212.
41 Alan Palmer, "The Construction of Fictional Minds," *Narrative* 10.1 (2002): 31.
42 For instance, Geoffrey N. Leech and Michael H. Short, *Style in Fiction: A Linguistic Introduction to English Fictional Prose* (London: Longman, 1981), 336–50.
43 Palmer, *Social Minds*, 181.
44 Jonathan Culler, "Omniscience," *Narrative* 12 (2004): 29; see also J. Hillis Miller, *Literature as Conduct: Speech Acts in Henry James* (New York: Fordham University Press, 2005), 105.
45 See Dorrit Cohn, *Transparent Minds: Narrative Modes for Presenting Consciousness in Fiction* (Princeton, NJ: Princeton University Press, 1978); as well as Seymour Chatman, *Story and Discourse: Narrative Structure in Fiction and Film* (Ithaca, NY: Cornell University Press, 1980), 173–94, 198–209; Leech and Short, *Style in Fiction*, 336–50; Helmut Bonheim, *The Narrative Modes: Techniques of the Short Story* (Cambridge: Brewer, 1982), 50–74.
46 For a critique of this association, see Meir Sternberg, "Point of View and the Indirections of Direct Speech," *Language and Style* 15 (1982): 67–117, and "Proteus in Quotation-Land: Mimesis and Forms of Reported Speech," *Poetics Today* 3.2 (1982): 107–56.
47 Palmer, *Fictional Minds*, 76.
48 Gérard Genette, *Narrative Discourse: An Essay in Method* (Ithaca, NY: Cornell University Press, 1980), 195–96.
49 Palmer, *Fictional Minds*, 131.
50 Cognitive narratologists implicitly acknowledge the existence and operation of these two planes (e.g. H. Porter Abbott, "Unreadable Minds and the Captive Reader," *Style* 42 [2008]: 448), but they are seldom theorized separately or suitably distinguished in critical discussion.
51 Uspensky, *A Poetics of Composition*, 85.
52 David Herman, "Hypothetical Focalization," *Narrative* 2 (1994): 230–53.
53 Uspensky, *A Poetics of Composition*, 86.
54 Lisa Zunshine, "Theory of Mind and Fictions of Embodied Transparency," *Narrative* 16 (2008): 73.

55 See, for instance, Henry James's *The Other House*, intr. Leon Edel (London: Rupert Hart-Davis, 1948), 29, 41, 19, 43, 98, 11, and "Covering End," in *The Two Magics* (London: Macmillan, 1898), 264, 284, 312, 328, 362, 277, 339, 392.
56 Palmer, *Fictional Minds*, 221–13.
57 Sharon Cameron, *Thinking in Henry James* (Chicago: University of Chicago Press, 1989), 32–82.

6

The Mind, "a Room of One's Own": An Epiphanic Moment in Virginia Woolf

José Ángel García-Landa

Virginia Woolf was a woman of momentous—and exquisite—moments, memorable moments that stand out in her novels in the form of epiphanies, as well as in the recollection and reworking of her own experience through memory and autobiographical writing. The intensity with which moments are experienced requires a fidelity both to the original experience and to the moment's return to light—to the narrative reworking that explores their significance.

Hermione Lee writes as follows of Woolf's return to her earliest recollections as a child:

> her most intense memories were of moments of rapture or of shock, cutting through the moments of "non-being," of everyday life. Only by being turned into writing, she says in her autobiography, can these moments be "made whole" or lose their power to hurt. This is her whole rationale for writing: all her life she gives herself pleasure by finding the "revelation of some order" through such "moments of being." So she masters her memories by structuring them like fictions.[1]

Recent research on the phenomenology of Woolf's narrative time has likewise emphasized the importance of moments in Woolf's narratives, and the distinctiveness of their articulation in the experiential frame of the novels. In "Exquisite Moments and the Temporality of the Kiss in *Mrs. Dalloway* and *The Hours*,"[2] Kate Haffey examines the way the remembrance of one "queer" kiss by Clarissa Dalloway by her teenage friend Sally Seton is an enduring and recurring moment of emotional significance, endowed with a peculiar kind of presence or presentness, "a moment of queer temporality; it hangs between life and death, between youth and adulthood, and crashes through all the barriers meant to keep the past and the present separate."³ What the moment disrupts is not just the emotional structure of the ongoing self (home, marriage, middle age, the routine expectations of daily life) but also the ordinary, orderly, and workaday flow of time. The significant moment recurs and is therefore no longer merely past; the unexpectedness and continuing significance of its return challenges the expectation of our experiential subordination to time as a series and to sensory experience as the locus of the present. There is a rather deadening element in the expectation of ordinary purposive action, a living-out of the everyday as a self-fulfilling expectation:

> It is the belief that the future will be merely a repetition of the past. The moment, however, is able to disrupt this kind of temporality, the temporality of cause and effect, of past projected into the future. For both Clarissa and Kitty, a kiss allows them to occupy the present momentarily and to feel the elation of a future that is on the horizon but is not yet decided.⁴

The epiphanic moment is experienced as an unexpected synthesis of multiple identities and experiences, a conjunction whose very contingency opens up unforeseen possibilities of creative experience. Creativity, openness, unexpectedness, complexity—no wonder memorable moments that make the most of this synthesis provide the experience of the subliminal or the unconscious coming to consciousness, and no wonder they tend to return to mind and to become milestones in personal development, and in the story of one's relation to oneself. The attention Virginia Woolf pays to the complexity and density of the moment is a tribute both to the present and to the mind—if the mind is to be defined, for the sake of this argument, as the management of emergent complexity, and the present as the locus not just of reality, but of the mental activity that synthesizes it.

The theoretical foundation for this notion of the mind and of the present can be grounded in a materialist conception of time as a mental construction, such as the one provided by the pragmatist philosophy of George Herbert Mead.⁵ Perhaps best known as the philosophical founder of symbolic interactionism ("social pragmatism" in his own terms), Mead provides a suggestive philosophy of the mind that, in its integration of time, consciousness, and self-interaction, can illuminate mental phenomena such as "bringing to consciousness," self-communication, and the reworking of memories, providing a perspective which can provide bridges between Woolf's attention to mental and reflective experience and a more general scientific conception of the mind as an evolutionary (and bodily) phenomenon. As a matter of fact, the mind is for Mead the locus of both the present and the most complex syntheses of evolutionary phenomena—of emergent complexity and creativity. Mead's approach provides a philosophical interface where a theory of the epiphany as emergent consciousness can be readily related to other relevant approaches to symbolic action we'll mention in passing,—for example, rhetorical analysis after Kenneth Burke, dialogical-Bakhtinian perspectives, or cognitive theories of imagery such as Fauconnier and Turner's conceptual blends. The element of synthesis and blending in symbol-making will indeed be especially relevant to our central passage here, but our discussion as a whole should be read as a claim for the present relevance of Mead's symbolic interactionism for understanding mental activity and its representation.[6]

An epiphany is a moment of emergence and synthesis, a significant "coming-to-consciousness," a mental state in which the subject becomes self-reflexively aware of his or her own sensibility and privileged perception. It may actually be a moment of topsight, the awareness of one's own cognitively dominant understanding and perspective.[7] In the epiphanic moment, reality is revealed both as a complex interaction of phenomena and as the possibility of coming to terms with it, through an integration in the surrounding world that may be felt in the body, but is vividly experienced as the mind's insight into the world as experienced, the mind's making a new acquaintance of itself through a sudden understanding of the way things hang together, with ourselves and our outlook in their midst. Many of Woolf's memorable moments, "moments of rapture or of shock, cutting through the moments of 'non-being,' of everyday life"[8]—have this epiphanic quality. It goes without saying that there may be different types of epiphanies—some have a more aesthetic, some a more emotional or even religious or mystical quality (there is quite often, indeed, an adumbration of an unexpected or hidden dimension of reality in such epiphanic moments—and some of them may have a more cognitive and interpretive dimension). There is a "family resemblance" between epiphanies, but surely the central, most distinctive ones evince a multidimensional synthesis of cognition, aesthetics, emotion, and revelatory insight.[9]

I want to focus on one epiphanic passage in *A Room of One's Own*,[10] a passage about—among other things—the mind, or perhaps *the androgynous mind*, androgyny being here a way of escaping predetermination, and experiencing the mental fluidity in which the mind is most at home with itself—in a familiar room, perhaps, but in an unexpected dimension too, one in which the present and reality are transformed through the sheer power of the mind's plasticity. Coming from a reflective essay with political overtones, it is perhaps to be expected that the cognitive elements will be prominent, blended with the aesthetic and emotional dimensions of experiential insight. Here we will re-experience this epiphany in slow motion, through a close reading of the passage.

As a critical mode, close reading is perhaps most associated to the New Criticism, the contemporary critical response to modernist literature. It is quite well attuned to a mode of writing that privileges immersion in a foreign consciousness—that of a reflecting character, or that of any writer's text experienced as view of another mind from the inside. It is with the modernists—Henry James, Joyce, Proust, Dorothy Richardson, or Woolf—that prose fiction fully discovers and explores its privileged position as regards the reading of minds, of other minds; its potential to invite us into the private room of the mind of the other, and get a glimpse of the world as seen through their eyes and sensibilities.[11] Film, a novel medium, would still take some time to explore its own potential in this area, and it would do so to a large extent by following the insights explored by modernist novelists. A close reading of Woolf's epiphanic moment will be our instrument of choice to experience the complexity of Woolf's own "cinematographical apparatus of the mind," to use the terminology of her contemporary, the evolutionary theorist Henri Bergson.[12]

This is the moment in question:

> Next day the light of the October morning was falling in dusty shafts through the uncurtained windows, and the hum of traffic rose from the street. London then was winding itself up again; the factory was astir; the machines were beginning. It was tempting, after all this reading, to look out of the window and see what London was doing on the morning of the twenty-sixth of October 1928. And what was London doing? Nobody, it seemed, was reading *Antony and Cleopatra*. London was wholly indifferent, it appeared, to Shakespeare's plays. Nobody cared a straw—and I do not blame them—for the future of fiction, the death of poetry or the development by the average woman of a prose style completely expressive of her mind. If opinions upon any of these matters had been chalked on the pavement, nobody would have stooped to read them. The nonchalance of the hurrying feet would have rubbed them out in half an hour. Here came an errand-boy; here a woman with a dog on a lead. The fascination of the London street is that no two people are ever alike; each seems bound on some private affair of his own. There were the business-like, with their little

bags; there were the drifters rattling sticks upon area railings; there were affable characters to whom the streets serve for clubroom, hailing men in carts and giving information without being asked for it. Also there were funerals to which men, thus suddenly reminded of the passing of their own bodies, lifted their hats. And then a very distinguished gentleman came slowly down a doorstep and paused to avoid a collision with a bustling lady who had, by some means or other, acquired a splendid fur coat and a bunch of Parma violets. They all seemed separate, absorbed, on business of their own.

At this moment, as so often happens in London, there was a complete lull and suspension of traffic. Nothing came down the street; nobody passed. A single leaf detached itself from the plane tree at the end of the street, and in that pause and suspension fell. Somehow it was like a signal falling, a signal pointing to a force in things which one had overlooked. It seemed to point to a river, which flowed past, invisibly, round the corner, down the street, and took people and eddied them along, as the stream at Oxbridge had taken the undergraduate in his boat and the dead leaves. Now it was bringing from one side of the street to the other diagonally a girl in patent leather boots, and a young man in a maroon overcoat; it was also bringing a taxi-cab, and it brought all three together at a point directly beneath my window; where the taxi stopped; and the girl and the young man stopped; and they got into the taxi; and then the cab glided off as if it were swept on by the current elsewhere.

The sight was ordinary enough; what was strange was the rhythmical order with which my imagination had invested it; and the fact that the ordinary sight of two people getting into a cab had the power to communicate something of their own seeming satisfaction. The sight of two people coming down the street and meeting at the corner seems to ease the mind of some strain, I thought, watching the taxi turn and make off. Perhaps to think, as I had been thinking these two days, of one sex as distinct from the other is an effort. It interferes with the unity of the mind. Now that effort had ceased and that unity had been restored by seeing two people come together and get into a taxi-cab. The mind is certainly a very mysterious organ, I reflected, drawing my head in from the window, about which nothing whatever is known, though we depend upon it so completely. Why do I feel that there are severances and oppositions in the mind, as there are strains from obvious causes on the body? What does one mean by "the unity of the mind," I pondered, for clearly the mind has so great a power of concentrating at any point at any moment that it seems to have no single state of being. It can separate itself from the people in the street, for example, and think of itself as apart from them, at an upper window looking down on them. Or it can think with other people spontaneously, as, for instance, in a crowd waiting to hear some piece of news read out. It can think back through its fathers or through its mothers, as I have said that a woman writing thinks back through her mothers. Again if one is a woman one is often surprised by a sudden splitting off of consciousness, say in walking down Whitehall, when from being the natural inheritor of that civilisation, she becomes, on the contrary, outside of it, alien and critical. Clearly the mind is always altering its focus, and bringing the world into different perspectives. But some of these states of mind seem, even if adopted spontaneously, to be less comfortable than others. In order to keep oneself continuing in them one is unconsciously holding something back, and gradually the repression becomes an effort. But there may be some state of mind in which one could continue without effort because nothing is required to be held back. And this perhaps, I thought, coming in from the window, is one of them. For certainly when I saw the couple get into the taxi-cab the mind felt as if, after being divided, it had come together again in a natural fusion. The obvious reason would be that it is natural for the sexes to cooperate. One has a profound, if irrational, instinct in favor of the theory that the union of man and woman makes for the greatest possible satisfaction, the most complete happiness. But the sight of the two people getting into the taxi and the satisfaction it gave me made me also ask whether there are two sexes in the mind corresponding to the two sexes in the body, and whether they also require to be united in order to get complete satisfaction and happiness. And I went on amateurishly to sketch a plan of the soul so that in each of us two powers preside, one male, one female; and in the man's brain, the man predominates over the woman, and in the woman's brain, the woman predominates over the man. The normal and comfortable state of being is that when the two live in harmony together, spiritually cooperating. (Virginia Woolf, *A Room of One's Own*, chapter 6)

This episode and this passage are, of course, highly characteristic of Virginia Woolf's sensibility, perceptions, and reflections. It is significant that the motif of a couple walking together in the city, as an image of precarious harmony between the sexes, was the intended opening of Woolf's first novel, *The Voyage Out*, surviving through many preliminary drafts of the novel.[13] As the novel stands, the couple get into a taxi, but the scene suggests disunion and confusion rather than unity. Still, we see Woolf coming back to the image in 1929, adding the cab as a rounding-off to the scene observed by the author in the street[14] in order to find in it a perfectly satisfactory resting place for the mind.

There is almost too much to comment on this moment that conflates stillness and a peculiar intensity, a moment of intuitive perception and its subsequent recollection and elaboration. I shall focus, therefore, on the second half of the passage, once the scene has been set by the epiphany itself, at that moment when time itself appears to stop, in a moment of insight and self-communication framed by the window frame. Woolf's written re-elaboration of the moment first, and then our close reading of each sentence, will provide us with a perspective twice removed on the workings of the author's—and the character's—thought processes.

> The mind is certainly a very mysterious organ, I reflected.

And this is the reflective attitude par excellence: reflection on the mind brings with it a suggestion of endless reflections, or an infinite regress. The organ (?) will remain mysterious after Woolf's reflections, or our own. As a matter of fact, it may become even more mysterious in the process, given that we may discover some depths or dimensions unsuspected by those who have never taken the time to pause and reflect on their own thoughts. And yet in some sense the mind will also get to be better known, taking a new acquaintance of itself,[15] observing itself in its processes, its associations of ideas, and its various simultaneous levels and intersecting planes of functioning. In her previous essays "Modern Fiction" and "Mr Bennett and Mrs Brown" Woolf had already drawn our attention to this strange quality of reality that emerges when we examine it in closeup and get to discover new hidden dimensions in it, through the mere procedure of not submitting ourselves to ready-made, hackneyed, or customary habits of perception or representation.

"The Mark on the Wall" is another insightfully subtle essay or story in which Woolf's mind observes its own processes. It is an essay on nothing, one might say—but it is a nothingness that is brimming with energy and productivity, like the quantum void of modern physics. Like the passage in *A Room*, it is yet another essay on a moment of self-absorption, with the author's mind a blank page, so to speak, or rather a palimpsestic blank. Moments of self-absorption are full of potentialities and of barely formulated thoughts milling under the empty surface. This kind of blankness contains the temptation and the potential of creativity, of the unexpressed. Just try to look for a moment at a blank page, and it is not whiteness that you will see. Or perhaps you will see a whiteness like Moby Dick's, challenging the mind, which is itself, to extract from "these waste blanks" that which nobody had seen but which was, somehow, already there. Or waiting to emerge, from the mind's inaudible workings, to consciousness.

> drawing my head in from the window,

This reflection (or this emergence from the deep) takes place at the moment when Virginia Woolf the character goes back into the room (a room with a view, a room of her own) after looking on the street through the windows of perception. Everything happens in this second, a London second dense like the ones we find in Joyce's Dublin, or in those slow-motion digressions of Sterne's in *Tristram Shandy*. The room is the offline mind turned on itself,[16] the Paleolithic cave of the Dream-time. The window is the window of perception, an opening on the external world ("the world outside your window" in Tanita Tikaram's song, or Bickerton's "online thought").

Through this window, Virginia Woolf (the character, and now the writer) has witnessed a scene that she will proceed to allegorize, or rather, a scene that has allegorized itself spontaneously in the back room of her mind, providing her with the image she needed in order to alleviate the strains tightening in her. In an ordinary and yet unnaturally quiet moment, a man and a woman get into a taxi, and the cab drives off. The whole is described within the image of a stream—the stream of time that carries all things within it, perhaps, or the stream of chance, of happenstance, the contingent flow of events and moments (they are the same stream, or at least they flow on the same river bed). The man, the woman, and the moment were being watched from a window by Virginia Woolf, who now turns her attention back to herself.

> About which nothing whatever is known, though we depend upon it so completely.

This is not wholly inaccurate. These were the formative years of psychoanalysis, of phenomenology, of modern experimental psychology—and of Mead's symbolic interactionism—long before cognitive neurology and the experiments on the theory of mind. What was known about the mind if we discount these contributions is really very little, and Woolf seems to have realized this. Her perceptions and intuitions will need an explanation, too; possibly, they will elicit explanations for quite some time to come. To say that "we depend upon the mind so completely" is, however, a slightly preposterous or ridiculous way of putting it. It would be more accurate to say that we live in a mental environment, or that we are mental beings first and foremost. Put in a different register, we are both body and soul, but it is our souls rather than our bodies that are most ourselves.[17]

There is a parallel, though, between the mind and the body, and Woolf seems to point to something like a corporeality of the mind—to certain joints or muscles or organic structures sustaining its morphology, and articulating it in ways that can be subject to tensions or strained postures and movements:

> Why do I feel that there are severances and oppositions in the mind, as there are strains from obvious causes on the body?

She feels it because she is a modern woman, living through the tensions of modernity, and the new woman is struggling for a new role in the public sphere. That is one reason why Woolf is writing, and that is one reason why she needs her room, her own private space. The tension between the masculine and the feminine spaces is given a memorable formulation in *A Room of One's Own* when the author is barred access to the university library because she is a woman. This strain in the public space is experienced by Woolf as an inner strain. (It is also a strain in her own marriage with her devoted, protective, and oppressive husband, Leonard.)

This underlying tension, both personal and political (*the personal is the political* would become a motto of the new feminist movement in the 1970s but is a living experience here), now finds an expression, and with it a relief, in the image of the man and the woman getting into the cab. Let us note in passing that the automobile is a product and a symbol of modernity, much more so for Woolf than for us nowadays.

> What does one mean by "the unity of the mind," I pondered.

A major modernist theme surfaces here—the multiplicity underlying the self that was being theorized at the time by the social psychology of Cooley and Mead, and their theory of the structuring of the self through roles.[18] Still, in the 1920s and the 1930s literary circles were more aware of psychoanalysis and often conceived of this multiplicity in terms of the tension between the unconscious drives of the id and the socialized, civilized self, or in terms of the repression of the pleasure principle (as Freud does in *The Ego and the Id*, 1923, or in *Civilization and Its Discontents*, 1930).

The modernist critique of the unity of the mind, and its denunciation as an illusion, finds a memorable expression in the following poem by E. E. Cummings:

> so many selves(so many fiends and gods
> each greedier than every)is a man
> (so easily one in another hides;
> yet man can,being all,escape from none)

> so huge a tumult is the simplest wish:
> so pitiless a massacre the hope
> most innocent(so deep's the mind of flesh
> and so awake what waking calls asleep)
>
> so never is most lonely man alone
> (his briefest breathing lives some planet's year,
> his longest life's a heartbeat of some sun;
>
> his least unmotion roams the youngest star)
> —how should a fool that calls him "I" presume
> to comprehend not numerable whom?[19]

The slightly anomalous typography is kept here as in the original, because in order to understand this poem in its full formal dimension one must take into account that Cummings (who often wrote his name "e. e. cummings") sometimes renounced using capitals, defying the orthographic conventions of English poetry (and prose) as he does in this poem. It is not by chance that the only capital letter here is ascribed to the overbearing and preposterous "I," a spelling anomaly in Cummings disguised behind a spelling anomaly in the English language, signaling here an over-ambitious conception of the self (compare to another spelling anomaly, "God" as "He"), and a pronoun often rewritten by *cummings* as a less ambitious "i"—that may also be read as Roman numeral for number one, but is itself graphically divided and is perhaps less optimistically Phallic.[20] The subdued or minor character of the self is thus expressed in this poem together with its precarious unity, or its dispersed diffusion through the universe, in keeping with Cummings's religious views.

Still there is an I in Woolf's text, the capital I of "I pondered," visible and intrusive in contradiction with the third person of the mind being reflected upon—somewhat like the predicament visible in Hume's argumentation while he deconstructs the self into a loose sequence of impressions—an excellent reasoning that is at odds with the continual presence of the argumentative and philosophical I, who did not refrain from signing the *Treatise of Human Nature* with his own name. An author must need be an I to some extent, or pass for one. Nay, an author is a privileged self, an authoritative I as a speaker, a focus of understanding or a point of view, even when discussing the dissolution and precarious structure of the self.

> For clearly the mind has so great a power of concentrating at any point at any moment that it seems to have no single state of being.

The mind appears here as the management of attention. The shifting of attention amounts to what Keats would call a "negative capability" of the mind—it becomes engrossed in its object; it is a fluid process of engaging different aspects of reality, giving access to subworlds within the world, or sub-moments within the moment (notice that *the moment* recurs again in this sentence of Woolf's text). Our plastic, Protean mind keeps us in a permanent state of potentiality, at a crossroads of infinite possibilities that were barely intuited at the moment it first began to turn back on itself and to study itself, "minding the mind."[21] Having (or being) a multidimensional mind makes the ability to focus attention all the more important. Woolf's experience of the London moment is an excellent example of the way in which these two aspects of the mind combine—its openness to the world and its multiplicity (the window) and its ability to center on itself, and, reflexively, transform itself and transform the world through the focusing of attention. Attention, and its selectivity, plays, of course, a central role in the articulation and fusion of images and representations in the process that Fauconnier and Turner call conceptual integration or blending.[22] Which is arguably, together with symbolism and narrative (and I do mean *together*), the most distinctive ability of the human mind?

> It can separate itself from the people in the street, for example, and think of itself as apart from them, at an upper window looking down on them.

In this sentence the reader's mind suddenly recognizes the scene narrated by Woolf, the setting for this excursus or incursion into the mind—both a setting and an example—a model of the functioning of the mind itself. It is also a model for perspectival and cognitive *topsight*, for the author's own superior cognitive prowess—and an expression of the misgivings elicited by such cognitive dominance, the danger of isolation within one's own frame, in an ivory tower away from common human concerns, as a misguided metaphysician looking down on the *hoi polloi*, an intellectual with delusions of grandeur building one of those idealistic edifices that rest on a negation of their material basis. Although, as a matter of fact, this sentence is already thought inside the room, and written on the desk, it contains therefore two distinct phases or moments: first, a vivid sensation (by Woolf the focalizer character) of a moment of contemplation standing at the window, where the image is first generated by perception and physical experience. Then, the internal dialogical reaction to that perception, leading perhaps to the subject's moving away from the window, but reaching full conscious expression back at the desk, when Woolf the narrator writes about her experience. It is now that the lived sensation of isolation can be fully expressed, the isolation that was experienced at the window in a dynamic tension with the observer's immersion in the quiet moment and the scene. The isolation and the incipient reaction to it find a more perfect expression in the deliberate solitude of the writer at her desk, in her room. This rounds off the writer's reaction to the impression and further shapes its symbolic meaning, the sense which is now being attributed to it. The mind is reacting to others, and thinking with others, even when most alone, and responding to its own promptings.

> Or it can think with other people spontaneously, as, for instance, in a crowd waiting to hear some piece of news read out.

We are individuals, we are a society of individuals, we contain multitudes, legion after legion.[23] We are one and many—the crowd inside—but in a crowd we can feel largely what others feel, and either through overt communication or through empathy, we can know that we partake of other people's experiences and that they also share much of what we feel, given that we live in a communal world shaped by shared symbols, values, and experiences.[24] Woolf was very much aware of this community of feeling and thought, as shown in the following passage from a 1903 journal:

> I think I see for a moment how our minds are threaded together—how any live mind is of the very same stuff as Plato's & Euripides. It is only a continuation & development of the same thing. It is this common mind that binds the whole world together, & all the world is mind.[25]

This passage comes close to the formulation of a universal intertextuality of mind and thoughts in intellectual terms, but there is also an empathetic and emotional dimension in Woolf's projecting herself into other selves and other minds, in reading, in writing or in observing experience. As a matter of fact, there is a moment of empathetic projection in the first earlier scene as well, the one recalled by the solitary writer which stands in contrast with her situation: from the window, Woolf also feels and lives by proxy what it is to meet one's partner, the other in the couple, and to get together into a taxi. The spontaneous union with others, in the collective experience of the waiting crowd, brings to my mind (and likely to that of other readers) Virginia Woolf's experience of political activism, her early experiences with the women's suffrage movement, fictionalized in *The Voyage Out* (1915). Without explicitly mentioning anything of the like, the example of the waiting crowd in *A Room of One's Own* makes us think of a group of people with similar expectations, taking part in a common situation, and waiting for some crucial piece of news, relevant to them all and to their projects—a moment of participation in the life of a community characteristic of a period in which such political emotions were especially intense and absorbing. The image may have been suggested in contrast to the solitary mind watching the view from the window, aloft from communal human concerns, even the most pressing ones, or those which have appeared to be pressing in another "moment of being."

> It can think back through its fathers or through its mothers, as I have said that a woman writing thinks back through her mothers.

Mental experience is not restricted to the present moment: it is an experience of time travel, as the mind (re)constructs past and future moments, always in some evaluative or emotional relationship to the present—and memories of personal experiences actually have a distinct neurophysiological basis of their own.[26] But the elaborate symbolic constructions of human culture allow us to travel to the communal past and future, moving through the worlds of history, art, and literature, and living through them other people's experiences that are also potentially our own—that are already in part our own. The literature inherited by Woolf is primarily that of the patriarchal Western tradition, that of her *fathers*—most prominently among them Leslie Stephen, the model for Mr. Ramsay in *To the Lighthouse*. Stephen was doubly a father, as a *pater familias* and as a man of letters, the guardian of patriarchal culture, the editor of nothing less than the *Dictionary of National Biography*, which is the closest thing to an official registry of the fathers of the English nation.[27] And of some of the mothers, too—as Virginia was particularly sensitive to the female tradition of forgotten and neglected women writers—or *invented* women writers, as in her counterexample concerning the outstanding genius Judith Shakespeare in *A Room of One's Own*.[28] Anglophone feminists of a later generation—like Ellen Moers in *Literary Women*, Sandra M. Gilbert and Susan Gubar in *The Madwoman in the Attic*, or Elaine Showalter in *A Literature of Their Own*[29]—will readily connect with Woolf in "thinking back through their mothers," rediscovering their experiences and conditioning circumstances, and developing an increased awareness of their own experiences and circumstances as women writers in the process. Woolf's writing, and texts like the present one, will provide a powerful inspiration for them in this process of "thinking back" through their intellectual mothers, even the childless ones—many major women writers are childless mothers, and many give birth to literary children that take decades, or centuries, to gestate. They change, too, in the process—Virginia Woolf herself, once reinterpreted along the lines suggested by herself, has turned out to be much more of a feminist theorist than she seemed to be in her own lifetime, and a figure of increasing complexity as her posthumous reputation developed.[30]

> Again if one is a woman one is often surprised by a sudden splitting off of consciousness,

An attention to the mind and to its workings—felt from the inside, as a split threatening the subject's own consistency, the mind divided against itself. The specific experience of being a woman involves these divisions or tensions the text mentioned earlier. Such tensions in an intersubjective mind amount almost to a double personality and a double allegiance: the sense of self inherited from the fathers, and the one coming from the mothers, perhaps one that is discovered in particularly significant moments. Because the allusion to the moment recurs here in the suddenness and surprise as, indeed, a split marks a moment as a special one, a moment of insight perhaps, when the tensions make themselves felt or a veil actually falls, transforming the stroller, or the street—

> say in walking down Whitehall, when from being the natural inheritor of that civilization, she becomes, on the contrary, outside of it, alien and critical.

Whitehall is the neural center of political power in Britain, still off limits to onetime suffragette activists. Woman appears now as *the other within* civilization, or perhaps *the other within herself*, because this societal division is interiorized and experienced from the inside—as a consequence of Cooley's "looking-glass self." It is not just a matter of a split between the "alien and critical" woman and patriarchal society (or between the "alien and critical" woman and other women); it goes deeper than that. The split is a "splitting off of consciousness" that takes place within the woman herself. We see Virginia as the frustrated suffragette, still furious at the limited role of women in the public sphere, living her discontent as a mental alteration, a recurrent schizophrenia (this moment is also *many moments*). A split of consciousness is a threat coming from the inside, from the outside that has become the inside and has structured it as this unstable system of tensions. The anger, the alienation, the tension are not so alien, maybe, to those voices that hounded Virginia occasionally and would not let her alone, invading the mind's private room.[31] Speaking of windows, and tensions, one must remember that Virginia Woolf had already tried to commit suicide once by jumping from a window, an episode displaced and fictionalized—in the sense of assimilated and exorcised through fiction-making— in *Mrs Dalloway*. And (fast-forward to the future, a future we now know) it was in part the threat and the torment of those alien voices she heard inside her head that made her opt once again for suicide in 1941. This is all to say that the feeling of defamiliarization and strangeness, the *Verfremdung* from the spectacle of life, was not new to her—and in her experience this feeling of alienation was joined, to a great extent, to the tensions involved in the female condition and the feminine social identity. Woolf found being a woman problematic, and not just in political terms. From a sexual point of view, she apparently never fully came to terms with her own sexual identity. She was never sexually attracted to her husband and apparently could not endure penetration during sex[32]—her relationship with Leonard developed into a mixture of companionship and patriarchal guardianship on his part, after her most serious nervous breakdown just after their marriage.[33] While never "coming out" as a lesbian, and often derisive of homosexuals, Woolf was more erotically attracted to women than to men. She seems to have had a strong physical aversion to heterosexual physicality, and she channeled this rejection through nervous breakdowns and hysterical countermoves, which fed into her panic attacks, bipolar oscillations, hypersensitivity, anorexic fixations, headaches, "voices in the head," and other disorders.

Psychoanalysis 101 would suggest a circulating association between this aversion to the penetration of the inner bodily space and her desire for *a room of her own* free from the intrusions of men. They soon had separate bedrooms. Virginia had also been Leonard's in-house landlady before their marriage—an experience of intimacy and separation that further overdetermines the loaded connotations of the staked-out private space of a writer's room.

Masculine prosaic priorities and their interruptions of the female train of thought are unwelcome in "The Mark on the Wall," in *To the Lighthouse*, and elsewhere. The integration with masculinity would have to be psychologically interiorized, as it could not be endured in the form of heterosexuality. Thence her interest in female rebelliousness and in androgyny, and her lesbian or transsexual fantasies, like the ones she imaginatively projected in *Orlando* (1928)—a novel written for her beloved Vita Sackville-West. Surely not all women share this impulse toward contentiousness or this sense of social and identitarian alienation, but Woolf posits herself, as an educated and thinking woman, as a role model for the typical woman, a role model who is also a social misfit or a marginal malcontent.

There is perhaps a deeper dissatisfaction here, beyond gender roles or inequalities, not least an acute sense that (in Luis Eduardo Aute's words) *el pensamiento no puede tomar asiento*, "thought cannot take a seat."[34] But this realization is experienced through the subject position of a modern woman in the 1920s and in the context of her own psychopathological dispositions and background. Woolf strives to imagine a way out—a nontraumatic, harmonious experience of herself and of society, an existence without divisions like the one she portrayed in part in *Orlando*, or the one the painter Lily Briscoe manages to imagine through her art in *To the Lighthouse*. The image of the integration of opposites, the reconciliation of the masculine and the feminine element, getting together into the taxi of the integrated self, and driving away to an optimistic future, is a tempting one—although neither her marriage with Leonard Woolf nor her personal experience was as harmonious and balanced as this symbol of smooth integration.

> Clearly the mind is always altering its focus, and bringing the world into different perspectives.

The mind re-presents the world, and in so doing it constitutes and transforms it—Bergson's notion of the *cinematic apparatus of the mind* is apposite here, as Woolf seems to be thinking as well of the world reshaped by the mind as a filmic narrative focalized by the camera from different angles, or perhaps as an object that can be photographed in a variety of ways, through the shifting lens of mental attention. Be as it may, the experienced world, phenomenal reality, results from or includes these perspectives, which give it the actual shape it takes.

> But some of these states of mind seem, even if adopted spontaneously, to be less comfortable than others.

Here we get to listen to the person with a personal experience of an ailing mind, subject to inner tensions, in pain because of the recurrent unnaturally stiff postures and repeated contortions interiorized by the self, a mind seeking first of all postural relief, a less forced positioning with regard to the world. Patriarchal culture is both spontaneous and compulsory; the order of the sexes ("heteropatriarchy" in the current language of the tribe) is both spontaneous and forced on the mind. Under different (constraining) circumstances, a different order might be spontaneously generated, too.

> In order to keep oneself continuing in them one is unconsciously holding something back, and gradually the repression becomes an effort.

Here the language of psychoanalysis appears: the Virginia who is familiar (not firsthand, but through her Bloomsbury acquaintances, and through Leonard) with Freud's psychoanalysis and his theories on repression and the unconscious. She does have firsthand knowledge, though, both of psychotherapy after her first suicide attempt, and she has become conscious of the weight of the Victorian repressions carried by herself and her class and culture; conscious, as well, of the need to refocus her attention, and the postural habits of the social world she inhabits, in order to alleviate the tensions undergone by the mind. Perhaps too in order to become aware of things about which she cannot think clearly at this point, since these tensions obviously prevent the mind from focusing on some issues with the clarity she requires.

> But there may be some state of mind in which one could continue without effort because nothing is required to be held back.

We find here a utopian moment: an intimation of a mental state without tensions, perhaps once the current sexual order has been transcended; something that would take us beyond evolution, or to the end of evolution—to the posthuman? This utopia may possibly never overrule (or dissolve) the present sexual or social order, but nevertheless it does exist, as a utopia—and crucially, too, as a lived experience, not in a life lived out as such, but surfacing to a glimpse in a transient moment.

The utopian order appears, therefore, as an epiphany, a state of mind or the sensation of one. Perhaps it is reworked through memory—like the remembered kiss in *Mrs Dalloway*—perhaps it will never materialize except as an enshrined memory or a passing epiphany, but this is more than nothing: it is a reality that has been inhabited. Hamlet said that nothing is good or bad unless our mind judges it to be such, and the mind constructs its own worlds—its own mountains and cliffs for Gerard Manley Hopkins, or Blake's *mind forg'd manacles*.[35] The mind can also build its own room as a stronghold, and its own utopia.

> And this perhaps, I thought, coming in from the window, is one of them.

This moment. A culmination of the passage lies precisely here: in becoming conscious of the present—*this present, this gift*—as it is now that the narrative structure of the passage makes us realize that the whole piece of stream of consciousness has taken place in an intense moment. But is that the case? Because there is the moment, and there is its reworking in thought, the retrospective reflection on the moment, which (as we have pointed out) is also visible in the writing of this passage, so that the moment is paradoxically both the moment lived in its immediacy and also explored and experienced as a recreation in thought.

> For certainly when I saw the couple get into the taxi-cab the mind felt as if, after being divided, it had come together again in a natural fusion.

It is clear that Woolf does not just experience the relief afforded by this image as a focalizing character at the window: she consciously reflects on it, and on the therapeutical import of the image, as a narrator; as the author of the book, in her notebooks, she further comments on the special emotional significance the image has for her, and she reworks it deliberately to suit her purpose, adding to the actual experience, in a fiction-making move.[36] The epiphanic experience and the subsequent reflection and re-elaboration of its symbolic sense through writing are segments of a continuum, moving from a spontaneous reaction of the mind to the threshold of allegory; they are ways of focusing on the relief and experiencing it with full consciousness, appropriating it to the extent of turning it into an allegory of the utopian androgynous mind: the masculine and the feminine halves of the mind, or of the human species, reconciled to one another, and setting off for the journey of life in a taxi-cab. This is an allegory, as well, of an ideally successful marriage, which is not perceived here as distinct from the satisfactory, non-repressive integration of the masculine and feminine elements in human nature.

> The obvious reason would be that it is natural for the sexes to co-operate. . . .

Human nature reappears here. But this nature, mediated or distorted by culture, does not dictate the exact way in which the sexes should cooperate, divide their roles, or indeed be structured. When we face the problem of gender and sexual difference, as any generation does, we drag along the whole of human history, and of biological evolution.[37] The dilemma does not disappear, as it seems obvious that human culture—human cultures—is not a free-floating construction that can get rid of, or freely rework, either human history or biology.

It is in this line where Nature reappears that we part with Woolf's text. Not all distributions of roles—whether internal to the mind or external ones, in society—are equally natural, and we have glimpsed the dangers and tensions produced by the enforced postural requirements and mental economies of specific cultural environments—those of Victorian England, most vividly, in the case of Virginia Woolf. She endured (and tried to think through) her own experience of androgyny in a relatively benign patriarchy and made a powerful contribution to the ongoing debate regarding what the "natural cooperation of the sexes" should be, both in the mind and in a society that is attentive to its own utopian impulse. Like the Brontë sisters before her, she expressed her own sensibility publicly, in a memorable and transformative way, in "a prose style completely expressive of her mind." Virginia Woolf's style is both an exercise in personal individualism and an act of political intervention; in her work these are inseparable from narrative self-fashioning and from aesthetic innovation on the way we perceive the mind, the world, and our own selves.

> I'll walk where my own nature would be leading;
> It vexes me to choose another guide.
>
> (Brontë, "Stanzas")

Notes

1 Hermione Lee, *Virginia Woolf* (London: Chatto and Windus, 1996), 106. Lee refers us to Virginia Woolf's own "Sketch of the Past" published in *Moments of Being*, ed. Jeanne Schulkind (1979; rev. ed. Sussex: Sussex University Press, 1985), 81.
2 Kate Haffey, "Exquisite Moments and the Temporality of the Kiss in *Mrs. Dalloway* and *The Hours*," *Narrative* 18.2 (May 2010): 137–62.
3 Ibid., 149.
4 Ibid., 154–55. The notion of reality as a self-fulfilling set of collectively constructed expectations is insightfully dealt with by Peter Berger and Thomas Luckmann in *The Social Construction of Reality* (New York: Doubleday-Anchor, 1967). Another take on the same and its implications for the structure of the self appears, via Erving Goffman's frame theory, in my paper on "Reality as self-fulfilling expectation and the theatre of interiority" ("Goffman: La realidad como expectativa autocumplida y el teatro de la interioridad"), online at *SSRN* (April 2008), http://ssrn.com/abstract=1124990.
5 George Herbert Mead, *The Philosophy of the Present*, ed. and intro. Arthur E. Murphy (1932; rpt. Amherst, NY: Prometheus Books, 2002). I comment further on Mead's views on time and consciousness in the notes to my Spanish translation of Mead's essay, *La filosofía del presente* (University of Zaragoza, 2009), http://personal.unizar.es/garciala/publicaciones/meadpresente.html—and in "George Herbert Mead y la complejidad del tiempo humano," in *Corporalidad, Temporalidad, Afectividad: Perspectivas Filosófico-Antropológicas*, ed. Luisa Paz Rodríguez Suárez and José Ángel García-Landa (Berlin: Logos Verlag, 2017), 151–71.

6 Besides *The Philosophy of the Present,* Mead's theory of mental representation and evolutionary cognitivism is to be found in another posthumous volume, *Mind, Self, and Society from the Standpoint of a Social Behaviorist,* ed. and intro. Charles W. Morris (1934; rpt. Chicago: University of Chicago Press, 1967). On "social behaviorism" or symbolic interactionism as an approach in social psychology, see Joel M. Charon's *Symbolic Interactionism: An Introduction, an Interpretation, an Integration,* 7th ed. (Upper Saddle River, NJ: Prentice-Hall, 2001). Kenneth Burke's theory of symbolic action is set out in *Language as Symbolic Action: Essays on Life, Literature, and Method* (Berkeley: University of California Press, 1966). For Fauconnier and Turner's "blending" or conceptual integration, see note 19.
7 For a further elaboration of the concept of topsight see my note "Panopticon of Topsight on *The Order of Things*," *Ibercampus* (June 12, 2015), available at http://www.ibercampus.eu/panopticon-of-topsight-in-the-order-of-things-3165.htm
8 Lee, *Virginia Woolf,* 106.
9 On modernist epiphanies and their romantic ancestry, see Charles Taylor, "Epiphanies of Modernism," in his *Sources of the Self: The Making of the Modern Identity* (Cambridge: Cambridge University Press, 1989), 456–94.
10 Virginia Woolf, *A Room of One's Own* (1929), in *The Norton Anthology of English Literature,* ed. M. H. Abrams, with Stephen Greenblatt et al., 7th ed. (New York: Norton, 1999), 2:2153–214.
11 On mental representations of consciousness and on "mind-reading" see Dorrit Cohn, *Transparent Minds: Narrative Modes for Presenting Consciousness in Fiction* (Princeton, NJ: Princeton University Press, 1978) and Alan Palmer, *Fictional Minds* (Lincoln: University of Nebraska Press, 2004).
12 Bergson, *L'Évolution créatrice* (Paris: PUF, 1959), 272ff.
13 Julia Briggs, *Virginia Woolf: An Inner Life* (London: Penguin, 2005), 1.
14 Ibid., 321.
15 Shakespeare, Sonnet 77:

> Look what thy memory cannot contain
> Commit to these waste blanks, and thou shalt find
> Those children nursed, delivered from thy brain,
> To take a new acquaintance of thy mind.

16 On "online" and "offline" modes of thought, see Derek Bickerton, *Adam's Tongue: How Humans Made Language, How Language Made Humans* (New York: Hill and Wang, 2009). A proper understanding of these modes of mental activity should be framed within Mead's theory of social interactionism and of the mind's self-interaction.
17 "Though I am parted, yet my mind, / That's more myself, still stays behind" (Thomas Carew, "To My Mistress in Absence," in *The Poems of Thomas Carew,* online edition at http://www.luminarium.org/sevenlit/carew/absence.htm

18 Charles H. Cooley, *Social Organization: A Study of the Larger Mind* (New York: Scribner's, 1909); see also Mead, *Mind, Self, and Society from the Standpoint of a Social Behaviorist* (1934).
19 "So many selves," in *XAIPE*, ed. with an afterword by George James Firmage (1950; rpt. New York and London: Liveright-Kindle edition, 2007). Available at https://www.amazon.com/XAIPE-Cummings/dp/0871401681
20 *i* is also the title of "six nonlectures" delivered at Harvard by Cummings between 1952 and 1955.
21 The mental capacity and intersubjective phenomenon of *joint attention* has been considered by Michael Tomasello one of the grounding elements of the peculiarly intersubjective human mind (see "Joint Attention and Cultural Learning," in his *The Cultural Origins of Communication* [Cambridge, MA: Harvard University Press, 1999], 56–93). Woolf's detailed description of the London moment can be read as an elaborate exercise in joint attention—and the same applies to our close reading of the passage. Further reflections on attention can be found in my paper "Atención a la atención (Sociobiología, estética y pragmática de la atención)," *Analecta Malacitana* 33 (December 2012): 3–27. Available online at http://www.anmal.uma.es/numero33/indice.htm
22 Gilles Fauconnier and Mark Turner, "Conceptual Integration Networks," expanded web version available at http://markturner.org/cin.web/cin.html
23 From Emily Brontë's "Stanzas" (*Poems by Currer, Ellis and Acton Bell,* 1846; in *Online Literature*, http://www.online-literature.com/bronte/1360/):

> To-day, I will seek not the shadowy region;
>   Its unsustaining vastness waxes drear;
> And visions rising, legion after legion,
>   Bring the unreal world too strangely near.

Brontë was another "wit woman" awed by the potential multitudes she contained. Brontë's poem (there is actually some debate as to the extent of her sister Charlotte's revision) is also a deliberate exercise in mental balance and integration through the conscious creation of symbols for the mind. It provides an account, too, of a woman writer's coming to terms with internal and external pressures on female self-fashioning, and with her own potentially threatening excess of sensibility and imagination.

24 The recent discovery of mirror neurons, which fire on watching common experiences of looking, moving, or grasping in other subjects, provides an additional neurobiological grounding for the well-established fact of the distinctive human sociality. See, for example, Daniel Lametti, "Mirroring Behavior: How Mirror Neurons Let Us Interact with Others," *Scientific American*, June 9, 2009. Available online at http://www.scientificamerican.com/article.cfm?id=mirroring-behavior

25 Quoted in Lee, *Virginia Woolf*, 171.
26 See Jérôme Dokic, "Voyages mentaux dans les temps," a lecture at the École Normale Supérieure (Les Lundis de la Philosophie) February 10, 2014. Online audio at *Savoirs ENS*: http://savoirs.ens.fr/expose.php?id=1655
27 Perhaps only rivaled by *Whitaker's Table of Precedency*, in "The Mark on the Wall."
28 The weight of the patriarchal past can also be detected between the lines in Emily Brontë's "Stanzas":

> I'll walk, but not in old heroic traces,
>   And not in paths of high morality,
> And not among the half-distinguished faces,
>   The clouded forms of long-past history.
> I'll walk where my own nature would be leading:
>   It vexes me to choose another guide.

29 Ellen Moers, *Literary Women: The Great Writers* (Garden City, NY: Doubleday, 1976); Sandra M. Gilbert and Susan Gubar, *The Madwoman in the Attic: The Woman Writer and the Nineteenth-Century Literary Imagination* (New Haven, CT: Yale University Press, 1979); Elaine Showalter, *A Literature of Their Own: British Women Novelists from Brontë to Lessing* (Princeton, NJ: Princeton University Press, 1977).
30 See, for example, Catharine R. Stimpson, "Woolf's Room, Our Project: The Building of Feminist Criticism," in *The Future of Literary Theory*, ed. Ralph Cohen (New York: Routledge, 1989) 129–43; Toril Moi, "Who's Afraid of Virginia Woolf? Feminist Readings of Woolf," in her *Sexual/Textual Politics: Feminist Literary Theory* (London: Routledge, 1990), 1–17.
31 There exists, however, a possible neurophysiological explanation for the "voices in the head" heard by so many unstable geniuses and original minds. See Charles Fernyhough, "The Science of Voices in Your Head" (video lecture), *YouTube (The Royal Institution)*, September 14, 2016, https://youtu.be/95otBlepVHc
32 Lee, *Virginia Woolf*, 331. Woolf's disgust with heterosexuality and penetration may partly originate in a childhood episode of sexual molestation by a half-brother of hers. See Lee, *Virginia Woolf*, p. 127: "Over and over again in her re-creations of the imaginative world of childhood, there is a moment of fear or shame or panic, the image of a safe private world being invaded, often with the strong sense of sexual threat."
33 See Briggs, *Virginia Woolf: An Inner Life*, 33; Lee, *Virginia Woolf*, 298–340.
34 Luis Eduardo Aute, "De paso" (from *Albanta*; Madrid: Ariola, 1978); lyrics in Música.com, http://www.musica.com/letras.asp?letra=1009738
35 See my note on "Prisons and Worlds of the Mind," *Ibercampus* (*Vanity Fea*), April 29, 2017, http://www.ibercampus.eu/prisons-and-worlds-of-the-mind-4645.htm

36 Briggs, *Virginia Woolf: An Inner Life*, 321.
37 See my introduction to *Gender, I-Deology*, ed. Chantal Cornut-Gentille D'Arcy and José Ángel García-Landa (Amsterdam: Rodopi, 1996). Woolf's ideal of androgyny was received favorably by many feminist critics, for example, Carolyn Heilbrun in *Toward a Recognition of Androgyny* (New York: Knopf, 1973). On the psychopathology of mental androgyny, see D. W. Winnicott, "Split-Off Male and Female Elements Found Clinically in Men and Women: Theoretical Inferences," in *Psychanalytic Forum* 4, ed. J. Linden (New York: International Universities Press, 1972). A neurological perspective on sexual difference in the brain can be found in Simon Baron Cohen's *The Essential Difference: The Truth about the Male and Female Brain* (New York: Perseus, 2003).

7

Complexities of Social Cognition in Dorothy Richardson's *Pointed Roofs*

Patrick Colm Hogan

Social cognition—the way our minds operate in relation to other minds—is among the most important areas of research in cognitive science.[1] This is because it is one of the most important areas of human life, underlying communication, cooperation, and the very possibility of culture. A key concept in social cognition research is "Theory of Mind" (ToM), our capacity to understand (in some degree) the intentions and experiences of other people.[2] ToM is sometimes referred to as "cognitive empathy," which is to say, sharing someone's thoughts, as opposed to "affective empathy," which is to say, "feeling what another feels."[3] In a more colloquial and hyperbolic idiom, it is called "mind reading." (I will use "ToM" and "cognitive empathy"—and, on occasion, "mind reading"—interchangeably.) As the present volume attests, ToM is important in cognitive literary study; it has been influentially developed by literary cognitivists, prominently Lisa Zunshine.[4]

Most cognitive literary study involves taking up concepts from cognitive science in order to illuminate literary structures or to explore individual literary works. In *What Literature Teaches Us about Emotion*, I have argued that the benefits of joining cognitive science and literature may go in both directions.[5] Successful and enduring literary works present us with detailed depictions of human thought and action; moreover, they do so in ways that readers find resonant and compelling, even across cultures and historical periods. The point is perhaps most obvious in relation to emotion, since literature tends to appeal to the recipient's emotions through the emotion-laden acts and experience of the characters, and the value we attribute to literary works is largely a matter of our (recipient) emotions. The value of literature for understanding simulation is only slightly less evident. Simulation is the process by which we imagine counterfactuals (what might have happened, but didn't), hypotheticals (what might still happen), and aspects of reality that we cannot experience directly (e.g., other people's thoughts and feelings). Literary authors appear to be particularly skilled at simulation. That does not necessarily suggest that authors will make any worthwhile, explicit comments about cognitive science and simulation. However, it does indicate that literary works are prime instances of complex, sharable, and effective simulation. As such, studying literary works should advance our understanding of simulation too—for example, the degree to which it is distinctively patterned for individual authors or what components it has and how those might be varied.

It seems clear that literary study is likely to prove fruitful for enhancing our general comprehension of ToM as well. ToM enters literature most obviously with the characters' understanding of one another. It enters also in the author's tacit understanding of his or her readership, his or her ability to anticipate emotional response or cognitive inference, thus knowing when to include information or leave it out. It enters in the reader's understanding of the author. It enters with the author's and reader's simulation of the characters (simulation being one of the two modes of ToM processing, the other being inference or "theory" proper).[6]

In the following pages, I would like to consider some aspects of Dorothy Richardson's *Pointed Roofs* in order to ascertain what it might contribute to our understanding of ToM. Specifically, Zunshine has argued that literature is characterized by an unusual degree of sociocognitive complexity. In connection with this, she has focused particularly on embedding, the ability of ToM to operate recursively. For example, suppose John understands that Jane imagines that Hamlet is considering suicide when he says, "To be, or not to be" (III.i.62). John applies ToM to understand Jane's application of ToM to Hamlet. Embedding is certainly important, and Zunshine is right to emphasize it. However, there are many other facets of sociocognitive complexity. These include the classes of targets for ToM, the means we use to understand those targets, and the functions served by such understanding. Of course, not all of these topics are likely to be addressed by a single author. But there are some authors who seem particularly well suited for research aiming to explore some of these areas.

This brings us to Dorothy Richardson and her novel. One reason to study Richardson in relation to ToM is that *Pointed Roofs* exhibits considerable interest in "psychology—that strange, new subject."[7] I am not referring here to any influence then-current psychological thought might have had on Richardson. Indeed, authors' attempts to conform their stories to prior theories are usually of little or no value for advancing our knowledge in a given area, since they commonly repeat both the insights and the errors of the theory they are drawing on. The value here is more general, deriving from the author's interest in the human mind.

In keeping with this interest, *Pointed Roofs* is a "stream of consciousness" novel, a work that systematically depicts the ongoing sequence of thoughts that occupy a person in waking life.[8] Indeed, the application of "stream of consciousness" was "first of all" to Richardson.[9] This is true literally, as Richardson's *Pointed Roofs* was the first literary work to be labeled "stream of consciousness."[10] As such, *Pointed Roofs* stands at the beginning of a series of novels that are almost definitive of High Modernism and therefore are likely to be central to a consideration of ToM and Modernism—James Joyce's *Ulysses*, Virginia Woolf's *Mrs. Dalloway* and *To the Lighthouse*, and William Faulkner's *As I Lay Dying* and *The Sound and the Fury*.[11]

Some Aspects of Theory of Mind

Before turning to Richardson, however, it is valuable to consider some different aspects of ToM. We may draw a broad distinction among three components of an account of ToM processing. First, there are targets (the persons whose thought we wish to understand); second, there are means (the procedures involved in coming to that understanding); third, there are functions (the ends served by ToM, understood in broad, principally evolutionary terms).

The targets of ToM processes are various and complex. The most obvious targets are other individuals, ranging from people we know well to people we do not know at all. We also use ToM processes on ourselves, most obviously when we try to imagine what we will do in the future or what we would do in counterfactual or hypothetical situations (on some of the errors we make in such imaginings).[12] As I have discussed elsewhere, there is also reason to believe that we engage in ToM processing with respect to social subgroups or even people in general.[13]

As to means, it is standard to distinguish two sorts of ToM processing—simulation and inference. Simulation involves, roughly, imagining oneself in another person's situation. Indeed, the relation between self-understanding and understanding others through simulation is very close. As Devos, Huynh, and Banaji explain, "Conscious attempts to adopt another person's perspective ... prompted individuals to engage cognitive processes typically reserved for introspection."[14] Inference—or "theory theory" as it is called—involves reasoned drawing of conclusions based on information about the other person. In each case, we may think about the process as involving some general principles with parameters or variables. When we engage in cognitive empathy, we set the variables differently from what they would be for us. The parameters are most significantly of two sorts: first, informational (allowing for differences in the target's perceptual perspective, and other relevant, particular knowledge); second, dispositional (allowing for differences in the target's propensities).

For example, if I eat cream, I suffer digestive distress. So, when I see an ice cream parlor, I have no particular reaction. Now, suppose I wonder what a particular four-year-old will do, if I do not manage to keep him from seeing the ice cream parlor. I think of his disposition (virtual mania for ice cream) and his situation (currently the ice cream parlor is not visible, but if we keep heading along this road it will appear before us, bright, glittery, and unmistakable). In other words, I take general principles—for example, that we tend to pursue opportunities for enjoyment and shun threats of pain—and alter such variables as "eating ice cream = threat" (for me) to "eating ice cream = opportunity" (for him). The difference between simulation and inference is simply that I "run" the procedure imaginatively in the former case, but reflect on the implications of the propositions in the second case. It seems clear that we engage in both simulation and inference in virtually every case of cognitive empathy.

Of course, none of this is simple, and we can specify further complications as we find necessary. For example, disposition is an extremely intricate construct. It involves the presence of concepts (will the boy recognize the building as an ice cream parlor?), reasoning capacities (if he does not recognize the building, will he draw the appropriate inference from the looming, plastic, ice cream cone on the building's roof?), abilities to distinguish short-term from long-term interests (e.g., what if he knows he won't be allowed to have cheese cake later if he has ice cream now? or what if he is lactose intolerant and will suffer digestive distress later?), capacity to modulate short-term impulses, and so forth.

Moreover, we may understand different sorts of target by reference to variables, and in some cases with respect to the simulation-inference division. For example, cognitive empathy with "anyone" (as in "anyone passing by would think I was yelling at him; they wouldn't know his hearing aid was on the fritz") assumes a sort of common, human disposition, with variation in information alone. It could readily involve simulation or inference. In contrast, social subgroups would often be based not only on differences in information but also on—often stereotypical—dispositional properties (e.g., that women are more empathic and men better at spatial rotation tasks). In addition, such groups may be "in-groups," with which one identifies, or "out-groups," with which one does not. In the case of out-groups, simulation is much less likely, largely restricting cognitive empathy to inference.[15] Finally, one might expect cognitive empathy with individuals to be primarily a matter of individually differentiating features, whether idiosyncrasies of personality or specific limitations on information. This would be in keeping with the general observation that specific-level information tends to drive out general, category-level information.[16]

The preceding references to in-groups and out-groups may serve to remind us of a distinction that is important in discussions of shared emotion, but as far as I can tell has not received as much attention with respect to cognitive empathy. I am referring to the distinction between spontaneous and effortful empathy. Spontaneous affective empathy is a sharing of a target's feelings that occurs automatically. Effortful affective empathy, in contrast, involves a decision to try to adopt the target's point of view and thus share his or her feelings. Spontaneous empathy is more likely to occur with in-group members, in part because group identification gives rise to a particular "interpersonal stance" or response orientation regarding another person's emotions.[17] If my interpersonal stance is *parallel* (or *congruent*) with the target, then I will feel the same sort of emotion as he or she feels—rejoicing in his or her triumphs and grieving over his or her losses. However, when my interpersonal stance is *antagonistic* (or *complementary*), I will respond with indifference, Schadenfreude, jealousy, or some other contradictory emotion. In principle, the distinction between spontaneous and effortful should arise in cognitive empathy as well, with similar inhibitions deriving from in-group/out-group identifications (the parallel versus complementary division may arise also, such that I might, for example, presume the validity or invalidity of the other person's beliefs).

Finally, ToM has several clear functions. The most obvious is the anticipation of causal sequences in a target's intentional behavior that may involve threats or opportunities. It has obvious adaptive value to be able to figure out that someone else is eyeing one's food covetously and picking up a sharp stick with the possible aim of using it as a weapon; it also has obvious adaptive value to be able to recognize that an attractive member of the opposite sex has undertaken extensive grooming suggesting that he or she is in the mood for love. Another obvious function is in the development of cooperative behavior. We may accomplish more when our efforts are coordinated with those of other people, and that coordination is pretty much impossible if we have no good idea of what other people are thinking. Of course, we may also wish to act in our own, individual interests at times. For example, I might wish to hide some fresh meat from my companions, saving it for myself. But to hide something, I need to have a sense of what other people know or might learn. ToM used to deceive or manipulate is referred to as "Machiavellian intelligence." (It has been treated extensively in literary study by Blakey Vermeule.)[18] A third, obvious function is in learning, thus the acquisition of individual skills as well as larger routines of cultural convention.

Dorothy Richardson does not present us with a systematic treatment of cognitive empathy. This is a novel, after all, not a psychology book. However, she addresses the nature and function of ToM processes in ways that are to some degree surprising and that may therefore be particularly valuable for advancing our comprehension of this complex and important topic.

Pointed Roofs and the Limits of Cognitive Empathy

When perusing *Pointed Roofs* with ToM in mind, perhaps the first thing that is likely to strike a reader is that Richardson—or at least her main character, Miriam—shows remarkably little interest in minds. The stream of consciousness in the novel tends to focus on perceptual features. Here is a typical stream-of-consciousness sequence from early on in the book:

> The organ was playing "The Wearin' o' the Green." It had begun that tune during the last term at school, in the summer. It made her think of rounders in the hot school garden, singing-classes in the large green room, all the class shouting "Gather *roses* while ye may," hot afternoons in the shady north room, the sound of turning pages, the hum of the garden beyond the sun-blinds, meetings in the sixth form study. . . . Lilla, with her black hair and the specks of bright amber in the brown of her eyes, talking about free-will. (*PR* 2–3; ellipsis in the original)

The sequence begins by actually occluding the person playing the tune, saying that "the organ was playing," not that a person was playing the organ, that "it had begun," not that someone had begun it. The reference to "singing-classes" stresses the perception of music and Miriam's own agency, but not that of anyone else; the heat of the afternoon and the shade in the north room are equally perceptual.

The reference to reading does not concern what the students are reading or what they think about it, but merely the sound of the pages turning. Other people's minds enter minimally at the end when we are informed about the subject of Lilla's speech. But even then it is only an abstract topic, presumably mentioned explicitly (e.g., "Consider free will"), not something that requires much exercise of ToM capacities.

The passage is not at all unique. It is part of Miriam's general attitude. For example, when she speaks with someone later, we read that she "noted the easy range of the child's voice, how smoothly it slid from bird-like queries and chirpings, to the consoling tones of the lower register" (*PR* 38). It is as if Miriam did not pay any attention to the meanings of the words, but only to their sounds. There is a hint of mind in the word "consoling" (and also "queries"), but it is not even clear that the consolation here is intentional, since it is the "tones" that are consoling (and in context "queries" seems to suggest pitch contours more than interest in information). She reflects on how she sits with someone and hears "her unchanged voice saying" something—not the person saying something, but the voice doing so. At another point, she thinks of a conversation with a character named Elsa; she "remember[s] monosyllables and the pallid averted face and Elsa's dreadful ankles" (*PR* 143) almost as if there is no person behind the monosyllables and ankles.[19]

Indeed, Miriam seems not to think much about other people's ideas and emotions. Just before leaving her family in England in order to travel to Germany, she reflects that "she had never once thought of their 'feeling' her going away" (*PR* 19). One might think that she suffers from some pathological inability to engage in cognitive empathy. However, that is not the case. There are moments where it is clear that she is perfectly able to infer intentions and interests, even embedded ToM processing. For example, when her father is speaking with someone about her situation in Germany, she immediately and easily recognizes that he "is trying to make the Dutchman think I am being taken as a pupil to a finishing school in Germany" (*PR* 24). Indeed, she is readily able to understand even more complex ToM sequences. For example, at one point she infers that Fräulein wishes Mademoiselle to engage in conversation that will help the girls learn French. Moreover, as part of this embedding, she recognizes that Mademoiselle might have understood Fräulein's "design," but does not; "she felt quite sure that Mademoiselle had no clear idea in her own mind that she was carrying out any design at all" (*PR* 142).

In part, the paucity of intersubjective understanding is simply a matter of Richardson being sensitive to the limits of "mind reading," her being aware that our abilities to understand other people's thought and emotion are highly fallible and are likely to be effective only in some circumstances. As Nicholson-Weir puts it, "Richardson acutely understands the difficulties of intersubjectivity."[20] We see Miriam facing the inaccessibility of other minds several times in the course of the novel. For example, at one point, she "wondered how [Gertrude] really felt. That, she realised with a vision of Gertrude going on through life in smart costumes, one would never know" (*PR* 131). The detail about "smart costumes" is revealing. Gertrude is aware of what sorts of outfit are in or out of fashion and will invariably wear the fashionable ones. But "costume" here also suggests pretense or concealment. Thus, one reason we will never know what other people think is that they are always capable of partially concealing it. This is merely a way of stating part of what is captured by the idea of Machiavellian intelligence. We find it again when Miriam "wondered intensely what was in Elsa's mind behind her faint hard blue dress" (*PR* 230).

But the problem is not confined to deceit. Sometimes even the most sincere efforts at conveying one's ideas and experiences fail. Miriam "felt that if only she could make her meaning clear all difficulties must vanish" (*PR* 262). So, she tries to convey the particularity of her ideas and experiences. But she cannot do it. Sometimes this results in gross misunderstandings that, despite their grossness, seem irreparable. After a joking comment, Miriam realizes that she has conveyed entirely the wrong impression. She then wonders, "How could Mademoiselle misunderstand her insane remark? What did [Mademoiselle] mean [by her response]? What did she really think of her?" (*PR* 271–72). In some cases, Richardson seems to imply that misunderstanding is inevitable because people do not even have underlying motives. They just act, perhaps imitatively. "Fräulein goes on having her school. . . . What does she really think?" she asks, answering her own question, "Out in the world people don't think" (*PR* 286; ellipsis in the original).

Part of the difficulty is with Miriam herself. As Mark Wollaeger points out, "Too often, it seems, Miriam is depth; everyone else, surface."[21] There are suggestions that she is inclined to engage in extensive out-grouping, and disinclined to engage in effortful cognitive empathy. As to the former, she reflects that she is "unsociable" and "could not think of anyone who did not offend her. I don't like men and I loathe women" (*PR* 31). The comment on men and women is particularly striking. It would initially seem that she must identify herself with one group or the other, but she does not really do so. Both are outgroups for her, apparently leaving her with no in-group, thus no class of people with whom she is likely to experience spontaneous cognitive empathy easily and routinely. As to effortful cognitive empathy, Miriam's employer, Fräulein, comments critically on Miriam's insensitivity and its effects on her teaching. Specifically, Fräulein remonstrates with her, saying that, if she continues her current practices, "you will neither make yourself understood nor will you be loved by your pupils" (*PR* 265). Instead, "you must enter into the personality of each pupil and must sympathise with the struggles of each one upon the path on which our feet are set" (*PR* 266). Such effortful perspective taking seems fairly rare with Miriam—except perhaps regarding a few figures, such as her father and Fräulein. These exceptions may be result from attachment feelings; perhaps attachment bonding increases the likelihood of effortful ToM processing.

On the other hand, Richardson may not be suggesting that Miriam is exceptional in her empathic limitations. It seems to me quite possible that Miriam is not less inclined toward cognitive empathy than the rest of us. In other words, the novel may indicate that Miriam is ordinary, and that we are inclined to overestimate the role of cognitive empathy in our social interactions. Perhaps we do not dwell as much on the inner lives of others as we imagine.

Pointed Roofs and the Means of Cognitive Empathy

A remarkable feature of this novel's treatment of ToM is the way Richardson spells out some of the more minimal and mechanical processes that constitute a great deal of spontaneous cognitive empathy. Specifically, Richardson suggests that much of what we think about other people's feelings and intentions is a direct result of simple expressive features. We perceive these features and experience our own response (whether parallel or contradictory) as information about the target's thoughts. The cases she mentions would often appear to rely on innate sensitivities, though they may involve learned associations as well. They are often a matter of our sensitivity to "unconditioned low-level perceptual information such as low spatial frequencies in fearful faces . . . , the sclera of fearful eyes . . . , or increasing sound intensity."[22]

In *Pointed Roofs*, as in life, many of these perceptual cues are a matter of facial expression. This is consistent with empirical research. Sapolsky notes that "though we derive subliminal information from bodily cues, such as posture, we get the most information from faces."[23] In keeping with this, many of the cases where Miriam has some sense of other people's interiority result from an apparently spontaneous response provoked by facial expression. Thus, she recounts the feelings of two companions with the image, "Emma shrinking back with a horrified face against Jimmie who was leaning forward entranced with watching." (Note that this is cognitive empathy, even though it concerns emotion, because it involves knowing what the target is experiencing, not sharing the feeling of the target.)

Moreover, a target's Machiavellian deceit may be foiled by his or her inability to adequately imitate an innately programmed expression, such as a smile. Thus, when Miriam recognizes falsity in "a little insincerely smiling man" (*PR* 255), it is by way of the smile. The point goes along with Richardson's suggestion that there is often no interiority that accompanies behavior; when people "don't think," they "grimace." Elsewhere, she explains that Fräulein "wanted me to grimace, simply. You know—be like other people" (*PR* 275). But, again, the falsity of the grimace is often palpable, due to the relatively automatic nature of a sincere smile and one's automatic emotional and cognitive response to sincere and false smiles.

Though smiles are important, the eyes are area of the face that is most expressive—as Sapolsky puts it, "Eyes give the most information";[24] therefore, eyes are the most consequential for this automatic ToM response. Richardson sometimes goes out of her way to convey the automatic triggering of basic understanding by way of a target's gaze. For example, she remarks on some items that "they were certainly not pretty hats," continuing, "she wondered at Mademoiselle's French eyes being so impressed" (*PR* 177). She senses interest directly from the eyes, so much so that she does not even say that Mademoiselle was impressed, but rather that her eyes were impressed. She senses this presumably due to gaze direction, pupil dilation,[25] and the extent to which the eyes are open. Construing this as "being . . . impressed" does involve some interpretation, but relatively little. The less directly communicated aspect of Mademoiselle's mind—why she was impressed— leaves Miriam bewildered. She considers another one of her companions similarly, explaining that "Millie looked pensively about her with vague disapproval. Her eyebrows were up" (*PR* 270). The eyes convey disapproval, principally through their wide parting and associated high eyebrows. But the disapproval is necessarily "vague," which is to say, its precise source and quality are not clear.

Miriam's interactions with Fräulein often involve concern over the latter's thoughts and feelings, both because Fräulein is her employer and because Miriam apparently has some attachment feelings for her, as already noted. Whether she is distressed or at peace with Fräulein's attitude, that attitude is regularly signaled through her eyes. Thus, she explains, "Fräulein's eyes had spoiled it. Fräulein was angry about it for some extraordinary reason." Or, at another time, "Fräulein had looked at her in that moment as an equal" (*PR* 210, 250). Like anger, disgust and contempt may be (partially) signaled through the eyes.[26] In keeping with this, Miriam ties her sense of Fräulein's disgust to her gaze as well, explaining that "her eyes were drawn to meet Fräulein's and she read there a disgust and a loathing such as she had never seen" (*PR* 259).

Other mechanical cues derive from other forms of physical expression, often innate. These include vocal tone (e.g., pitch contour), volume, and other sound features.[27] For example, Miriam finds one character sad as "her little voice [was] filled with tears" (*PR* 39). The comment may be roughly literal (if she actually choked up when speaking) or it may mean that the sound quality suggested sadness. In either case, it is a mechanical, perceptual trigger of ToM understanding. Similarly, she remarks on how "Fräulein's voice had thickened and grown caressing" (*PR* 150). She had worried her tone might indicate anger, but it does not. She concludes that "perhaps no one was in trouble" (*PR* 150). Elsewhere, she refers to voices that are "thick and plaintive" or "thin and cold" (*PR* 247). In these and other cases, it is again purely perceptual features that elicit a sense of the target's attitude.

Unsurprisingly, posture and touch enter as well.[28] At one point, she finds someone's "shape, all miserable and ashamed" (*PR* 221). Here, she is responding to postural cues of shame. At another point, she refers to the way a girl hugs her. She characterizes the "contact" as "more motherly than her mother's" (*PR* 39). She finds herself surprised "that a human form could bring such a sense of warm nearness, that human contours could be eloquent" (*PR* 39). Touch is one of those mechanical signals to which we are perhaps particularly sensitive in childhood, when a parent's touch can be "eloquent" in conveying an attitude that it is important for the child to recognize. But such emotional conveyance is not confined to childhood or parent-infant contact.[29]

Of course, not all Miriam's means of achieving cognitive empathy are mechanical responses to expressive signals. Another very striking feature of Richardson's novel is the degree to which the understanding of other people's thoughts is a function of identity categories. Indeed, there is very little ToM processing in the novel that appears to bear on individual features. Moreover, even Miriam's self-understanding is to some extent mediated by categorization. Here too one might wonder if this is best understood as an idiosyncrasy of Miriam's or as a generalizable pattern, suggesting that we all pay less attention to individuating features than we commonly believe.

More exactly, there are moments when Miriam apparently operates on more individuating presumptions, as with her father, or her imagination of what her mother would say to her in a particular circumstance. But these are a very small minority of cases. She also sometimes thinks in more general terms about just anyone. For example, at one point, "She almost laughed once or twice when she met an eye and thought how funny she must look 'tearing along' with her long, thick, black jacket bumping against her" (*PR* 203). Clearly, she is referring here to common responses differentiated only by information, not by the varying dispositions of the people involved.

Nonetheless, identity categories are, in this novel, far more common means of inferring the thoughts and feelings of other people. Moreover, it is not a matter of any such category. Miriam does draw on a number of categories locally, as when she wonders, "did elderly people fear cancer all the time" (*PR* 287), basing her ToM reasoning on properties attributed to the group of elderly people. But she draws on two sets of categories most frequently and most consistently.

The first of these sets defines national identity. The stress on national identity is almost certainly a product of historical contingencies. Indeed, it may suggest something about the way many people in England or perhaps Europe more broadly were thinking about identity in the time leading up to the First World War. This historically and culturally specific identity categorization is subdivided by a second, cross-cultural identity categorization—that of sex. Thus, when seeking to understand psychological states or explain behavior, Miriam commonly categorizes targets as English or German (or French), sometimes going on to subdivide those groups into male and female. Of course, at times she does also draw on sex categorization independent of nationality.

It is worth noting that Miriam has an unusual relation to identity categories. She sees the world in terms of social identity categories and socially defined membership in those categories—for example, English and German, with Miriam herself categorized as English. However, she feels an affinity for her socially assigned out-group, whom she tends to value more highly than the socially assigned in-group (e.g., in her early thoughts about "wonderful Germans"). On the other hand, this out-group enthusiasm is not stable. Indeed, we see that she can be shifted out of her out-group idealization, adopting a more usual preference for the in-group—the English, for example. I imagine that this is a fairly common pattern with a certain sort of identity-defined liberalism, which maintains identity-group divisions, but asserts the superiority of the out-group; a more effective and enduring solution to identity-group antagonisms would almost certainly involve undermining the identity-based divisions, rather than reversing their hierarchy, especially as the reversal may be insecure and easily reversed again.

In any case, Miriam's thoughts about other minds are dominated by national categories. In her new home, she encounters some English and some German girls. At times, she considers herself English and wonders whether this means other English women have the same thoughts and feelings. For example, "She glanced towards the two tables of English girls in the centre of the room wondering whether they felt as she did" (*PR* 135). In this case, she is seeing not only the others in terms of national categories but herself as well.

More often, however, she seems to dissociate herself from the identity group to which she would be socially assigned. For example, she reflects on the girls' attitude toward herself, thinking "they did not dislike her. Of that she felt sure. She could not say this for even one of the English girls. But the German girls did not dislike her" (*PR* 67). This is significant in two ways. First, she understands and tacitly explains the feelings of all the girls by reference not to individual dispositions, but to national character. Second, that national character is, from Miriam's perspective, superior on the German side—since one typically prefers those who like one to those who do not. On the other hand, this idealization is itself partially qualified by the extent to which Miriam reflections are guided by national categories. Thus, she subsequently thinks that "those German eyes did not criticise her" (*PR* 67). This is already interesting, since it combines the perceptual and categorical processes that we witnessed earlier in the case of Mademoiselle's "French eyes." But the more surprising point comes just after. She is considering the German girls' thoughts about herself, and she thinks that their ToM processes must be categorical as well: "Perhaps, she suggested to herself, they thought a good deal of English people in general" (*PR* 67). In other words, it was not that they understood and approved of Miriam as an individual; it was rather that they understood and evaluated English people in positive ways, just as she is doing with the Germans. Elsewhere in the novel, Richardson suggests that ToM processing based on national categorization is indeed common among the Germans in the novel, though not necessarily in a way that idealizes a national out-group. For example, Bertha complains that she cannot "explain the peculiarities of the French temperament" (*PR* 273). When Miriam says she cannot talk about her mother, Fräulein Pfaff accounts for this reticence (or delicacy, or refinement) with the words "That is English" (*PR* 309).

Thus, Miriam tacitly assumes that the German girls share national category-based ToM processing with her. This is consistent with her (partial) identification with the Germans. That sense of identification with the socially defined out-group is presumably the result of feeling ill at ease within her own group, feeling an irreconcilable dissociation between her "practical identity"[30] and that of the English more generally. Practical identity is the range of preferences, interests, capacities, and so on, that underlie one's modes of acting and interacting in the world. It may or may not be consistent with the norms and expectations carried by one's categorial identity, thus the groups to which one is socially assigned (e.g., "English"). In keeping with this practical-categorial incompatibility, Miriam thinks about "a little gathering of English people"—the congregation in an English church. "Probably they were all Conservatives," she reflects; "that was part of their 'refinement'" (*PR* 102). In connection with this, she first reflects that she must be a "radical" rather than a conservative, thus a nonconforming English person. However, she concludes that she should think of herself rather as connected with the Germans. Conversely, the continuity of her practical identity with that of the Germans is suggested elsewhere. For example, worried about other people's attitudes, she thinks, "It was all right. No one had noticed her—or if either of the Germans had they would not think like that [i.e., critically]—they would understand—she believed in a way, they would understand."

Again, this is not to say that national categories are the only ones that are important for ToM inference in *Pointed Roofs*. In keeping with cross-cultural patterns, sex categorization is deeply consequential for Miriam's cognitive empathy. But, here too, the identity categorization operates with at least a superficial reversal of valuation. Thus, recurring to the perceptual-mechanical signals of interior states, Miriam reflects on what smiles show about women. "Those women," she thinks, "would smile those hateful women's smiles—smirks—self-satisfied smiles as if everybody were agreed about everything. She loathed women" (*PR* 13). Similarly, when she reflects on aspects of her mother's behavior—behavior that many of us would be inclined to view as parental (if we were to categorize it)—Miriam defines that behavior as female. For example, she realizes that she is not always inspired to play the piano well.

Thus, she is angry "when her mother and a woman here and there had taken for granted one should 'play when asked'" (*PR* 79). Miriam mutters "Women" in response to this recollection, implicitly explaining their incomprehension—thus inferring the mental state of her mother and the other person and accounting for their inability to understand Miriam's mental state—by reference to their sex category.

But, as already noted, cross-category identification is unstable. The instability seems to be based principally on sex. This is what one would expect, given the strength of sex categorization, which is almost certainly innate or innately prepared (therefore particularly easy to acquire socially). Thus, taking up a stereotype about men, Miriam thinks that "men's sermons were worse than women's smiles" (*PR* 107). More significantly, she comes to be disillusioned with Germans due to sex relations. "German men," she thinks, "despised women." In contrast, "her masters" at schools had been more "respectful than these Germans were" (*PR* 117). Her disapproval of gender relations in Germany serves to dispel her prior enthusiasm for the national out-group and to prepare her to return to England.

Pointed Roofs and the Functions of Cognitive Empathy

The most obvious functions of cognitive empathy concern isolating threats and opportunities with respect to other people, with particular attention given to cooperation, communication or deception, and learning. In other words, cognitive empathy serves one's own needs and interests, but it would appear to do so principally through what it tells us about other people. In contrast, Richardson seems to present ToM processes as operating mainly to inform us about ourselves. This necessarily involves understanding (or misunderstanding) other people. But in Richardson's depiction that understanding of others is much more directly self-involved than we commonly imagine. Even in cases where there is an issue of opportunities or threats (more often the latter than the former), Miriam's attention is ego-centered. For example, when she "felt she was in disgrace with the whole table" (*PR* 212), her concern seems to be more a matter of the shame she is currently experiencing, rather than any likely consequences in the thoughts and actions of others.

The idea that ToM bears on self-understanding is familiar in general terms. For example, Alicke, Guenther, and Zell explain that "self-concept construction and maintenance is a dynamic process of acquiring feedback from the environment and from other people."[31] However, Richardson's depiction suggests a more insistent self-focus such that a fuller development of self-conceptualization becomes a primary function of cognitive empathy.

More exactly, we may divide the principal functions of Miriam's ToM into self-understanding (or self-misunderstanding) and self-evaluation. To some extent, Miriam may arrive at a certain degree of self-understanding via understanding other people's understanding of herself. For example, she discusses her trip to Germany with Eve. Against Miriam's own apprehensions, Eve says that Miriam will "simply love" the "lectures" and will find her experience there "new and jolly." Miriam protests that Eve would "feel ill with fright." But Eve counters that "for you" (i.e., for Miriam), things will be different, "once you're there" (*PR* 7). In this exchange, Richardson at least allows the possibility that Eve understands the future Miriam better than the present Miriam does. In keeping with this, Miriam seems to achieve greater accuracy in cognitive empathy with herself through her ToM processing of Eve's cognitive empathy.

Of course, other people are not always more accurate in their understanding of Miriam (or any of us), and Miriam is not always open to their views either. For example, when faced with patriarchal stereotypes or role expectations, she rebels, as when we learn how "it filled her with fury to be regarded as one of a world of little tame things to be summoned by little men to be well-willed wives" (*PR* 208). In this case, she is very far from accepting another person's cognitive empathy with her—and rightly so, since the idea of her interlocutor does not fit her practical identity at all.

Indeed, Miriam's self-confident independence may lead us to expect that she would not frequently draw her self-understanding from other people—and that expectation is correct. But it does not follow that her self-understanding is immediate and effortless. It sometimes takes effort and experience of just the sort needed to understand other people. We see this, for example, in a passage we considered briefly before. In Germany, Miriam "discovered she could not always 'play'—even the things she knew perfectly" (*PR* 79). She needed to be in the proper mood, feel the right degree of inspiration, perhaps even feel adequately limber, in order to perform at her best. As a result of comprehending this fact about her performance capabilities, "she began to understand the fury that had seized her when her mother and a woman here and there had taken for granted one should 'play when asked'" (*PR* 79). The suggestion is that Miriam had found herself angry before, but had never really understood her own anger.

Now, she has learned enough to be able to infer the sources of her feelings; she has improved her cognitive empathy with her past self. We see another example of the same sort when her experiences in Germany lead her to reflect back on "all these years at the good school" in England. The contrast of her "masters" with (misogynistic) German men led her "bit by bit to understand her agony on the day of leaving" the old school (*PR* 121).

To at least some extent, Miriam improves her cognitive empathy for herself by induction from individual experiences. On the other hand, even this personal knowledge is never far removed from identity categories. The first case, concerning requests to play the piano, gives rise to her disdainful dismissal of "Women," noted earlier. The second treats national differences in male behavior. Moreover, Miriam sometimes understands even herself in terms of national categories, as when she thinks, "She was English and free. She had nothing to do with this German school" (*PR* 303).

Again, Miriam draws on ToM not only for understanding herself but also for evaluating herself. That self-evaluation often involves judging herself on the basis of other people's responses to her. A simple, perceptual case of this comes early in the novel, when Harriett assures Miriam that she is "*not* plain" (*PR* 17; italics in the original). As a result, Miriam "murmured" to herself, "I'm pretty—they like me" (*PR* 18).

On the other hand, like her self-understanding, Miriam's self-evaluation is limited in the degree to which it responds to the actual thought processes of other people. Indeed, Miriam's self-understanding and self-evaluation are often the result of what we might call *free simulation*, simulation that is not founded upon some particular event, such as a specific interaction with the other person. Sometimes such simulation does not involve even particular people that Miriam knows. For example, before going to Germany, she dreams of the people there. In the dream, "they came and stood and looked at her, and saw her as she was, without courage, without funds or good clothes or beauty, without charm or interest, without even the skill to play a part. They looked at her with loathing" (*PR* 13). Here, again, we find Miriam responding to a perceptual trigger—the expression of the other people's eyes. But in this case the eyes are in the heads of wholly fantastical people.

The point is not confined to dreams. On her way to take up her post, she imagines "one of the rooms at the old school, full of scornful girls. . . . They would laugh at her" (*PR* 26–27). In this case, the perceptual-expressive cue is in the vocalization of the imaginary observers, but the general situation is the same.

In both cases, then, the source of Miriam's understanding of herself is almost entirely unrelated to other people; it is almost entirely her own invention. Here, once again, we face the question of whether this is peculiar to Miriam or more general. If the latter, it suggests that what we learn about ourselves from other people may frequently have very little to do with those other people, since it is necessarily a matter of our own understanding or imagination of them. This also raises the issue of the degree to which shame is particularly consequential for such imaginations, since an enduring sense of shame is evidently the most important feeling underlying Miriam's free simulations in these cases. Indeed, shame is prominent even in cases where a real individual is the target. For example, her sense of shame is clear when she reflects that "she felt sure that if Fräulein Pfaff had been invisibly present at any one of her solitary conversational encounters with these German girls she would have been judged and condemned" (PR 143).

Richardson indicates that such imaginations are important. There is empirical research supporting the point. For example, Aron and Nardone explain that "undergraduate participants primed with the representation of their mother outperformed those who did not receive the prime on an academic achievement task."[32] Similarly, Schlenker writes that "people often imagine audiences that can serve as significant positive or negative reference groups for conduct."[33] The idea is more fully elaborated and specified in Richardson, with clearer implications for the functions of ToM processing.

Conclusion

In sum, we may distinguish numerous targets, means, and functions for ToM or cognitive empathy. Dorothy Richardson's novel points toward a number of possible qualifications of and extensions to the means and functions in particular. Most broadly, Richardson's representation of Miriam's stream of consciousness may suggest that our concerns with other people's interiority may be neither as pervasive nor as deep as we are often inclined to imagine. Indeed, in Richardson's novel, the concern with other people's minds occurs, at best, on an "as-needed" basis; moreover, it appears to be quite shallow even when it does appear.

Richardson's treatment of the means of achieving cognitive empathy is consistent with this limitation on ToM processing. Specifically, Richardson stresses the importance of mechanical triggers for our simulative understanding of other people's feelings. These are largely perceptual-expressive outcomes of emotion that are innate or easy to acquire, such that a particular emotion will tend to result in a particular facial expression, vocalization, or posture. We may respond to that facial expression, vocalization, or posture in either a parallel or a complementary way. In any case, our awareness of the source of the expression—thus the internal state of the target—is to a great extent automatic.

In addition to indicating the centrality of perceptual-expressive cues for ToM (perhaps especially ToM simulation), Richardson stresses identity categories as a key factor in ToM inference. Among identity categories, she places special emphasis on national categories, in part (one imagines) for idiosyncratic reasons, but in part for historical reasons relating to the development of nationalism in Europe.[34] These historically determined categories are subdivided by reference to universal and presumably innate sex categories. In treating both sorts of identity category, Richardson suggests that our relation to identity may be more complex than is often thought. Specifically, it may involve an out-group preference based on a sense of misalignment with one's socially defined in-group. However, that preference may be unstable and readily overturned, leading to a reestablishment of socially normative, in-group preference.

Richardson's novel also has implications for our understanding of the functions of ToM. First, the most obvious functions of cognitive empathy are focused on the target, even though they ultimately serve one's own purposes. For example, they might involve concerns about cooperation or communication. Richardson's presentation, however, indicates that the functions of cognitive empathy are more narrowly egocentric. Specifically, she suggests that they might principally concern self-understanding and self-evaluation. The self-evaluation may involve other peoples' verbal statements, but they may also result from one's own efforts at simulating or inferring one's own internal states, based in part on accumulating experience. The self-evaluation is likely to involve perceptual-expressive signals from others, such as particular ways of looking. On the other hand, a great deal of both self-understanding and self-evaluation appears to result from what we might term the "free" and "generalized" simulation of other people's responses. ("Free" simulation is not guided by any particular interactions and "generalized" simulations are not indexed to particular individuals.) In this way, the effects of other people on one's cognitive self-empathy may be quite limited even in cases where ToM embedding is involved (i.e., when one's self-evaluation derives from one's sense of the target's response to oneself). In cases of this sort, the simulated response of others may be principally a matter of one's own, underlying sense of shame (or, in some cases, pride).

Notes

1. This chapter also appears in Patrick Colm Hogan, *Personal Identity and Literature* (New York: Routledge, 2019). Reproduced with permission of the Licensor through PLSclear.
2. The concept is not uncontested; for critical views, see Ivan Leudar and Alan Costall, *Against Theory of Mind* (New York: Palgrave, 2009).
3. Martin Hoffman, "Empathy, Justice, and the Law," in *Empathy: Philosophical and Psychological Perspectives*, ed. Amy Coplan and Peter Goldie (Oxford: Oxford University Press, 2011), 230.
4. See Lisa Zunshine, *Why We Read Fiction: Theory of Mind and the Novel* (Columbus: Ohio State University Press, 2006) and "Sociocognitive Complexity," *Novel* 45.1 (2012): 13–18. See also the various contributions to Paula Leverage, Howard Mancing, Richard Schweickert, and Jennifer Marston William, eds., *Theory of Mind and Literature* (West Lafayette, IN: Purdue University Press, 2011).
5. Patrick Colm Hogan, *What Literature Teaches Us about Emotion* (Cambridge: Cambridge University Press, 2011).
6. On these as two modes of ToM processing, rather than two mutually exclusive accounts of such processing, see Martin Doherty, *Theory of Mind: How Children Understand Others' Thoughts and Feelings* (New York: Psychology Press, 2009), 48.
7. Dorothy Richardson, *Pointed Roofs* (London: Duckworth, 1921), 119. Hereafter cited in the text as *PR*. On Richardson's ambivalent relation to psychology, see Meghan Hammond, *Empathy and the Psychology of Literary Modernism* (Edinburgh: Edinburgh University Press, 2014), 60–62.
8. On the term "stream of consciousness" and its different uses, see Alan Palmer, "Stream of Consciousness and Interior Monologue," in *The Routledge Encyclopedia of Narrative Theory*, ed. David Herman, Manfred Jahn, and Marie-Laure Ryan (New York: Routledge, 2015), 570–71.
9. Katie Wales, *A Dictionary of Stylistics*, 3rd ed. (Harlow: Pearson Education, 2011), 394.
10. See Sydney Kaplan, "'Featureless Freedom' or Ironic Submission: Dorothy Richardson and May Sinclair," *College English* 32.8 (1971): 914–15.
11. Despite this, there has been relatively little treatment of Richardson drawing on ToM research or other ideas from cognitive science, leaving aside an occasional tantalizing aside, such as Dan Lloyd's brief comment on the relevance of Richardson and others to some aspects of neuroscientific research. See Dan Lloyd, "Neural Correlates of Temporality: Default Mode Variability and Temporal Awareness," *Consciousness and Cognition* 21 (2012): 702n5. There is some valuable, related work on phenomenology and Richardson, such as Rebecca Davis, "Stream

and Destination: Husserl, Subjectivity, and Dorothy Richardson's *Pilgrimage*," *Twentieth-Century Literature* 59 (2013): 309–42. The major exception is the work of Meghan Hammond. Hammond's study is complementary to the present chapter. She is concerned about cognitive empathy with the focalizer, Miriam, the way Richardson's work provides access to her mind.

12 Daniel Gilbert, Elizabeth Pinel, Timothy Wilson, Stephen Blumberg, and Thalia Wheatley, "Durability Bias in Affective Forecasting," in *Heuristics and Biases: The Psychology of Intuitive Judgment*, ed. Thomas Gilovich, Dale Griffin, and Daniel Kahneman (Cambridge: Cambridge University Press, 2002), 292–312.

13 Patrick Colm Hogan, "*Persuasion*: Lessons in Sociocognitive Understanding," in *Jane Austen and Sciences of the Mind*, ed. Beth Lau (New York: Routledge, 2017), 180–99.

14 Thierry Devos, Que-Lam Huynh, and Mahzarin Banaji, "Implicit Self and Identity," in *The Handbook of Self and Identity*, ed. Mark Leary, 2nd ed. (New York: Guilford, 2012), 158.

15 J. N. Gutsell, and M. Inzlicht, "Empathy Constrained: Prejudice Predicts Reduced Mental Simulation of Actions during Observation of Outgroups," *Journal of Experimental Social Psychology* 46 (2010): 841.

16 John Holland, Keith Holyoak, Richard Nisbett, and Paul Thagard, *Induction: Processes of Inference, Learning, and Discovery* (Cambridge, MA: MIT Press, 1986), 219, 221.

17 This is indicated by research reported in Michael Gazzaniga, *Who's in Charge? Free Will and the Science of the Brain* (New York: Ecco, 2011), 164; Machiel Keestra, "Bounded Mirroring: Joint Action and Group Membership in Political Theory and Cognitive Neuroscience," in *Essays on Neuroscience and Political Theory: Thinking the Body Politic*, ed. Frank Valk (New York: Routledge, 2012), 237; Grit Hain et al., "Neural Responses to Ingroup and Outgroup Members' Suffering Predict Individual Differences in Costly Helping," *Neuron* 68 (2010): 155; and Olga Klimecki and Tania Singer, "Empathy from the Perspective of Social Neuroscience," in *The Cambridge Handbook of Human Affective Neuroscience*, ed. Jorge Armony and Patrik Vuilleumier (Cambridge: Cambridge University Press, 2013), 542.

18 Blakey Vermeule, *Why Do We Care about Literary Characters?* (Baltimore: Johns Hopkins University Press, 2010).

19 As we will see, sound qualities of speech can have consequences for cognitive empathy. However, they offer very limited information. Thus, a critic such as Frattarola is right that Richardson makes use of sound to link characters, but the link is highly restricted. Moreover, as we will discuss, vision provides considerable ToM connection, contrary to Frattarola's discussion. See Angela Frattarola,

"Developing an Ear for the Modernist Novel: Virginia Woolf, Dorothy Richardson, and James Joyce," *Journal of Modern Literature* 33 (2009): 132–53.
20 Rebecca Nicholson-Weir, "Beyond Solipsism: Narrative and Consciousness in Dorothy Richardson's *Deadlock*," *The Space Between: Literature and Culture, 1914–1945* 11 (2015), unpaginated. Available at http://scalar.usc.edu/works/the-space-between-literature-and-culture-1914-1945/vol11_2015_nicholsonweir
21 Mark Wollaeger, "Richardson, Woolf, Lawrence: The Modernist Novel's Experiments with Narrative (I)," in *The Cambridge History of the English Novel*, ed. Robert Caserio and Clement Hawes (Cambridge: Cambridge University Press, 2011), 610.
22 David Sander, "Amygdala," in *The Oxford Companion to Emotion and the Affective Sciences*, ed. David Sander and Klaus Scherer (Oxford: Oxford University Press, 2009), 28–32.
23 Robert Sapolsky, *Behave: The Biology of Humans at Our Best and Worst* (New York: Penguin, 2017), 88.
24 Ibid., 89.
25 See, for example, Peter Lang and Margaret Bradley, "Reflexes (Emotional)," in *The Oxford Companion to Emotion and the Affective Sciences*, ed. Sander and Scherer, 336, on "the extra widening of the pupil to . . . attractive stimuli."
26 Paul Rozin, Jonathan Haidt, and Clark McCauley note that research shows that "some of the muscles around the eyes" are involved in "the disgust face." See their "Disgust," in *The Handbook of Emotions*, ed. Michael Lewis, Jeannette Haviland-Jones, and Lisa Feldman Barrett, 3rd ed. (New York: Guilford, 2008), 759.
27 See Patrik Vuilleumier, "Attention and Emotion," in *The Oxford Companion to Emotion and the Affective Sciences*, ed. Sander and Scherer, 55, on "vocal . . . sounds with emotional significance . . . such as prosody." For a fuller discussion, see Keith Oatley, Dacher Keltner, and Jennifer Jenkins, *Understanding Emotions*, 2nd ed. (Oxford: Blackwell, 2006), 102–3.
28 The former is suggested by Hammond's observation that "we often find Miriam frantically and unsuccessfully scanning the bodies around her for clues about the thoughts they hide"—though the scanning is not as frantic or unsuccessful as Hammond indicates. Hammond, *Empathy and the Psychology of Literary Modernism*, 77.
29 See Oatley, Keltner, and Jenkins, *Understanding Emotions*, 106–7, on communicating emotion through touch.
30 Patrick Colm Hogan, *Sexual Identities: A Cognitive Literary Study* (New York: Oxford University Press, 2018), 12–14.
31 See Mark Alicke, Corey Guenther, and Ethan Zell, "Social Self-Analysis Constructing and Maintaining Personal Identity," and William Swann and

Michael Buhrmester, "Self-Verification: The Search for Coherence," both in *The Handbook of Self and Identity*, ed. Leary, 292 and 406–8, respectively.

32 Arthur Aron and Natalie Nardone, "Self and Close Relationships," in *The Handbook of Self and Identity*, ed. Leary, 521–22.

33 Barry Schlenker, "Self-Presentation," in *The Handbook of Self and Identity*, ed. Leary, 554.

34 See Benedict Anderson, *Imagined Communities: Reflections on the Origin and Spread of Nationalism*, rev. ed. (London: Verso, 1991) on spontaneous and "official" nationalisms in the decades before the action of the novel.

8

Atmospheric Changes: Proust, Mind-Reading, and Errancy

Paul Sheehan

On the face of it, literary Modernism is inordinately well suited to embrace and even enlarge the possibilities of the psychological novel. The radical *inwardness* that has come to define the modernist project—in which characters' deepest, most innermost thoughts and sensations are depicted with cartographic precision—dovetails with the aims of psychologically oriented fiction. For Fredric Jameson, it is stylistic ingenuity that enables modernist interiority to plumb the depths of the psyche so effectively. He writes: "The most influential formal impulses of canonical modernism have been strategies of inwardness, which set out to reappropriate an alienated universe by transforming it into personal styles and private languages."[1] The "transformation" to which Jameson refers is thus oriented around the question of form. In large part, this can be attributed to a panoply of well-known literary techniques, some borrowed from earlier models (free indirect discourse, interior monologue), others more or less concocted by Modernism (stream of consciousness, fractured, nonlinear narration).

Yet acute or extreme inwardness does not define the psychological novel form, as it develops across the nineteenth century. From Jane Austen to George Eliot and Henry James, writers use modes of interiority in notably contrapuntal ways. Mental activity is prudently shaped to fit the contours of social reality, and to map out the detailed intimacies of human relationships. To capture thought, emotion, and desire with any degree of accuracy, in other words, means plotting the outcomes or effects of these operations in the external world. Some novelists, in fact, went even further: more than just exploring the contours and rhythms of the inner life, they engaged closely with contemporary theories of psychology.

George Eliot and Henry James were two such exemplars. Eliot showed a keen early interest in phrenology and was acquainted with George Combe, the leading English advocate of that particular mind-science.[2] And she adopted from the work of her partner, the philosopher George Henry Lewes, the notion that psychologically complex characters could be fashioned from the union of biology and sociology.[3] Henry James, for his part, adopted psychological ideas from his older brother William's radical approach to consciousness—principally, in the challenge he issued to the "idea of a buried self with a fixed fate."[4] The younger James's solution to these psychic and intermutual constrictions was to show individuals bound to more open-ended and desultory social matrices.[5] Victorian science of the mind, such as it was, therefore provided useful models of human behavior for both Eliot and James.

The thread that binds inside and outside in the Victorian psychological novel also provides a channel for narrative movement—*thought* as a prelude to *action*, the former giving impetus to (and raising the stakes of) the latter. This is partly the result of a judicious narrative technique. As Sigmund Freud notes, in "Creative Writers and Day-Dreaming" (1907): "It has struck me that in many cases of what are known as 'psychological' novels only one person—once again the hero—is described from within. The author sits inside his mind, as it were, and looks at the other characters from outside."[6] As a result of this tactic, the stabilizing procedures of Victorian realism could be maintained (even amid the commitment to mental activity), and storytelling logic preserved.

With the modernist turn, however, psychological inwardness (as noted earlier) is paramount, but the result is nothing less than a frontal assault on the Victorian novelist's faith in the powers of storytelling. The modernist impatience with narrative orthodoxy—famously summarized by Virginia Woolf as "this appalling narrative business of the realist: getting on from lunch to dinner"[7]—feeds directly into the concern with tracking the patterns and caprices of the mind and its contents. What emerges, then, is a manifest antinomy: the spirit of the psychological novel is kept alive in modernist fiction, through the continuance or retention of many of its essential features; but these features are now set firmly against, rather than in the service of, the "well-made" narrative.

The resolution to this antinomy lies in the fact that the Victorian novel of psychological realism is intensely social, and intensely moral. It depicts a psychology of the self in the context of—and often in conflict with—the demands of liberal society. This means that knowledge of others' motivations, beliefs, perspectives, and so on, has moral ends—namely, how to conduct one's social relations wisely and responsibly. Understanding subjectivity is thus consanguine with intersubjective decision-making; knowledge and virtue go hand in hand. The modernist novel of introspective counter-realism, by contrast, is not concerned with questions of moral or social obligation, nor is it invested in preserving the illusion of outward stability. And insofar as it is inflected or mediated by contemporary psychology, it valorizes sense-experience and the reality of consciousness, and the uncertainties of wavering or vacillating subjectivities.[8]

In his essay on creative writing, Freud alludes to an "eccentric" subclass of psychological novels. "In these," he writes, "the person who is introduced as the hero plays only a very small active part; he sees the actions and sufferings of other people pass before him like a spectator. Many of Zola's later works belong to this category."[9] Large portions of Marcel Proust's multivolume novel, *In Search of Lost Time* (1913–27), could also be put in this category. Proust's narrator, whom he suggests that we refer to as "Marcel," devotes much of his energies to observation, to reflection, and to deduction: in a word, to mind-reading. All observable human behavior possesses an obscure underside, and it is the narrator's task to trace these often-perverse or confounding actions back to their psychic origins.

At the same time (and moving beyond the "eccentric" category adumbrated by Freud), Proust's prodigious feats of mind-reading are at their keenest when the mind that he is attempting to fathom is his *own*. The "actions and sufferings" that are the narrator's alone are not imparted to us as confessions, exactly, nor as self-analyses (which are usually accompanied by some kind of diagnosis). What takes place is more like internal self-reading, as Marcel scrutinizes the flow and tempo of his own thoughts, probing the mental architecture that regulates and facilitates their efficacy. This self-reading operates in tandem with outward, observational mind-reading of other people—which could be seen as a modern(ist) update of the "inner-outer" dyad bracing the nineteenth-century psychological novel.[10]

Insofar as my object in this chapter is mind-reading as exercised by Proust, I approach it via narrational representation. This is in contrast with a great deal of cognitivist criticism, which is focused on the reader and his or her capacity to understand fictional minds. Indeed, for Lisa Zunshine, the simple act of reading/studying fiction is founded on this capacity. She writes:

> The very process of making sense of what we read appears to be grounded in our ability to invest the flimsy verbal constructions that we generously call "characters" with a potential for a variety of thoughts, feelings, and desires, and

then to look for the "cues" that allow us to guess at their feelings and thus to predict their actions.[11]

This form of mind-reading is, in short, directed from reader to character. I am considering Proust, by contrast, via intratextual Theory of Mind (ToM): Marcel's propensity to read his own and other people's behavior in terms of thoughts, feelings, desires, and intentions.

The *Search* is not only a psychological novel, albeit one of a highly unusual (not to mention elongated) cast, but also a philosophical novel. It expounds and dramatizes a philosophy of mind, from which, I argue, it is possible to extract a ToM. I show how this ToM is articulated via different forms of mental "errancy": those moments or scenes when cognitive processing is confounded in some way. In the course of doing so I explore, by turns, the role of the intellect in thought-processing, the construction of mental models, an outline of the infirmities of the mind, and a brief foray into cognitive framing.

Illuminating Blindness: The Malady of Miscognition

Just as Eliot and James took a number of cues from contemporary psychology, so too does Proust engage with (but also, ultimately, overcome) certain aspects of nineteenth-century French thought. For some critics, the notion of "involuntary memory"—Proust's most celebrated concept, and the theoretical backbone of the narrative—is sufficient for the *Search* to qualify as a psychological novel. Before Proust, the term "affective memory" was used to describe a similar phenomenon: when particular sensations are experienced, they can act as triggers to recall earlier emotional states. The most noteworthy French study in this vein, a few years before Proust began work on the *Search*, was Théodule Ribot's *The Psychology of the Emotions* (1896). Ribot, however, attests to the phenomenon of "intellectual memory," which conveys a "vague affective trace"[12] of the past event—a milder and more volitional form of experience than Proustian *memoire involuntaire*.[13]

Proustian ToM could also be considered in light of Associationist philosophy, which sees mental states and processes as intimately entwined with past experiences—although the emphasis on empirical methods situates it squarely in the Anglo-American context. Within the French tradition, Proust has closer ties to the influential work of Hippolyte Taine, the critic and historian. In his 1869 study *On Intelligence*, Taine treats memory as something that is subject neither to the will nor to inclination:[14] an approach that anticipates Proust's depiction of spontaneous unbidden memories rising up to renew and revivify the past. However, as the title of his book indicates, Taine gives pride of place to the intelligence or intellect, which he equates with the "faculty of knowing," and thus pursues in order "to examine our knowledge, that is to say our cognitions."[15]

A similar focus on "intellect" is more or less how cognitive psychologists and cognitive literary critics today see knowledge acquisition. Alan Palmer, for instance, begins theorizing about the mind in terms of the "relationship between knowledge and its representation in the brain."[16] He differentiates between *immediate* mental phenomena—which include such things as moods, desires, emotions, sensations, visual images, and so on—and *latent* states of mind—which encompass not just knowledge but also such "tendencies of thought" as attitudes, evaluations, dispositions, beliefs, skills, imagination, and intellect.[17] In a similar fashion, Monika Fludernik argues that consciousness itself comprises one's "mental center of self-awareness, *intellection*, perception and emotionality" (emphasis added).[18]

Proust's priorities are somewhat different, as he makes clear in volume five (*The Fugitive*). If pride of place is given to the intellect, it is only as a starting point, and not because it plays any special role in the acquisition of knowledge. Recovering from an emotional crisis (a condition that Michael Taussig calls "cardiac fatigue")[19] Marcel reflects on his own wayward impulses: "The fact that the intellect is not the most subtle, powerful and appropriate instrument for grasping the truth is only one more reason in favour of starting with the intellect rather than with the intuitions of the unconscious or with unquestioning faith in our premonitions."[20] By attending to experience, says Proust, we can see that what most influences our thoughts and feelings is not reason, but "other powers." He adds: "And then it is the intellect itself, which, recognizing [these other powers'] superiority, uses its reasoning in order to abdicate in their favour and accepts the rile of collaborator and servant. It has 'experimental faith.'"[21] Proust, then, challenges many of the psychological verities of his time, including affective memory, Associationist theory, and the Tainean emphasis on "intelligence." To get to grips with Proustian ToM, I suggest, we might better look to an alternative strand of Continental thought.

In the mid-1960s, the French theorist Paul Ricoeur coined the term "hermeneutics of suspicion," to describe a theory of interpretation that sought a "reduction of the illusions and lies of consciousness" via a "method of demystification."[22] The three great exemplars of this propensity, in Ricoeur's view, were Marx, Nietzsche, and Freud, whom he dubbed the "masters of suspicion." Of course, says Ricoeur, all three are "seemingly mutually exclusive,"[23] given the breadth and reach of their projects, which encompass political, economic, cultural, linguistic, and libidinal matters. It is also the case that these three thinkers are generally excluded from ToM discussions, not least because their work is seen as speculative and critical rather than empirical. I suggest, however, that by following Ricoeur's lead on consciousness and its deceptions, it is possible to discern a significant area of *psychological* overlap in these diverse bodies of thought.

In a nutshell, Marx, Nietzsche, and Freud believe that our cognitive abilities are severely compromised, and that this prevents us from grasping the true nature of our being in the world—socially, politically, and psychologically. Of the three "masters" Marx is the most controversial, because the term often used by his followers to describe this cognitive deficit, "false consciousness," is not one that he devised.[24] Yet despite this, many Marxian thinkers use it to describe the epistemological (rather than purely political) consequences of ideology—the chief of which is that it distorts or obscures what is understood as "reality." For Nietzsche, cognitive distortion is another name for the "necessary illusions" that cushion and sustain the human race—the compulsion to deceive oneself in order to uphold certain metaphysical tenets. Logic, free will, agency, causation all these necessary illusions are *consolatory*, first and foremost, but also life-preserving and culture-enhancing. As Nietzsche writes in 1872: "Illusion necessary for the sentient being to live. Illusion necessary for progress in culture."[25]

Freud's entire project, by contrast, is oriented around mankind's seemingly limitless appetite for illusion. And unlike Marx's and Nietzsche's, these illusions neither are necessary nor do they presuppose a "true consciousness." In *The Future of an Illusion* (1927), Freud examines the deep psychic background of religious belief (the "illusion" in question), and locates it in the elemental clash between a destructive instinct and a vitalizing, but prohibitive, civilization.[26] Human thought processes thus tend toward wish-fulfillment and a disregard for reality, as a way of tempering, if not relieving, this terrible bind. Unlike Marx and Nietzsche, Freud stresses that "illusion" is not synonymous with "error";[27] but in terms of the psychological outcome, all three are consentient. Eagleton's bleak overview of Freud's philosophy could therefore be applied just as readily to Marx's or Nietzsche's. He writes: "For Freud, all cognition contains miscognition, all illumination is overshadowed by a certain blindness. Wherever we uncover meaning, then we can be sure to find non-meaning at its root."²⁸ In that regard, Ricoeur's proponents of suspicion are also the masters of misrecognition, pursuing a "negative hermeneutics" based on demystification and willful disillusionment.²⁹

Proust was writing immediately after Marx and Nietzsche, and alongside Freud. Without necessarily embracing any of their methods, or even their idioms, his views on consciousness and cognition are closely attuned to theirs. Indeed, the *Search* could be seen as both exemplifying and working through different modes of miscognition. At the broadest level, it is fundamental to the novel's structure. Although the story is a retrospective, first-person narration, events are often relayed in the text as if they have just happened. The effect is of having two narrators that somehow coexist within a single voice, one of them "innocent," the other "experienced." And so even though the latter is always present, the tale is nonetheless driven by, as Sara Danius notes, the "narrator's fear that he might not become what he so desperately wants to be—an artist. Year in and year out, the narrator is burdened by his own utter incompetence."³⁰ That vocational incompetence is reflected in Marcel's tendency to miscognise events, people, motivations, and suppositions.

Vincent Descombes describes a similarly bifurcated design and sees in it the "Proustian theory of the novel": on the one hand, the bird's-eye view of a broad social phenomenon, the well-bred bourgeois (Marcel) entering "high society"; on the other, the individual's perspective on his own experience. Descombes writes: "The transposition of the 'social phenomenon' into 'individual circumstances' gives us the subject of a psychological novel."³¹ Thus, it is not Proust's ruminations on involuntary memory that give the *Search* its most indicative psychological dimension, but the more prodigious feat of aligning the individual with the social. At the same time, Proust also moves *beyond* the conventional psychological novel, by dramatizing the "conflict between the inner version of the hero and the bird's-eye-view of the neutral observer."³² Such a conflict signifies that Marcel's errors are not fatal or even lamentable, but part of a larger dramatic schema that comes slowly into view.

Before turning to an example of Proustian miscognition, let us first note that ToM has a *projective* quality, based on the building of mental models. As Keith Oatley puts it, we build such models of people or characters "from their utterances, from their behavior, and from what other people say about them."³³ This projective quality subtends a *predictive* quality, a way of anticipating how someone might react or proceed in a given situation. The temporal aspect is crucial; for a model to have any efficacy, it must be built up from multiple encounters over the medium or long term. Yet even allowing for this, the mental models that Marcel builds are often markedly flawed. Any knowledge that he gains from them is only provisional, and any advantage he enjoys from "projecting" (much less predicting) someone's actions is limited or nonexistent.

An episode from volume two, *In the Shadow of the Young Girls in Flower*, illustrates this condition. At the heart of it is Albertine Simonet, who dominates Marcel's thoughts throughout the later volumes of the *Search*. He first becomes aware of her in Balbec, a fictional seaside town in the Normandy region, where she is part of the "little gang" of girls that stirs his imagination. It is in Balbec that Marcel also makes the acquaintance of Elstir, a portrait and landscape painter, who has already become one of the narrator's three totemic artist-figures (along with the novelist Bergotte, and the composer Vinteuil).[34] "There's hardly a day," Elstir casually mentions to Marcel, "when one or other of [the gang of girls] doesn't come down that lane and drop in to pay me a little visit."[35] Marcel seeks, then, to make Albertine's acquaintance through the intercession of Elstir. He takes the painter on a walk along the esplanade, stalling for time in the hope that they might encounter Albertine and her friends.

Eventually they do appear, but only in the distance. And it is not the whole gang, but "a few of the stars from the zoophytic cluster of young girls, who, although they looked as though they had not seen me, were without a doubt at that very moment making sarcastic remarks about me."[36] Marcel sees himself in terms that echo Huysmans's debilitated aesthete, Des Esseintes: possessed of a "feebleness" and an "excess of painful sensitivity and intellectuality."[37] The young girls, by contrast, exude an "almost barbaric and cruel vitality"[38]—the basis for Marcel's belief that they must be passing derisive remarks about him. This is a kind of mind-reading by reversal, or inference by contrast. Because the girls' temperaments and physical dispositions are so different from his own, by implication they must (he believes) see him in a critical light.

Marcel's next move is also predicated on an act of mind-reading. Now that the girls are visibly present, and believing that Elstir will carry out the introduction he has been so carefully "staging," Marcel casually saunters away, affecting interest in the window of a nearby antiques shop:

> I went on gazing into the shop-window, waiting for the moment when Elstir would shoot my name at me, like a harmless, expected bullet. The certainty of being introduced to the girls had made me not only feign indifference towards them, but feel it. The pleasure of their acquaintance, having become inevitable, was compressed and reduced. . . . I could recognize neither my desire nor its

object; I was almost sorry to have gone out for a walk with Elstir. But the main reason for the shrinking of the pleasure to which I had been so looking forward was the knowledge that nothing could now prevent me from enjoying it."[39]

Knowledge and its object suddenly become a problem, when they are attached to certainty, to inevitability, to an event that, no matter how desirable, can (apparently) no longer be prevented. And as a result, knowledge and pleasure are in conflict, the one tarnishing and despoiling the other. Marcel, then, seems to be afflicted with a chronic psychic condition, one in which the only thing worth having is that which cannot be had: a particularly dispiriting condition, to which we will return in a moment.

In any case, Marcel's "reading" of Elstir is awry. Despite his careful engineering of circumstances—the outdoor stroll, the stalling for time, the lingering at a certain spot—it does not go as planned. For when he turns back around, "Elstir parted from the girls without calling me over. They turned up a side-street and he came towards me. It was a fiasco."[40] The painter's explanation for this turn of events is nothing if not plausible. "What did you stand miles away for?" he asks Marcel. "Anyway, they were in a hurry."[41] The critic Roger Shattuck notes that, by the final volume of the *Search*, "Marcel has lived through a whole series of misapprehensions, which occur when he tries to verify the present against past experiences or expectation."[42] This is one such "misapprehension," with the narrator's understanding of people and environment (based on "past experiences") unable to be projected onto the present with sufficient acuity.

Yet nowhere are Proust's qualities as a scenarist more evident than in this episode, a non-encounter stretched across twelve pages of text. The scene is a suspenseful micro-drama of contrivance, expectation, disillusionment, and final, crushing defeat. For even though the initial impetus is the narrator's confidence in his mind-reading abilities ("knowing that Elstir will call me over,")[43] it is in direct competition with his control over the shape and pace of the narration. Thus, immediately after he realizes that Elstir is parting company from the group of girls, Marcel turns his attentions elsewhere—to the face of the girl standing closest to the painter. "For an instant her eyes passed across mine, like those flowing skies on stormy days when clouds moving at different speeds come close, touch, then part.... In a momentary intersection of eyes we stood there, each in ignorance of the promises or threats for the future that the other silent passing continent might contain."[44] Marcel's recognition of his folly is momentarily suspended, making this adventitious exchange of glances—as penetrating and poetic as any in Virginia Woolf, as detached as that of a *nouveau romancier*—a rejoinder to the slowly building drama, which is about to reach its climax.

Proust's novel, writes Richard E. Goodkin, "reminds us repeatedly of the need to be sidetracked."[45] He calls this willful swerving or deviating "Proustian error" and describes it as "missing the mark, not reaching the goal, or even being disappointed if ever one does arrive at it."[46] Regarding the scene with Elstir on the esplanade, Proustian error could be enlarged to take in not only the novel's boundless capacity for digression but also the narrator's ongoing tendency to miscognise situations and eventualities. Once this allowance is made, error conjoins with something more psychologically demanding.

Intermezzo: In Praise of Infirmity

The need to be sidetracked—to miss the mark, to bypass the goal—suggests that indirection can yield benefits that would otherwise not be available. A similar kind of counter- or para-logic underlies Marcel's espousal of infirmity. The sound sleeper, he muses, has little to tell us about processes of sleep, whereas the insomniac presents rich observational material for examination. "This malady alone," says Marcel, "causes us to take notice of and to learn, and enables us to analyse, the mechanisms of which we would otherwise be ignorant."[47] This can be applied to Marcel's infirmity, at least insofar as it is physical. As we have just seen, with the episode at Balbec, he is painfully aware of his own neurasthenic condition. Lydia Ginzburg suggests that this is what makes Marcel the perfect narrator: being effectively free of personality, "his personality consists merely of hypertrophied nervous reactions to any influence."[48] By the same token, nervous distemper and exhaustion also reduce Marcel's role as a participant, creating space for his observational and mind-reading activities.

As for mental infirmity, we have already seen a clear-cut example of it, in the moment when Marcel seems almost certain to be introduced to Albertine and her friends. Knowing that it is about to happen causes him to hesitate, to feel indifferent, to begin even to regret what must surely follow. Roger Shattuck terms this, after Montaigne, "soul error" (*une erreur d'âme*): "The incapacity to give full value or status to one's own life and experience. [. . .] Whatever bends to our desire *disqualifies* itself by becoming a part of ourselves."[49] It is not the object or occurrence that is the problem, then, but one's ownership of it, which diminishes its value. Insofar as there is a solution to this "incapacity," it involves the re-routing of desire through a different medium—the medium of art, as we will see.

After neurasthenia and "soul error," there is a third kind of infirmity. To look beyond mind-reading, for the moment, and consider literary Modernism in a cognitivist framework, one issue becomes paramount: mental competence. It subtends a scale of debility, at one end of which belong those narrators and characters that are mentally impaired in one way or another. Faulkner's Benjy (*The Sound and the Fury*), Woolf's Septimus Smith (*Mrs Dalloway*), Fitzgerald's Nicole Diver (*Tender Is the Night*), and Conrad's Stevie (*The Secret Agent*) all suffer from diagnosable mental disorders, which have some bearing on the narrative procedures that govern the novel in question. This has been a recognized part of modernist literary poetics, at least since Louis Sass (*Madness and Modernism* [1992]) plotted the metaphorical pathways between modernist aesthetics and the schizophrenic condition.[50] At the other end of the scale, and more relevant for questions of cognition and errancy, is a group of characters (and sometimes narrators) whose psychological dysfunction is much less extreme, though still noteworthy.

This second group itself has two sides. Consider, for example, Ford Madox Ford's John Dowell, narrator of *The Good Soldier*, whose ailment, if he has one, is willful blindness. Dowell's capacity for self-deception—his signature refrain, as his narration begins, is "I just don't know"—leads him to miscognise characters, events, and his wife's fidelity for almost the entire novel.[51] By contrast, a different kind of mental malady afflicts the vengeful Captain Ahab in *Moby-Dick*, who has lost a limb, before the story begins, to the albino whale of the title. Ahab is so consumed with chasing and killing the whale that he leads his crew, his ship, and himself to total destruction. Proust's Marcel warrants comparison with both these figures. He is Ahab-like in his monomania, though driven by sexual jealousy rather than bloody revenge. And he has a compulsive tendency to overthink everything, almost to the point of paralysis. Yet Marcel is, by turns, just as confounded mentally as John Dowell, albeit more tormented by unreliable and unstable knowledge.

In the two "Albertine" volumes, *The Prisoner* and *The Fugitive*, Marcel comes close to joining that first group of modernist characters, the ones with certifiable mental disorders. In the former volume he is living with Albertine in Paris and becomes obsessed with uncovering the "truth" of her sexuality—namely, if she is, or is not, involved in clandestine lesbian affairs. His mind-reading abilities, pushed to the limit, fail to yield a definitive answer. Christine Cano identifies here a striking parallel: Proust's compulsive manuscript revisions, which cause the text to sprout "morbid outgrowths," warrant comparison with Marcel's obsessive investigations. She writes: "What destroys the ostensible coherence of the primary [i.e., unrevised] text, growing out of proportion to the rest of the story, is the insatiable desire to know."[52] Indeed, even after he receives the news of Albertine's accidental death, in *The Fugitive*, Marcel continues his investigations, only reaching a state of peace once he is able to forget. Those endless textual revisions, says Cano, highlight two distinct narratives: one rational and proportional, the other "placed under the sign . . . of excess and even dementia."[53] In such a climate, where doubt, suspicion, and jealousy cannot be quelled, narrative closure becomes all but impossible. I suggest, however, that Proust's interests lie elsewhere: that he is more concerned with *origins* than with *endings*.

Dramatizing the Mind: Two Myths of Origin

In *Reading for the Plot*, Peter Brooks argues that repetition is fundamental to narrative per se. Repetition can shape in a text in a variety of ways, such as a "retelling" of events that have in some sense already happened; a form of uncanny remembering that invokes the primitive and instinctual; or a way of imposing structure and meaning on a story, using "all the mnemonic elements of literature."[54] Repetition also creates a movement of *return* in a text, a doubling-back whose outcome is unclear: "We cannot say whether this return is a return *to* or a return *of*: for instance, a return to origins or a return of the repressed."[55] Regarding the latter, it is apparent that Proust is not especially interested in how memories and feelings get repressed or "buried"; as Leo Bersani notes, his real concern is with the "unconscious as an extension of being."[56] It is, then, the former of Brooks's two "doubling-back" outcomes that drives the *Search*: textual repetition as indicative of a concern with origins.

Nicola Luckhurst finds in the *Search* a concern with biological origins, and with splitting and reproduction. Repetition, she posits, is "at the origin of life itself,"[57] conveyed through the language of heredity with its basis in modern genetic theory. Furthermore, this concern assumes a structural importance, as the novel unfolds. Luckhurst writes: "Repetition in *A la recherche* simply recurs; there is no release into some final moment of recognition. Moreover, what is repeated, and indeed repeatedly revealed, pertains in some way to origins. We might even say that origins in *A la recherche* signify as such because of their capacity to repeat or replicate."[58] As we will now see, Proust's reflections on origins do not just pertain to the science of biology, but also have points of contact with science of mind—with emergence of ToM, in the first example, and with the onset of sexual jealousy, in the second. What is striking about both instances is that they directly involve other people, affirming Proust's tendency to *dramatize* his narrator's psychological condition, rather than simply elucidate it.

Having a ToM means, at the most basic level, being able to impute mental states to oneself and to others. More than this, it means being aware of the relationship that oneself and others have to certain mental states, and being able to *represent* these relationships explicitly—that is, to have a capacity for meta-representation. This capacity underlies such things as moral responsibility, self-consciousness, and social interaction. As far as mental development goes, cognitive psychologists observe emergence of ToM in children four years of age and older, when they are able to set the "wrongness" of someone else's belief in light of their own knowledge of a situation.[59] There is also the question of "pretense" in slightly younger children (around two years of age), and how playful pretending indicates an early ability to understand mental states.[60]

Marcel presents his own "myth of origins" of ToM in volume three (*The Guermantes Way*), which he attributes to Françoise, his family's maid. For Marcel, it has the transformative power (though not the trauma) of a primal scene, as if readying him for future neuroses. Although he does not reveal how old he was, the question of "pretense" does arise—only not as a form of play, but as a defense or protective measure. Most of all, Marcel recalls being aware of Françoise's mental state, and also her unerring ability to "read" him in a certain way, and see through his pretense:

> I have never once experienced a humiliation without having seen beforehand on [Françoise's] face the signs of condolences held there in readiness; and when in my anger at the thought of being pitied by her I tried to pretend that I had in fact done something successful, my lies broke pointlessly against her respectful but quite obvious disbelief and her awareness of her own infallibility. For she knew the truth; she kept it back and confined herself merely to a slight movement of the lips.... At least this is what I believed for a long time, for in those days I supposed that it was through words that the truth was communicated to other people.[61]

Mind-reading works here as a kind of circuit. Marcel sees pity in the "signs of condolences" that Françoise evinces. And when he attempts to cover up the "humiliation" that she can detect in his face and actions, Marcel detects further indications of her mind-reading at work in her "quite obvious disbelief" and "awareness of her own infallibility." This kind of process is aptly summed up in George Butte's pithy formulation: *I know that you know that I know.*[62] Or as Keith Oatley puts it, we don't just make mental models of others; we also make, "recursively, mental models of others' mental models."[63] In an intersubjective world, one's own act of knowing can itself become an object of knowledge, giving rise to a kind of feedback loop of mental absorption and readjustment.

Marcel's awareness of this looping effect leads him to rethink his idea of truth, principally by understanding that it can be read in semiotic traces—facial and bodily gestures—as well as in words. He goes on to suggest that this other kind of truth might actually be more reliable than linguistic utterance or inscription, gathered as it is "from countless external signs, even from certain unseen phenomena, analogous in the world of human character to atmospheric changes in the physical world."[64] Yet being aware of such "atmospheric changes" does not make the truth about mental phenomena any easier to grasp. For the minds behind the faces and bodies, the cognitive processes that underlie the physical signs and the "unseen phenomena" continue both to captivate and perplex Marcel.

The second "origin" scene can be read in light of an earlier encounter, which shows Marcel as a kind of mental assailant. It takes place in volume two, after he visits a Romanesque church in Carqueville (a fictional town not far from Balbec), to admire its architectural subtleties. As he walks out, and espies some local village girls, the sacred space of the church is traduced by Marcel's profane longings. His eye is drawn to one of the taller girls, who is sitting beside a jar full of fish that, he presumes, she has just caught. This "fishergirl" is given neither a name nor much of an identity. But unlike the "bird-girl" in Joyce's *Portrait of the Artist*, whom Stephen uses to plot a course between the physical and the spiritual (thereby forging a schema for aesthetic experience), Proust's fishergirl brings together, via Marcel's yearnings, the physical and the mental:

> My eyes rested on her skin and my lips could almost believe they had done likewise. It was not only her body I was after, it was the person living inside it, with whom there can only be one mode of touching, which is to attract her attention, and one mode of penetration, which is to put an idea into her mind.[65]

Although he downplays any *exclusive* interest in the fishergirl's body, Marcel's turn of phrase is distinctly carnal, even sexual. So he attempts to "put an idea into her mind," but it comes to naught: "The inner self of the beautiful fishergirl seemed to remain closed against me; and I doubted that I managed to gain entry to her, even after I had seen my own image furtively reflected by the mirror of a look she gave me."[66] Rather than sexual innuendo, this is the language of a military offensive, the object of which is a kind of mental takeover.

To find a way into the girl's inner self, then, Marcel changes tack. Instead of meaningful looks, he uses money (a five-franc coin) and his social status, asking the fishergirl to locate for him a two-horse carriage containing a marquise. She is, Marcel believes, suitably impressed; he has managed to insinuate himself into her mental space. But this "conquest" of her mind has the effect of dampening his desire, as he ruefully notes: "It felt as though I had touched her person with invisible lips and that she had liked it. As happens with physical possession, this forcible insertion of myself into her mind, this disembodied possession of her, had taken away some of her mystery."[67] Again, there are sexual overtones here, but the outcome is not fulfillment, or even momentary enjoyment, but disillusionment. The girl's all-important aura of mystery has been partly dispelled, now that his ploy of "disembodied possession" has succeeded. So for Marcel, the pleasure of mind-reading-as-knowledge is counteracted by the pleasure of *not knowing*, of sensing (and enjoying) the many possibilities that inhere in the inner lives of others. The shadow of "soul error" is also apparent here, and the ruinous cycle of wanting, having, and devaluing.

In this instance, Marcel is the protagonist of his desires, the aggressor who seeks to dominate, however momentarily, another's mind. Two volumes later, in *Sodom and Gomorrah*, we see the other side of the coin: Marcel as a helpless victim of his own overwrought mental projections. To take account of this next episode, I want to consider it in light of a psychological technique, cognitive framing, to show the effect that this can have on knowledge and interpretation. Frames, in brief, are interpretive tools, helping us to ascertain contexts and understand "knowledge representations," even if only provisionally; for one frame can be readily replaced by another, as contexts and knowledge change. In addition, notes George Lakoff, "many frame-circuits have direct connections to the emotional regions of the brain," and hence can take effect almost immediately. By the same token, although "words themselves are not frames," says Lakoff, "under the right conditions, words can be chosen to activate desired frames."[68] Both of these elements, emotional immediacy and linguistic activation, can be seen at work in this next scene, one of the novel's most celebrated.

It takes place at a casino near Balbec, where Albertine and her girlfriends have gone for a night out. Marcel is initially reluctant to join them, but at the entrance he meets Doctor Cottard, a Parisian acquaintance. So they enter the casino together and see some of the girls in front of a piano:

> "There, look," [Cottard] added, pointing to Albertine and Andrée, who were waltzing slowly, pressed one against the other, "I've forgotten my eyeglass and I can't see properly, but they're certainly at the height of arousal. It's not sufficiently well known that it's chiefly through the breasts that women experience it. And look, theirs are touching, completely." Indeed, those of Andrée and Albertine had not ceased to be in contact.[69]

Cottard's attempt at mind-reading is based, we might assume, on obscure medical knowledge ("It's not sufficiently well known..."), even as it is undercut by his status as onlooker (he admits that he "can't see properly"). Nevertheless, Cottard is constructing a frame for Marcel, an interpretive schema to decipher the meaning of the scene. He is inferring that not only are Albertine and Andrée sexually attracted to one another but they are also—wittingly or unwittingly—"performing" this attraction, through an impromptu waltz. Unlike the "mind-rape" of the fishergirl, this is a form of "mind-contamination"; later, Marcel even compares it to being poisoned.[70]

As a primal scene, seeing Albertine and Andrée dancing in this way confirms what Marcel learned from Françoise, how truth is not dependent on words—even though it is Cottard's remark that initiates his response. For the effect that it has on Marcel is electrifying: already troubled by Albertine's furtive behavior, from this point on he is beset by suspicion and mistrust. Cottard's "frame," his casually barbed remark, thus provides the ignition-point for the narrator's jealousy, out of which are generated the next two volumes of the *Search*: Marcel's virtual imprisonment of Albertine, precipitating her abrupt departure (*The Prisoner*); and the book-length reflection on time, habit, and forgetting that succeeds it (*The Fugitive*). It is only by the end of the latter volume that Cottard's frame—which has become for Marcel more like a prison—can finally be lifted, and succeeded (or displaced) by a resounding affirmation of the supreme efficacy of art.

Conclusion: The Other Side of Error

In February 1914, as the *Search* was undergoing expansion from its projected three volumes, Proust wrote a letter to his friend, the editor and critic Jacques Rivière. Describing his plan for the book as the "evolution of a mind," Proust goes on to say: "I have chosen not to analyze [this mind] in an abstract way, but rather to recreate it, to bring it to life. And so I am forced to depict errors, but without feeling bound to say that I hold them to be errors."[71] We have seen this strategy played out in various ways throughout the *Search*, from miscognition, mental infirmity, and "soul error" to Marcel's fraught relationship with knowledge. On the one hand, he is driven by an insatiable desire to know, a monomania that takes him (and the text) to the edge of dementia; on the other, and in different circumstances, he recognizes the pleasures and charms that come with not knowing. Torn between the two, Marcel seeks to find a way of not having to make this impossible choice.

Fundamental to Proust, then, is what we might call the *truth of miscognition*: a keen awareness that error cannot simply be bypassed but must somehow be absorbed and assimilated. For error, in Proust, has a powerful association with the novel's anchor-point. As we saw in the fishergirl scene, Marcel momentarily sides with "non-knowing" so that the elation of desire can be prolonged, and not overtaken by disappointment. This is also the side of art—the side of suggestion, allusion, ambiguity and intuition, the generative and the creative, rather than the constraining intelligibility that accompanies "knowing." When Proust raises those "other powers" above the intellect, as he does in *The Fugitive*, it is the operations of art that he is implicitly aggrandizing.

To see how this conflict resolves itself, let us return to Proust's "myth of origin" of ToM. He recalls hearing from another servant that Françoise had made a stinging remark about him, thereby sowing the seeds of doubt and confusion. Marcel concludes from this that people do not present themselves to us with clarity and fixity, but rather

> as a shadow we can never penetrate, of which there can be no direct knowledge, about which we form countless beliefs based upon words and even actions, neither of which give us more than insufficient and in fact contradictory information, a shadow which we can alternately imagine, with equal justification, as masking the burning flame of hatred and of love.[72]

This could be seen as the originating force for Marcel's mind-reading compulsion, with its bleak prognosis that "there can be no direct knowledge" of other people—Albertine's closedness, her mental "unreadability," being a case in point. Nevertheless, Proust uses it to explore the destructive side of passion, to show how mental-state inferences can precipitate an almost-lethal infatuation, alternating between the "burning flame" of love and suspicion, desire, and mistrust.

By the end of the *Search*, this flame has abated. Indeed, in an extended critique of realism and habit, in the final volume (*Finding Time Again*), Marcel recognizes a way around the "unknowable other." He says: "It is only through art that we can escape from ourselves and know how another person sees a universe which is not the same as our own and whose landscapes would otherwise have remained as unknown as any there may be on the moon."[73] Because we all inhabit different universes, errancy is our natural state. But the medium of art subdues and palliates those differences. By embracing errancy, rather than trying to "correct" it, Marcel realizes that art can provide what mind-reading cannot: a way to truth that obviates the contingencies of time and psychology.

Notes

1 Fredric Jameson, *Marxism and Form: Twentieth-Century Dialectical Theories of Literature* (Princeton, NJ: Princeton University Press, 1971), 2.
2 See Diana Postlethwaite, "George Eliot and Science," in *The Cambridge Companion to George Eliot*, ed. George Levine (Cambridge: Cambridge University Press, 2001), 104–5.
3 Ibid., 115.
4 Harvey Cormier, "Jamesian Pragmatism and Jamesian Realism," *Henry James Review* 18 (Fall 1997): 295.
5 Some James scholars question Henry's affinities with his brother's psychological philosophy. Sharon Cameron, for example, argues that Henry James parts company with William James on the question of consciousness, reaching different philosophical conclusions. See Sharon Cameron, *Thinking in Henry James* (Chicago: University of Chicago Press, 1989), 80.
6 Sigmund Freud, *The Penguin Freud Library*, Vol. 14: *Art and Literature*, trans. James Strachey, ed. Albert Dickson (London: Penguin, 1990), 138.
7 Virginia Woolf, *The Diary of Virginia Woolf*, Vol. 3: *1925–1930*, ed. Anne Olivier Bell (London: Hogarth Press, 1980), 209.
8 See Judith Ryan, *The Vanishing Subject: Early Psychology and Literary Modernism* (Chicago: University of Chicago Press, 1991), 2, 19.

9   Freud, *Art and Literature*, 138.
10 David Herman attempts to show how, in literary Modernism, "minds at once shape and are shaped by larger experiential environments" ("1880–1945: Re-minding Modernism," in *The Emergence of Mind: Representations of Consciousness in Narrative Discourse in English*, ed. David Herman [Lincoln: University of Nebraska Press, 2011], 249–50.) However, it is not clear if this approach can be applied to modernist writers other than Joyce and Woolf, Herman's two exemplars.
11 Lisa Zunshine, "Theory of Mind and Experimental Representations of Fictional Consciousness," *Narrative* 11 (October 2003): 274.
12 Théodule Ribot, *The Psychology of the Emotions* (1896; rpt. London: Walter Scott, 1897), 152.
13 Proust's first English biographer, George D. Painter, notes that he read an earlier Ribot work, *Les Maladies de la volonté* (1883), in 1905. See *Marcel Proust: A Biography*, 2 vols. (London: Penguin, 1990), 2:52.
14 Hippolyte Taine, *On Intelligence*, Vol. 1 [1870], trans. T. D. Haye (New York: Henry Holt, 1875), 91–92.
15 Taine, *On Intelligence*, vii. Looking outside the French tradition, the experimental psychology of Hermann Ebbinghaus conducted in the 1880s first identified what are now known as IAMs (Involuntary Autobiographical Memories) as a particular type of memory; see Hermann Ebbinghaus, *Memory: A Contribution to Experimental Psychology* (1885), trans. H. A. Ruger and C. E. Bussenvis (New York: Dover, 1964). See also Rosemary J. Bradley, Chris J. A. Moulin, and Lia Kvavilashvili, "Involuntary Autobiographical Memories," *The Psychologist* 26.3 (March 2013): 190. And for an informed philosophical discussion of Proust's psychological predecessors, see Miguel de Beistegui, *Proust as Philosopher: The Art of Metaphor*, trans. Dorthée Bonnigal Katz (London: Routledge, 2013), 27–28.
16 Alan Palmer, *Fictional Minds* (Lincoln: University of Nebraska Press, 2004), 4.
17 Ibid., 58, 81.
18 Monika Fludernik, *Towards a "Natural" Narratology* (London: Routledge, 1996), 58.
19 Michael Taussig, *What Color Is the Sacred?* (Chicago: University of Chicago Press, 2009), 201.
20 Marcel Proust, *In Search of Lost Time*, Vol. 5: *The Prisoner*, trans. Carol Clark, and *The Fugitive*, trans. Peter Collier (London: Allen Lane, 2002), 391.
21 Ibid.
22 Paul Ricoeur, *Freud and Philosophy: An Essay on Interpretation*, trans. Denis Savage (New Haven: Yale University Press, 1970), 32. "Suspicion" as a critical method has itself been subjected to critique, in a number of recent works. Affective involvement and an emphasis on constitutive and "creative" textual analysis inform,

for example, commentaries by Bruno Latour and Rita Felski. See Latour, "Why Has Critique Run Out of Steam? From Matters of Fact to Matters of Concern," *Critical Inquiry* 30 (Winter 2004): 225–48; and Rita Felski, *The Limits of Critique* (Chicago: University of Chicago Press, 2015).

23 Ricoeur, *Freud and Philosophy*, 32.
24 For a succinct discussion of how useful "false consciousness" is, in terms of understanding Marx's beliefs about ideology, see Jorge Larrain, *Marxism and Ideology* (London: Macmillan, 1983), 109–13.
25 Friedrich Nietzsche, *Writings from the Early Notebooks*, trans. Ladislaus Löb, ed. Raymond Geuss and Alexander Nehamas (Cambridge: Cambridge University Press, 2009), 112.
26 Sigmund Freud, *The Future of an Illusion*, trans. and ed. James Strachey (New York: Norton, 1961), 7–8.
27 Ibid., 30–31.
28 Terry Eagleton, *Ideology: An Introduction* (London: Verso, 1991), 176.
29 See Jameson, *Marxism and Form*, 119.
30 Sara Danius, *The Senses of Modernism: Technology, Perception, and Aesthetics* (Ithaca, NY: Cornell University Press, 2002), 117.
31 Vincent Descombes, *Proust: Philosophy of the Novel*, trans. Catherine Chance Macksey (Stanford, CA: Stanford University Press, 1992), 155.
32 Ibid., 155.
33 Keith Oatley, "Theory of Mind and Theory of Minds in Literature," in *Theory of Mind and Literature*, ed. Paula Leverage, Howard Mancing, Richard Schweickert, and Jennifer Marston William (West Lafayette, IN: Purdue University Press, 2011), 16.
34 A potential fourth artist-figure, La Berma the actress, does feature intermittently throughout, but is much less of a model or guide for Marcel than the three male artists.
35 Marcel Proust, *In Search of Lost Time*, Vol. 2: *In the Shadow of the Young Girls in Flower*, trans. James Grieve (London: Allen Lane, 2002), 426.
36 Proust, *In the Shadow of the Young Girls in Flower*, 434.
37 Ibid., 433.
38 Ibid.
39 Ibid., 434–35.
40 Ibid., 435.
41 Ibid., 438.
42 Roger Shattuck, *Proust's Binoculars: A Study of Memory, Time, and Recognition in A la recherche du temps perdu* (London: Chatto and Windus, 1964), 26.
43 Proust, *In the Shadow of the Young Girls in Flower*, 434.

44 Ibid., 435.
45 Richard E. Goodkin, *Around Proust* (Princeton, NJ: Princeton University Press, 1991), 28.
46 Ibid., 28.
47 Marcel Proust, *In Search of Lost Time*, Vol. 4: *Sodom and Gomorrah*, trans. John Sturrock (London: Penguin, 2002), 57.
48 Lydia Ginzburg, *On Psychological Prose*, trans. and ed. Judson Rosengrant (Princeton, NJ: Princeton University Press, 1991), 310.
49 Roger Shattuck, *Proust's Way: A Field Guide to* In Search of Lost Time (New York: Norton, 2001), 84–85.
50 Louis Sass, *Madness and Modernism: Insanity in the Light of Modern Art, Literature and Thought* (New York: Basic Books, 1992).
51 Although this is the most widely accepted critical reading of Dowell's psychology, some Ford scholars regard the character as an arch-manipulator, *à la* Nabokov's Humbert Humbert, who conceals his true understanding of people and events. See Diane Stockmar Bonds, "The Seeing Eye and the Slothful Heart: The Narrator of Ford's *The Good Soldier*," *English Literature in Transition (1880-1920)* 25 (1982): 21–27; and Frank G. Nigro, "Who Framed *The Good Soldier*: Dowell's Story in Search of a Form," *Studies in the Novel* 24.4 (Winter 1992): 381–91.
52 Christine Cano, *Proust's Deadline* (Urbana: University of Illinois Press, 2006), 104.
53 Ibid., 104.
54 Peter Brooks, *Reading for the Plot: Design and Intention in Narrative* (Cambridge, MA: Harvard University Press, 1994), 97, 98–99, 99.
55 Ibid., 100.
56 Leo Bersani, *Marcel Proust: The Fictions of Life and of Art*, 2nd ed. (New York: Oxford University Press, 2013), 256.
57 Nicola Luckhurst, *Science and Structure in Proust's* A la recherche du temps perdu (Oxford: Clarendon Press, 2000), 198.
58 Ibid., 198–99.
59 Heinz Wimmer and Josef Perner, "Beliefs about Beliefs: Representation and Constraining Function of Wrong Beliefs in Young Children's Understanding of Deception," *Cognition* 13 (1983): 105–6.
60 Alan Leslie, "Pretense and Representation: The Origins of 'Theory of Mind,'" *Psychological Review* 94 (1987): 420–21.
61 Marcel Proust, *In Search of Lost Time*, Vol. 3: *The Guermantes Way*, trans. Mark Treharne (London: Allen Lane, 2002), 62.
62 George Butte, *I Know That You Know That I Know: Narrating Subjects from Moll Flanders to Marnie* (Columbus: Ohio State University Press, 2004).
63 Oatley, "Theory of Mind and Theory of Minds in Literature," 17.

64 Proust, *Guermantes Way*, 63.
65 Proust, *In the Shadow*, 295.
66 Ibid., 295.
67 Ibid., 296.
68 George Lakoff, "Why It Matters How We Frame the Environment," *Environmental Communication* 4.1 (March 2010): n.p.
69 Proust, *Sodom and Gomorrah*, 197.
70 Ibid., 199.
71 Quoted in Descombes, *Proust*, 5.
72 Proust, *Guermantes Way*, 64.
73 Marcel Proust, *In Search of Lost Time*, Vol. 6: *Finding Time Again*, trans. Ian Patterson (London: Allen Lane, 2002), 204.

9

Weimar Cognitive Theory: Modernist Narrativity and the Metaphysics of Frame Stories (After *Caligari* and Kracauer)

David LaRocca

In questioning the significance of the frame story (*Rahmenerzählung*) in *The Cabinet of Dr. Caligari* (*Das Kabinett des Doktor Caligari*, 1920, dir. Robert Wiene), I will not seek a historiographical interpretation of who did or did not introduce the idea of implementing the narrative device; this aspect has been debated expertly and extensively.[1] Rather, in what follows, I wish to address the philosophical and filmic effects of the frame story itself for (a) establishing the cognitive space of the film's mise-en-scène (in order to assess "where" it is we can say the images—within the frame—are taking place). By this point, nearly a century after it was released, and given its cultural prominence and artistic impact, I may not need to announce a spoiler alert when I say that we learn, by the film's end, that the interstitial segment is a flashback (and of a special sort, namely, a madman's fantasia)—and thus is not part of the time beyond (viz., before and after) the frame story. For this reason, I wish to consider (b) how the time *within* the frame story should be understood. If it is part of the mental experience of a character, to what extent are we to treat its status as a cognitive projection (e.g., being "in the mind" of the person recollecting)? What happens when we go from seeing a person with an unstable mind to, as it were, *inhabiting* that mind in cinematic time and space? And most crucially, how do replies to these questions help us sort the innovations of the narrative shape of the film itself: namely, (a) present-day forward-bracket (viz., the beginning of the "frame story"), (b) body of film as flashback/fantasy/mental construct, and (c) present-day end-bracket?

To reply to these questions, I will draw inspiration and orientation from another modernist work (about modernism): Siegfried Kracauer's essential and still-pertinent *From Caligari to Hitler: A Psychological History of the German Film* (1947), though not so much to ratify Kracauer's critique of the frame story (which he thinks ruined the potential of the film, turning it from "revolutionary" to "conformist"—because, like so many cinematic denouements, it ended with a take-back or negation of reality: some variation of "it's all a dream"), but instead to re-engage his observations on the cognitive nature of the film, especially in so far as it relies on distinctive traits of the film's narrative construction.[2] As Kracauer noted, "The settings amounted to a perfect transformation of material objects into emotional ornaments," which means, again, that they turned actual depictions of a "revolutionary" sort, with potentially grand political significance, into something more akin to emotional projections (viz., "ornaments")—tricks of light and shadow, angle and exaggerated action, and thus amount to little more than dreams and nightmares. More recently, Susan Hayward remarked on Wiene's film that "set design, lighting, and the [human] body are all interrelated squeezings-out of a psychology."[3] Even as Kracauer's and Hayward's comments abide, I wish to ask more specifically how the frame story effects and transforms our sense *of* that mise-en-scène; how its emotional and psychological status depends on the existence and content/context of the frame (front and back), the dreamy/mental middle, and thus, together, the narrative shape of the film as a whole.

Looking back to Wiene's film, then, we could say that the middle portion of *Caligari* is meant to be a "picture" of consciousness—in the sense that it provides an image of what a mind is experiencing, a scenario that is dominated by a dynamic visual orchestration. The "ornamental" would then bear, and contain, its resemblance to, or isomorphism with, the mental. As in the current serial, *Westworld* (2016–, dir. Jonathan Nolan and Lisa Joy), consciousness is not understood to be the location of narrative lives (e.g., the site of personal identity, memory, dreams) but rather is constituted *by* narrativity; we are shown (yet again) how consciousness is an emergent condition awaiting narrative imposition. Thus, by way of Wiene's film and *Westworld*, even as we acknowledge film's capacity to picture thinking, to depict consciousness, we are reminded anew of film-as-a-medium—especially as a medium that affords narrative structuring (e.g., by means of the modalities and techniques of *syuzhet*). The awareness is troubling, though, since it suggests that with *Caligari*, as with so many films since, and including *Westworld*, we are uncannily receptive and often unaware of the extent to which we treat a movie (or some portion of it) *as* consciousness. Whenever a film makes recourse to the position "everything you've seen on screen is, in fact, all in a character's mind," we know we are being subjected to a kind of visual (or later audiovisual) legerdemain that argues for a special attribute of the medium itself. It is a peculiar sort of trick, to be sure, since it is a coupling of a take-back and a giving over; what we thought was real and material (i.e., part of the reality of the shared world on screen) is traded for something mental (i.e., part of the reality of individual consciousness—a private, unshared world).

Kracauer's critique of cognition and narrativity suggests to us that Wiene and the several collaborators on *Caligari* (including Fritz Lang, who was replaced late by Wiene, and not long after created the exceptional parallel film, *The Testament of Dr. Mabuse* [1933]—the second in a trilogy beginning with *Dr. Mabuse the Gambler* [1922] and ending with *The Thousand Eyes of Dr. Mabuse* [1960]) were—nearly a century ago—already ensconced in the distinctively modernist project of destabilizing the location of the subject and, along the way, questioning his or her sanity. Just as viewers were learning to treat film projections as images of people, places, and things, filmmakers—and this is a key intervention of German expressionist cinema at this decisive, modernist moment between the wars in the Germany of the Weimar Republic—were trying to lend credence to the psychological and psychoanalytic dimension of the screen: that it was *itself* a projection, that it was like a dream or nightmare (or as the case may be, akin to the mental state of a lunatic).

Caligari, as a film, obsessively explores where the mind is and how its imaging—*of* consciousness, or *as* consciousness; and whether as index or dream or nightmare or hallucination or recollection from memory—might be represented. Film, as a medium, provided the occasion to absent the protagonist and shift viewers' attention intensively and entirely into a realm of representations made available for cognitive assessment (what we usually just call spectatorship); and yet, in *Caligari*, it was not solely through aspects of representation (mise-en-scène, lighting, set design, acting styles, etc.) but through narrative construction that the story (*fabula*) was subverted by the plot (*syuzhet*).[4] I wish to articulate how we learn from this piece of modernist cinema about the relationship between narrative (e.g., framing techniques) and the meaning of cinematic representations (e.g., what kind of image we can claim to see within the mise-en-scène, and between the familiar frames—or more linear end-caps of "beginning" and "ending"). Among other theories and theorists, I will assess the extent to which Noël Carroll's concepts of "criterial prefocusing" and "vectorially converging states" might apply to Wiene's film.[5] I will subsequently engage Kracauer's reflections *From Caligari to Hitler*, then, finally, I will assess how the legacy of *Caligari* is pertinent to our contemporary debate in cognitive cultural studies—especially in the constellation of issues (and reports) it offers on narrativity.

Caligari provides a worthy case for adjudicating that, and how, framing may give rise—and thus life—to the creation of multiple layers or levels of (cognitive) abstraction from the original (or originary), indexical image. Memories, daydreams, nightmares—and cinema itself—seem to depend on such framing, but *Caligari* helped to realize the affective potential of this narrative technique very early in cinematic history, in the midst of a roiling modernism, and with lasting implications into present-day cinema practice and film theory. In many ways, the following remarks are meant to assess the lasting pertinence of *Caligari*—both for our thinking about modernism and for our sense of inheriting its claims and preoccupations in an age of cognitive studies (e.g., for among other reasons, its depiction of an inner life, mental reality, and the ways film [re]presents a striking "picture" of mind). Moreover, contemporary filmic instances are folded into the conversation about mental pictures and (moving-image based) portraits of mind as a way to mobilize texts that may be more familiar to us. We shall find that *Caligari*, like so many cinematic frame stories since, compels a viewer to ask how movies think. *Caligari*, in a bit of modernist fervor, reveals a cinematic exhibition that is itself nothing short of thinking—in effect, the very depiction of thought on film.[6]

* * * *

In his contribution to *The Oxford Companion to Cognitive Literary Studies*, the celebrated and influential film theorist Noël Carroll takes up an inquiry into the relationship between "Theater and the Emotions."[7] Not surprisingly, given Carroll's pronounced contributions to film studies, and his philosophical finesse with the subtleties of the medium of film, selected moments from his discussion of theater, I should wish to suggest here, bear meaningfully on our thinking about the kinds of cognitive and emotional effects we can expect from cinema. I have in mind, then, to convey two signature concepts from Carroll's discussion of theater, to the present discussion of film.

When we come to watch a film, such as *Caligari*, we do not encounter it as we might an experience in our own personal lives, since part of what we have come to expect—and enjoy—about film is not just the art of representation (in its metaphysical sense) but also its modes of presentation. While we may still marvel at the mimetic powers of cinema (powers, no doubt, that continue to evolve and some may reasonably argue, expand or intensify—as with 3D, CGI, VR, AR, and related innovations in high-definition "immersive cinema"), an important and even essential part of our pleasure derives from the way representations are put together—presented to us. Instead of a story, we can speak of *syuzhet* (or discourse), which David Bordwell has described, after the Russian theorists, as the manner of composition, a method for creating a document of potential emotional impact that may be at odds with fidelity to the presumed linearity of time and space.[8] When a storyteller denies her listeners immediate satisfaction by saying that "before I tell you how the soldier died, I must first tell you how he came to be a soldier," she is shuffling the story elements to augment the story's affective tonality. In *Eternal Sunshine of the Spotless Mind* (2004), screenwriter Charlie Kaufman and director Michel Gondry give you tears upfront—in the opening credit-sequence, the filmmakers, the storytellers, begin at the end, or at *an* end—and then go back to sort out how Joel Barish (Jim Carrey) reached the point of emotional catastrophe. Joel's story with Clementine (Kate Winslet) does not *begin* with tears, but this application of *syuzhet* technique makes it so.

As the language and practices of theater have been translated to cinema for more than a century—indeed, mise-en-scène is but one among many medium-specific borrowings that have gone on to become central attributes of cinema—what Carroll says of the work of theater, we can, once again, map onto cinematic labors:

> In the theater, the playwright, the director, the actors, and so on have already done a great deal of the selection necessary in order to sculpt the scenes before us emotionally. Much of the selection that the emotions do for us in daily life has been done by the dramatist and the production team. That is, they have criterially *prefocused* the fictional events before us in such a way that the emotions the scene calls for—the emotions the creators of the play desire—emerge smoothly and reliable, at least in the ideal case.[9]

When Carroll adds "costuming, lighting, scenography, music" to the qualities that "can also contribute to the criterial prefocusing of scenes," the parallels and relevance to cinema should be overt. The film theorist may point out ways in which criterial prefocusing is accomplished by cinematic means—for example, by way of cinematography, production design, lighting, and editing. The point, to be sure, is neither to reduce theater and cinema to a common form nor to equate their work one way or another. Rather, with circumspection, I am much more simply asking that the adoption of Carroll's criterial prefocusing for thinking about film's effects helpfully illuminates an aspect of cinematic experience that we are already familiar with (but may not yet have a reliable term for). If *syuzhet* and criterial prefocusing provide a vocabulary with which to speak of narrative techniques in cinema, and in our case of *Caligari*, consider also Carroll's phrase for addressing cognitive effects of that arrangement:

> In virtue of criterially prefocusing, we can explain how it is that spectators and characters can share the same emotional states without enlisting the concept of identification. Identification presumes a causal relation between the character's inner states and that of the viewer. However, by means of criterial prefocusing, we can elucidate how the shared states can be related coincidentally rather than causally.[10]

Carroll concludes that the coincidence can be described as "vectorially converging" emotional states.[11] Or, drawing from Robert Sinnerbrink's distinctions, we can say that criterial prefocusing enables a robust activation of sympathy, but not empathy.[12] Carroll himself is attuned to this distinction and resists calling the "emotional relationship between the audience and character" one of empathy.[13] As Carroll glosses the phenomenon, the emotions of character and viewer "converge on the distressful pole of affect without ever becoming identical"; "the audience's affect is not identical with the character's, but only similar in valence, or vectorially convergent."[14]

Carroll's resistance to empathic identification (of, say, audience with character) is instructive because it underscores a crucial point about our cognitive relationship to presentation *and* representation (either in theater or on film), namely that "if we are want to account for what generally it is that brings about the audience's similarly valenced feelings toward the character, we need not invoke some mysterious process of identification. Once again, the audience's mental state is due to criterial prefocusing."[15] If we cannot be said, as viewers, to feel empathy for characters (in the technical, or, oddly, as the case may be, colloquial, sense that the audience member feels *the same* as the actor), then, we are positioned to speak of our emotional and cognitive experience as laying in parallel—or in some kind of "vectorially convergent" relationship—to that of what we see and hear: viewers of film, therefore, inhabit an analogical relationship with the characters being screened.

David Denby has remarked that "the great achievement of modernism was its union of the discordant and the metaphysical."[16] *The Cabinet of Dr. Caligari* would seem a fitting illustration of this conjugation of traits, since its discordance, what we have been describing in terms of techniques of *syuzhet* and criterial prefocusing, is thought to deliver us to metaphysical insight. Consider how this is accomplished. In the opening shots of *Caligari*, the audience is introduced to a conversation in medias res. Then, in a scenario familiar to fairy tales, the time register is interrupted by a spell-casting once-upon-a-time invocation. The conversant becomes a narrator, and we viewers are sent back (as we just saw in *Eternal Sunshine*) in order to find out how these characters arrived on this bench. The listener is promised something like a circular path: go back, follow the steps, and they will lead you here, to me, at this place (discovering when or where or what precisely is this place becomes part of the invitation's allure).

Yet, by the film's end, the circular shape is withdrawn. A viewer does not "end up" where she began, on the bench, beside the narrator. Rather, the viewer is not present at all, really, but instead may be taken to be part of the narrator's mental landscape. The frame story, in short, has evacuated the familiar present/past/present sequencing that was, it seemed at the time, promised at the beginning of the film. Indeed, it may be the case that "frame" is the wrong—or at least a misleading—metaphor, since we are not talking about a structural effect that *surrounds* a story, but something that appears at the *beginning* and the *end* of a story.[17] Perhaps a better, more accurate, trope for such narrative organization would be "book-ending."

Two decades after Conrad Veidt played Cesare in *Caligari*, a film whose frame story (and structure) is a signal part of its legacy, Veidt portrayed Jaffar in *The Thief of Bagdad* (1940, dir. Berger, Powell, et al.), a film whose frame story is more straightforward in that it conjures a story book; with this iconic illustration at hand, the image of book-ends seems much more apt for understanding the interior space of *The Thief of Bagdad* as occurring, for example, "between two covers."[18] And this re-orientation by comparison may suit our thinking of *Caligari*, perhaps to the point of revising the very language the film has customarily been described with—in effect, shifting our practice from "frame story" to "book-ending." Still, with a century's worth of pronounced usage, conceptual pushback on the metaphor of the frame may be less fortuitous than trying to understand better its philosophical implications, including its implementation (and variations) in cinema since 1920. And conversely, the way this century of inventive imitation may draw us closer to an appreciation and understanding of the modernist innovations of the Weimar Republic's indelible *Caligari*.

In our own day, Wiene's framing trick, we might say, remains familiar to us in the guise of various M. Night Shyamalan entertainments, for example, *The Sixth Sense* (1999), in which Dr. Malcolm Crowe (Bruce Willis), by film's end, cannot be said to exist in the film in the same way we presumed he did (or could). He is dead. More proximate to our reflections on *Caligari*, however, is Martin Scorsese's *Shutter Island* (2010), a story that borrows self-consciously from, and with a cineaste's love of, *Caligari*, to say, by the film's conclusion: beware the killer, he might be you. Teddy Daniels (Leonardo DiCaprio), like Cesare (Conrad Veidt), was literally looking out for the killer, but that would not resolve the case, since the killer was, as it were, inside. Here is a first indication of how the *syuzhet* of the frame story critterially prefocuses our attention, but on the wrong thing! Hence the trick, or as it is often called "twist." Wiene, like Shyamalan and Scorsese and Nolan (Jonathan *and* Christopher) and many others, can use narrative techniques to mislead the viewer, thus increasing the chances for the thrill of the unexpected denouement.

As in *Caligari*, so in *Inception* (2010, dir. Christopher Nolan), the framing—indeed, with many layers of framing—leaves us wondering, at the end, if Cobb (again, DiCaprio) is still "in a dream" or if he has, at last, emerged from it: if he is awake, alive, and in the present. This brief link to Nolan's film is significant not because it shows Nolan's modernist credentials, but instead, the way in which *Caligari*'s preoccupation with the screen-as-dream is a *legacy* of modernism (and modernist cinema) that we are still contending with nearly a century later. Even as we have entered (and perhaps passed through postmodernism), our contemporary preoccupation with the cinematic screen as a dream space remains as intact and as insoluble as ever. (A reader of Plato's *Republic* must resist the temptation to point out the ways in which this preoccupation with the screen-as-false-reality is, in fact, a stubborn hold-over from pagan antiquity. Modernism's contribution, then, would be to formalize this conundrum—to stage it, to screen it—using the day's latest technology, projections of light through celluloid.)

If at the end of *Inception*, we are left wondering if Cobb is (still?) dreaming or not, I want to pick up the idea that if, in *Caligari*, we were critterially prefocused to identify with Francis (Friedrich Feher)—as a man who has undergone a terrible ordeal, and yet, in the end, because of the narrative intervention of the frame, we are told to believe *he* is mentally ill—what do we do with our vectorially converging states (those, namely, that we viewers are said to share with characters—not, again, as identical states, but as analogical relations)?

When the end-frame is revealed, it would seem that the psychological, political, moral, and emotional bottom drops out of the film. Such a result, we are told to understand, is what Kracauer means by the frame story enacting a shift from "revolutionary" to "conformist," of which more is discussed later in this chapter. For now, let us dwell on the way we have been trained (by means of criterial prefocusing) to feel "coincidentally" that Francis has been telling us the truth, namely, that the recollected story is a verity. And yet, as the other (back) side of the frame emerges, in the last moments of the film, the story is reconfigured as the projection of an ill mind.

When looking to Siegfried Kracauer's landmark study, *From Caligari to Hitler: A Psychological History of German Cinema* (1947), we should attend to his observation that "technical peculiarities betray peculiarities of meaning" (74). It is a poetic and portentous remark and yet provides a clear and effective context for thinking through the reasons why the frame story in *Caligari* (and for that matter in other films and fictions) is a philosophically and artistically consequential apparatus. The frame story does not contribute to the furtherance or velocity of vectorially converging states, as we might expect of the forward-moving dramatic energies of fiction, but instead stands ready to *undermine* the credentials of the very content we have been criterially prefocused to believe in and build upon. Hence the evisceration of the various powers—emotional tensions, somatic effects, conceptual puzzles, and the like—that the "middle" of such films are commonly so capable of achieving in us, for us. The frame story, then, is tantamount to a fraud—albeit one so familiar that we often shrug in bemusement, as the credits roll, rather than furrow our brow in distress.

But then fiction is, as again Plato was among the first to declare, a variant of fraud, so what precisely does this deceit make possible—especially in its preclusion or suppression of anticipated meaning, or the dissolution of actualized meaning—remains of vital intrigue. Kracauer notes that the source material for the film, Hans Janowitz and Carl Mayer's manuscript, was an "outspoken revolutionary story" (64).

> The character of Caligari embodies [the fatal tendencies in the German system]; he stands for an unlimited authority that idolizes power as such, and, to satisfy its lust for domination, ruthlessly violates all human rights and values. Functioning as a mere instrument, Cesare is not so much a guilty murderer as Caligari's innocent victim. This is how the authors themselves understood him. According to the pacifist-minded Janowitz, they had created Cesare with the dim design of portraying the common man who, under pressure of

compulsory military service, is drilled to kill and to be killed. The revolutionary meaning of the story reveals itself unmistakably at the end, with the disclosure of the psychiatrist as Caligari: reason overpowers unreasonable power, insane authority is symbolically abolished. (65)

Both authors protested when first Fritz Lang, and then Wiene, planned to introduce a framing device. "The original story was an account of real horrors," notes Kracauer, while "Wiene's version transforms that account into a chimera concocted and narrated by the mentally deranged Francis" (66). Kracauer emphasizes that Janowitz and Mayer "raged against the framing story" because "it perverted, if not reversed, their intrinsic intentions." Consider the end of the film, where far from confirming "real horrors," the director of the mental asylum surmises that he will be able to cure his patient—and "[w]ith this cheerful message the audience is dismissed" (66). Janowitz and Mayer had written a story whose elements would criterially prefocus the audience to respond to dire and *genuine* social ills and threats, where the framing device vitiates this charged critique by invalidating its reality (or perhaps better, its *allusions* to reality, which in turn would have reinforced the story's cinematic efficacy and salience), leaving viewers in a position to reject the critique as the delusion of a madman. "While the original story exposed the madness inherent in authority," Kracauer observes, "Wiene's *Caligari* glorified authority and convicted its antagonist of madness" (65–66). And it is for this reason that Kracauer concludes: "A revolutionary film was thus turned into a conformist one" (66).

More recently, Friedrich Kittler has accused Kracauer of mounting a "simplified sociological reading" of the film, and yet, it could be argued that though the frame story repeals its so-called revolutionary content, the revolutionary proposal is *still there* for audiences to admire and perhaps take up as a banner or as a critique (146).[19] In short, even though a director announces that "it was all in a character's head," it remains that it is now (also) all in ours. If one were trying to program a (tacit) counterpropaganda, *Caligari*'s framing device might be just the tool to employ. On this line of reasoning, the realistic credentials of the film would be a *liability* to political and ideological critique, and so it is precisely the evaporation of these images—and their implications—as frauds of the mind, of an ill mind at that, which stands as a provocation to the viewer, who, we are prone to think (at least, of ourselves), possesses a sane mind. We need not panic or protest at the "take-back" inaugurated by the end-frame, but instead be attuned to the way expressions of "revolutionary meaning" may require indirect methods—including the (now) conventional frame story.

As we are considering the perhaps unexpected political and ethical impact of *syuzhet*, namely, that the ordering and bracketing of content can transform—and even invert—meaning, so we can marvel at the effects of mise-en-scène on our hermeneutics.[20] Scores of books have been written about the modernist aesthetics of expressionism in German cinema of the Weimar period.[21] But we needn't rehearse this lively, enriching, conversation in its breadth and depth to notice the uncanny ways in which two characteristic features of mise-en-scène—the set decoration and the lighting—are rendered with forceful exaggeration (striking contrast, prominent distortion, and the like). As a result of the framing device, the audience has already been granted criteria for writing off the flashback as a lunatic's hallucination. The expressionistic attributes of the mise-en-scène, however, provide a surplus of evidence to reinforce and ratify that dismissal. Here is how Kracauer interprets the moment:

> Wiene's version [of Janowitz and Mayer's story] disavowed [the] revolutionary meaning of expressionist staging, or, at least, put it, like the original story, in brackets. In the film *Caligari* expressionism seems to be nothing more than the adequate translation of a madman's fantasy into pictorial terms. This was how many contemporary German reviewers understood, and relished, the settings and gestures. One of the critics stated with self-assured ignorance: "The idea of rendering the notions of sick brains . . . through expressionist pictures is not only well conceived but also well realized." (70)

While Kracauer's use of the word "brackets" sends us back to my earlier notes suggesting that "frame story" might be replaced by some variation on "book-ends"—and "brackets" would do fine (as shown by their elegant, understated, and illustrative typography: [ ]), Kracauer seems giddy to point out the inconsistency, and apparent lack of nuanced interpretation on offer, evident primarily in the praise issuing forth from the agog contemporary German critics:

> In their triumph[,] the philistines overlooked one significant fact: even though *Caligari* stigmatized the oblique chimneys as crazy, it never restored the perpendicular ones as the normal. Expressionist ornaments also overrun the film's concluding episode, in which, from the philistine's viewpoint, perpendiculars should have been expected to characterize the revival of conventional reality. (70)

Kracauer's amplified condescension is not gleeful, though, but defeatist, as he continues: "In consequence, the *Caligari* style was as far from depicting madness as it was from transmitting revolutionary messages" (70). Here, according to

Kracauer, *syuzhet* and mise-en-scène have conspired to undermine both the political and the psychological import of the film. Criterial prefocusing leads us to a conclusion that is at once lackluster and incoherent. In the wake of Kracauer's assessment, a careful student of film (with a sense of humor) might be tempted to call the film's effect maddening. Yet, as Kracauer laments, the effect on the contemporary German viewer seemed anything but; this vision of madness, and madness contained (and perhaps even cured), was a reassuring fiction, and therefore was inert and enervating when it should have been the opposite. One might even say the film, as if by design, left viewers as it found them.

* * * *

In the second part of this chapter, I wish to process the insights about *Caligari* made possible by Carroll and Kracauer by turning to recent developments in cognitive cultural studies—a domain that readily and compellingly includes overlaps in philosophy, literature, and cinema (and thus "cultural" may be subdivided into cognitive *literary* studies, cognitive *film* studies, etc.). Given the foregoing, I will attend especially to the way we may understand the modernist narrative techniques of *Caligari* as they can be set in relief by critical developments happening in cognitive narratology nearly a century after the film's first screening.

Narratology has become, as Lisa Zunzhine has noted, "multimodal" and "transmedial," which is to say that it has evolved into *cognitive* narratology; and further, it has, as David Herman remarks, become "the study of mind-relevant dimensions of storytelling practices wherever—and by whatever means—those practices occur."[22] In the remarkable, blossoming literature in cognitive cultural studies, we can readily find many innovations that would provide new in-roads into our thinking about *modernist* narrative as well as expressionist cinema (such as we find it in the heyday of the Weimar Republic). I wish to draw from Alan Palmer's research, and in particular, his depiction of a "storyworld" and its relationship to the "fictional minds of characters" (176); Daniel Yacavone's innovative account of "film worlds"—by way of Nelson Goodman's *Ways of Worldmaking*—should be invoked, but for space constraints, analysis and comparsion will be left for another occasion.[23] We are, as Palmer shows, familiar with the notion of fictional characters in literature, as the saying goes, "having minds," but we can readily transfer such attribution to cinematically projected characters—and perhaps even more easily since film can be said to capture the image of thinking; a character may not say any words and yet the medium enables a representation of thought. We might turn also to Stanley Cavell's description that, when watching a film, a "human something" presents itself/is presented "as 'in our presence while we are not in his' (present *at* him, because looking at him, but not present *to* him)" (26–27).[24] In this light, it seems intelligible and meaningful to say that what we are seeing and hearing—upon there, on screen—is thinking.

Palmer draws from our accustomed habits of describing characters in fictional worlds in terms that suggest we believe they have a "mental network"— what we usually regard as "intentions, purposes, motives, and reasons" for action. He calls this habit an "exercise in attribution": "You were attributing a series of mental states and events to the characters. If my guess was right, then it suggests that narrative is, in essence, the description of fictional mental functioning. In my view, readers enter the storyworlds of novels primarily by attempting to follow the workings of the fictional minds contained in them" (177). Palmer's account of a storyworld is particularly useful when reflecting on Kracauer's claim that "technical peculiarities betray peculiarities of meaning" (74). For one thing, it appears that Wiene's introduction of a frame story (a function of *syuzhet*) coupled with his inconsistent application of German expressionist set design (a matter of mise-en-scène), has generated, for lack of a better word, a muddled storyworld. For one thing, a viewer may not be in a position to determine as it were the "inside" and the "outside" of the various worlds we have been presented with, and thus discern their order or adjacency in time and space. For instance, until the end-frame is revealed (in the last minutes of *Caligari*), we may think ourselves part of a flashback, but not, that is to say, party to someone's private memory. Our sense that we are not watching something taking place *in* a mind is partly owing to habits of viewership, but also to qualitative attributes of cinema-as-medium (e.g., that even when "in" a flashback, we can see the person who may be remembering, or we can see cuts in the film—from one shot to the next—which mark out the language of film but do not issue forth mental projection or recollection).

To underscore the troubled status of the storyworld in *Caligari*, consider a much more contemporary series of films featuring the character Jason Bourne (portrayed by Matt Damon, viz., *The Bourne Identity* [2002], *The Bourne Supremacy* [2004], *The Bourne Ultimatum* [2007], and most recently, if most disappointingly, *Jason Bourne* [2016]).[25] I do not mean to undertake a review of the relative merits of these films, but instead wish to concentrate our attention on one consistent attribute of their making or construction, and at that, by two different directors (Doug Liman for the first, founding installment, and thereafter Paul Greengrass).

In the *Bourne* series, we become accustomed to the alignment between *flashbacks* and *memory*. Jason Bourne sometimes expresses a pained facial grimace, but more often embodies a brilliantly affectless mask animated mainly by a stare of introverted reflection, both of which appear to the audience as cues that he has seen or felt something within—for example, remembered something of his own past, made a connection, sketched a plan for immediate implementation. But and this is the case throughout the three principal films that compose the initial trilogy (2001–2007) as well as the eponymous 2016 film (and even to an appreciable extent by Tony Gilroy's stand-alone spin-off, *The Bourne Legacy* [2012]), the flashbacks/memories are *never from Bourne's point of view*. Put colloquially, he is always "in the picture" (i.e., within the boundaries of the film frame—and thus very much part of the mise-en-scène). By means of a shift in film stock or shutter rate, camera motion, adjustments of aperture or coloration, the film trains us to recognize these moments as ones of "remembering," but, of course, this is *not* how personal memory works: each of us looks out from within, not, as in these films, at ourselves from some distant position or external perspective. We are not characters in our memories but agents of them, and therefore perceive the world from the vantage (in film language, pov) we think of as our own. The *Bourne* series—a credit to its cinematic innovations—inverts this commonplace. When this structure is noted (viz., that the character Bourne is "in" his memories, seen "in" them from some non-Bourne perspective), and we return to the films anew, we seem to be watching all of Bourne's private mental and emotional life *in the third person*. That is to say, though Bourne is meant to be the source of these flashbacks/memories, even *he* sees his own past from the point of view of another—namely, our position. Yet another trick of *syuzhet*, albeit a wonderfully clever and entertaining one. Still, for all the innovation, the ontological problems it entreats (e.g., with respect to frame stories and storyworlds) feel decidedly familiar—of a piece with thinking about *Caligari* since its first critical inheritance.

Even if we put aside the German expressionist qualities of the final minutes of *Caligari* (viz., the end-cap of the frame story), the persistence of which drove Kracauer to conclude that the film does not understand itself—and we, instead, strictly focus on the framing device, which is, we could say, less polemical and more identifiable as a narrative technique—we may, as in the *Bourne* series, discover that we do not have a clear sense of *where* or *when* the happenings on screen can be said to take place.

Since we are already in trouble with respect to what may be called the storyworld(s) of *Caligari*: is the story *between* the frames a flashback, or a memory, or a derangement of memory, or a hallucination (i.e., a projection of things that never were), or something else altogether? Peter J. Rabinowitz, who himself has contested Palmer's definition of narrative given just earlier (e.g., as being too sweeping, too essentializing), also pushes back on the "stress on sequence" that is, perhaps not surprisingly, a hallmark of narrative theory (86–87). "Yes, sequence is crucial," admits Rabinowitz, "but we read and enjoy narrative for other reasons, too, reasons often obscured by the stress on sequence" (86). Rabinowitz's point might be made with reference to a film that will, no doubt, stand out against the types and genres noted earlier (*Caligari*, of course, but also *The Matrix, Memento, Mulholland Drive, Inception, Westworld*, and the *Bourne* series), namely, *The Family Man* (2000, dir. Brett Ratner). Despite innumerable differences between *The Family Man* and these other works, the film, like *Caligari*, makes prominent use of a framing device. Indeed, *The Family Man* is drawing from what may be deemed a subgenre of framing-device-based narratives, especially, those emerging in the aftermath of Charles Dickens's *A Christmas Carol* and aimed a certain achievement of a "glimpse" into the different lives one does not live in order to reconfigure one's relationship to the life one is, in fact, living; we might annoint this subgenre *the cinema of the counterfactual*—and once pointed out, examples call out to us: from *Back to the Future* (1985, dir. Robert Zemeckis) to *Groundhog Day* (1993, dir. Harold Ramis) to *About Time* (2013, dir. Richard Curtis). Frank Capra's *It's a Wonderful Life* (1946), to be sure, is an iconic and enduring representative example of both an inheritance of Dickens and a template for *The Family Man*.

My point here, as it was earlier with the *Bourne* series, is not to judge the relative merits of these films (e.g., the directorial styles and pedigrees of Brett Ratner vs. Frank Capra; or the figuration of a CIA black-ops assassin opposite a middle-aged dad and tire salesman from New Jersey), but rather to offer an illustration of Rabinowitz's point, at least in so far as I am adopting and adapting it here: namely, that the content of the frame story in *The Family Man* is at once very brief (in terms of total running time) and tragically at odds with the sentiment of the core narrative contained within the frame.

To underscore the tragedy, recall how after Jack Campbell (played with customary feeling and fervor by Nicholas Cage) falls in love with lost love, Kate

Reynolds (Téa Leoni) after a dozen years apart, he *also* falls in love with their two young children. What's the problem, then? When Campbell re-awakens—having gone back to the future (i.e., to his present), and finds himself returned to his "old life"—he can go to the West Village and find Kate before she moves to Paris. And as it was in *An Affair to Remember* (1957, dir. Leo McCarey), the couple reunites, after some initial trepidation, in gratitude and relief. But, in *The Family Man*, at the end, where are the children? And for that matter, when Jack finds Kate in the West Village, how can we believe that this single, city-living, professional woman on the cusp of another big promotion is *anything like* the warm, wonderful New Jersey mom and contented nonprofit lawyer that we fell in love with, as Jack did (in the life lived between the frame story)? In short, the end-cap of the frame story in *The Family Man* is *devastating*, since we must fathom that Jack looks at Kate with his memories of *some other woman* (as created by his experience with the Kate he lived with and loved during his "glimpse" of what might have been).

Nor for that matter is Jack *Jack*. At the end, back at the airport, Jack is just a single millionaire who had a "glimpse," we (the audience, not Kate) lost the guy who became a loving dad and husband, and who found a way to his calling while having a family. The trick of the "glimpse" ending is that the old Jack is suddenly the new Jack, yet *with no experience* in the world as the new Jack; Kate isn't looking at the dad from New Jersey, but a tycoon who has spent thirteen years on Wall Street—as an inveterate bachelor—but only a few "mental" or "emotional" weeks with a wife and family. Jack may have had a glimpse, but in what sense is it plausible that he could be the dad and husband he was? Perhaps this question underwrites the emotional tonality of this subgenre, which encodes hope as a mastertone of its sensibility.

Moreover, the glimpse is complicated by the doubling it creates: Jack-as-New-Jersey-dad and Jack-the-bachelor-Manhattanite "in the body of" the New Jersey dad. Jack admits his knowledge on this score—namely, his understanding of the metaphysics of the glimpse—when he contemplates having an affair with his infatuated neighbor, Evelyn (Lisa Thornhill), since he figures that his marital status, like his ontological status, is special (read causeless, or without effect)—and so likewise, for an affair. Jack informs his confounded friend, Arnie (Jeremy Piven), that "it really wouldn't be cheating.... It's complicated.... Those rules don't apply to me." (One is reminded here of another frame story with a similar metaphysical setup—*Groundhog Day*, in which Phil [Bill Murray] tells Rita [Andie McDowell]: "I don't even floss.")

These men—Jack and Phil—leave their audiences (on-screen and off) in a state of envy and bewilderment.

Hearing Jack narrate aloud a proposed infidelity, Arnie, playing the role of the audience in this scene, recoils in confusion. But Jack, channeling his Wall Street bravura, is untroubled by Arnie's consternation. The scene plays as a comic send-up of the debate about "what counts" as cheating in a relationship, in a marriage, and yet, it masks the deeper question posed by the glimpse: in what sense does Kate even exist, or exist for Jack? Kate herself draws our attention to the freshness and depth of Jack's infatuation when she asks him a variant of these questions: "How can you do that? . . . —Look at me like you haven't seen me every day for the last twelve years." The screenplay glosses Kate's look this way: "There's love in her eyes but it's not meant for him." I wish to counter this reading—and invert it, for it is precisely Jack from Wall Street, and thus *not her husband*, who looks at Kate this way. The love in her eyes is meant for the man who does in fact look at her the way Jack does in this moment—and we know that this Jack is a visitor, an imposter, a confidence man, and "an alien" (as identified by his daughter). That Kate's New Jersey tire salesman, and husband of a dozen years, didn't look at her this way is part of the pain we must feel for her, even if for this figment Kate, a proxy for all the spouses of a dozen years or more who fail to be seen—to be truly looked at: desired, admired, listened to, and loved. Bringing Jack's distraction by Evelyn together with Jack's intense wonderment at Kate underscores a central figuration of marriage in this film, but also marriage as such, namely, what does it mean *to exist* for another, for one's spouse?

Jack's willingness to risk his marriage to Kate is one among many instances that remind the viewer that Jack is experiencing "a glimpse"—what we may call a dream. A similar shock is presented to us in *Back to the Future*, when Marty McFly (Michael J. Fox) finds himself alone, in the dark, in his underwear, with his mother, Lorraine (Lea Thompson), and later, in a car, on the cusp of making out with her. The events in *Back to the Future*, unlike *Caligari* and *The Family Man*, are said to be real—just operating in a different time register; thus, an affair with his teenage mother would actualize the Oedipal (and Freudian) terrors inherent to the story's threat, and thus, its drama. In *The Family Man*, by contrast, the frame is established by two shots of Jack: sleeping (early) and falling asleep in a chair (late), with a slow, roving camera moving up to rest upon his face—thus creating, in both cases, a mise-en-scène that presents us with the location of Jack's glimpse, namely, a space inside his head. During the middle portion of *Eternal Sunshine*, a similar attention to cognitive space is reinforce by a bird's-eye view of Joel sleeping in bed (with a Lacuna, Inc. helmet in place) and playfully expanded by an eye-line match that comes in and out of focus—thus, showing us Joel's point of view, in effect, him waking from his dream, emerging out of his memories.

Back at JFK airport, again, with Jack and Kate on the other side of the end-frame, as the snow falls portentously on their rekindled romance, all we can think is: those beautiful kids don't exist and, it would seem given the logic of the frame story, can't; and who is this woman in the airport—she's not Jack's wife, that is, the woman he is (and we are) thinking about (namely, the one he might have seen "every day for the last twelve years"). When George Bailey (James Stewart) is returned to *his* present, in *It's a Wonderful Life*—back from his glimpse with Clarence (Henry Travers), and bursts into the lively holiday domestic space, his children are alive and well—healed and happy and hurling themselves into his arms. And Mary (Donna Reed) is there too, very much herself. Not so for Jack Campbell's wife and children; the frame story in *The Family Man*, as it does in *Caligari*, renders the middle—the very meat and marrow of Jack's insights gleaned from his glimpse—an apparition of the mind. Jack is no family man, after all, just a guy at the airport, trying to make big life decisions.

Though this comparison of "high" and "low" art, film archive and mainstream—and especially in the juxtaposition of *Caligari* with *The Family Man*, a cinematic work of world historical significance and a passing popular holiday morsel—may seem an odd methodology (let's call it a modernist one), perhaps it can bear up, and bear out, if we consider how the case study of *The Family Man* amply illustrates Rabinowitz's point that "to the extent that we *do* read for sequence, there may be types of sequence that are not widely recognized—types of sequence that are, in fact, tied to those special spots.... Attention to favorite moments can reveal previously unrecognized alternative structures that exist in contestatory counterpoint with the more familiar structures we usually see in our favorite texts. (86)

Applying this logic to *The Family Man*, we can concurrently admit that we adore the story that is inside the frame even as we lament (loath!) the content and implications of the framing device (i.e., for what it means or does to the enframed time and space). How do we know, recognize, or articulate this confusion, this "contestatory counterpoint" that may summon revulsion? Partly by the effects of the framing device, since it turns what might have been a fantasy of a man falling in love with his wife and children (not unlike *It's a Wonderful Life*) into a perverse, if gently rendered and slyly inconspicuous, imposition of prolicide and uxoricide. The director must presume, must hope, that as Kracauer said above, with the "cheerful message" of the film's end-cap, "the audience is dismissed" (66) and thereafter won't look back or think back about the implications of the conclusion. It would seem that, coached by the filmmakers, we viewers don't (or don't want to) notice such things—namely, that the framing device has generated a nauseating predicament: the evisceration of the possibility of having (again) what was had (viz., this wife, these children). At the end, Jack and Kate are smiling together, looking longingly into one another's eyes as they reunite; the hope of their *shared* future suddenly put back into the realm of possibility, but Jack knows—or perhaps only *we know*, or can acknowledge—that the kids are gone, and in very real sense, Kate is gone as well. No wonder we aren't granted access to their re-kingled conversation; for what could they say to make sense of their reunion and its existential and metaphysical implications? This isn't a case where revolutionary content becomes conformist, as Kracauer saw in *Caligari*, but where the framing device *undermines* the love story (of both wife and children). The too-pronounced emphasis on the narrative sequencing (including the framing device) in *The Family Man* corrupts the entire work and leaves us unable to draw a meaningful, lasting moral, whereas an allowance for the "contestatory counterpoint" that forms the casually brilliant *interior* of the film—its ethical and emotive core—provides as satisfying a culmination as one could expect from the genre *and* the subgenre.

In the wake of some engagement with cognitive cultural, literary, and film studies, we can return anew to *Caligari*, especially to the effects of narrative method on our habits of visual attribution—and in particular, in this case, to the question of *where* we can say the story (between the frame) takes place. At the end of *Caligari*, when the end-frame is announced, we are returned to the time register that opened the film, but now with new information about *who* is telling the story; in this old, as it were originary position, we are coaxed (again by means of narrative sequencing) to appreciate how we went (suddenly!) from seeing *a depiction of a story* (our usual mode of address toward fiction film, and our expectation from it) to a by-the-way prompt that we were (in the middle of the film), in fact, seeing *the content of a mind* (and at that, a mind that is ill). The point seems at once blunt and subtle: blunt because it is so obvious, given the narrative intentions of the film (viz., to have viewers read it this way, as a mental projection), and subtle because our habits of viewership are so well hewn that it may be difficult for us to appreciate what has happened—in effect, to rethink or remember what it is we thought we saw. The "contestatory counterpoint" that transforms the middle of *Caligari* may simply go unrecognized; the viewer may neither catch the ontological redescription of the middle portion nor, perhaps more likely, succeed in drawing out the many charged ramifications of the change (such as we find in the spirited, frustrated comments by Kracauer).

At this point, one may be tempted to draw on the literature of aspect-seeing (as it comes to us primarily through reflections by Ludwig Wittgenstein, and by others on his work)—in short, to say that the end-frame makes the bracketed portion of the film "dawn" under a different aspect: that a story we thought was about our world (or, at least, existed in the diegetic time and space of the film) becomes, instead, a vision from a mind.[26] As with *Caligari*, then so again with *Eternal Sunshine of the Spotless Mind*, as pointed out by William Day, "the kaleidoscopic center of the film"—namely, the scenes that exist between the beginning- and end-frames—"take place in Joel's head"; what we see is not purported to be filmed events from our world (fiction in the form of Charlie Kaufman's screenplay, and fact in the shapes and tones that Jim Carrey and Kate Winslet provide as the actors performing the roles of Joel and Clementine), but, instead, phantasms of Joel's own memory—as if these scenes conjured by his mind, from his memory, were something or somewhere altogether different from the world we are used to facing when we face the movie screen (135).

I wish to continue this line of thinking—redescription, reassessment of cinematic form and content—by drawing still further from the currents of cognitive studies, and in particular, from the work of Lisa Zunshine, since in *Why We Read Fiction* and *Getting Inside Your Head*, we are treated to investigations that bear uncanny relevance to our preoccupations with *Caligari*. Consider the opening sentence, written with characteristic charisma and poetic flourish: "We live in other people's heads: avidly, reluctantly, consciously, unawares, mistakenly, inescapably" (xi). She continues:

> Cognitive scientists have a special term for the evolved cognitive adaptation that makes us attribute mental states to ourselves and to other people; they call it theory of mind or mind reading. Though it may sound like telepathy, theory of mind is actually its opposite. Telepathy implies perfect self-conscious access to someone's thinking. Mind reading is approximate guessing and imperfect interpretation, most of it taking place below the radar of our consciousness. (xi)

When Zunshine adds that "we live in other people's heads yet have no direct access to their thoughts and feelings," a viewer of *Caligari* may feel eager to raise her hand to say otherwise—since the film's frame story seems to insist that we have just such access. But, as Zunshine follows up, so would we be reminded that our "fantasy of perfect access to mind through body"—even if it be the "body" (or medium) of film—is, and must remain, at the level of fantasy (xi). And moreover, to simply underline her own gloss on "mind reading" [my emphasis], that phantasm will stand in need of *interpretation*, and in these transmedial terrains, a canny *translation*. (I will leave for a later time a necessary assessment of the "reading" metaphor as such, for if we are now all-too familiar with another Germanic modernist proposition—namely, Ludwig Klages's notion of logocentrism [and later, Jacques Derrida's critique of it], we must also—especially in our approach to cinema [a dual body of motion picture *and sound*, and perhaps, in time, a hydra of other attributes as well] appreciate the lectiocentrism of our accounts. If we are sure that films can be read, let us also *hear* them—and "read" them accordingly. While Emily Apter has ably enriched our thinking about the relationship between "the reading" and "the looking," there is a call—and the sonic trope seems fitting here—to add "the listening" [149].)

In the aftermath of watching *Caligari*, perhaps casting about to make sense of how the framing device alters our relationship to the content of the bracketed proceedings, Zunshine's cognitive cultural studies approach allows us to summon a fresh take on the film—namely, that "we *assume* that there must be a mental state behind an observable behavior" (xi). Our immersion in the story Francis is said to relate, putting ourselves in the position of the person who sat beside him on the bench and listened intently to him recount a personal memory, reinforced just this kind of assumption in our relationship to the characters "on" film, "in" the film, in his "mind." In a word, we were *reading* them—or, in Zunshine's phrase, undertaking a practice of "mind reading."

Yet, when we reach the end of the film, we might see ourselves as victims of a fraud—the madman has played a trick on us. That was no memory! Unlike in the *Bourne* series, where we are meant to *allow* Bourne's memories into the (present-day) narrative even if, as noted earlier, they are peculiarly third-person instead of point-of-view memories; and unlike *Eternal Sunshine*, where the memory status of the middle is dramatized and thus reinforced by a kind of sonic and visual erasure (made possible by the invasive technologies of Lacuna, Inc.)—in *Caligari*, the "take-back" of the end-frame disables our habitual, well-honed practice of mind-reading for, properly speaking, we cannot be said to read the minds of the characters (e.g., Francis, Cesare, et al.), but instead to be presented *with a mind*. It is precisely for this reason that so many fans and critics have a difficult time figuring out how Clementine knows that she can find Joel at Montauk because, after all, "Meet me at Montauk" was something she said to him in his own mind. Indeed, the line also does not appear to have come from the mind of Charlie Kaufman, either, since it is absent from the shooting script (Day, 132). The labors of transmedial reading—interpretation and translation—appear to be as vexing as they are endless.

In many of Zunshine's examples and case studies, she describes how people—how people's bodies—can be read, and in particular, how such readings of bodies may allow access to thoughts.[27] For those "moments in fictional narratives when characters' body language involuntarily betrays their feelings, particularly if they want to conceal them from others," she offers the notion of "embodied transparency" (23). If we draw from Zunshine's use of Jane Austen's novel *Persuasion*, we can readily—and without loss—turn to Roger Michell's film adaptation from 1995, starring Ciarán Hinds as Captain Wentworth. In both cases—novel and film—we can read *into* the mind of Wentworth, according to Zunshine, by means of studying his body language (either as described by Austen or as enacted/embodied by Hinds).

Yet *Caligari* provides the viewer with something else. Our habit of mind-reading does not work, or is undermined, when we are told that the film we have seen did not have characters with minds of their own, but, instead, that *the film*—the space between the frames—*is* mind. The "fantasy of perfect access to mind through body" seems to be replaced by the actuality of perfect access to mind through film—in film, as film. The film just is this mind. To be consistent, then, perhaps we should call the case of *Caligari* "disembodied transparency."

* * * *

The Cabinet of Dr. Caligari, as it now attains its centennial, is, for narrative theory, at least, still cutting-edge. Imbued with modernist preoccupations characteristic of the time—among them, the nature of personal psychology, mass psychology, psychiatry, psychoanalysis, psychosis, madness, deception, distortion, and especially, the very metaphysics of the film medium itself (is it all a dream? is the medium all mind?)—*Caligari* stands as a testament to anxieties and preoccupations that found able criticism in reflections by Siegfried Kracauer, and quite fittingly, belong, one should think, to the emerging domain of cognitive cultural studies (as exemplified earlier by Palmer, Rabinowitz, Zunshine, and others).

Among the ways one could end a brief study of modernist narrativity as expressed, or embodied, by *Caligari* would be to point out (or point up) that, as Kristin Thompson puts it, *Caligari* was "the first widely seen commercial film to incorporate a radical avant-garde visual style" (123). We are perhaps over-familiar with the film's activation of a style essential to Weimar expressionism of the 1920s, but drawing in the film's avant-garde credentials seems at once to have a sanative and salutary effect. Could it be that this assignation—of *Caligari*-as-avant-garde—helps us think through what modernist narrativity in *Caligari* may have accomplished (then and since), and why (or whether) it remains a charged and enlightening provocation all these years later? Have we, as readers of bodies (hoping to read minds), as viewers of films (and bodies and "minds" on film, in film), advanced beyond the modernist narrative tactic of the frame story (and its attendant defeat of embodied transparency)? *Caligari*, in light of the foregoing, might be counted as a cognitive theory in its own right: a way of understanding the collision of the film medium with its representations, and thereafter, a way for appreciating the salient modes through which film does not only (or merely) present us with bodies for our reading pleasure (and the assurance of our epistemic claims), but may also *bypass* bodies altogether—the avant-garde move—and render the mind for us in shimmering transparency and terror.

Notes

1 For representative works, see Mike Budd, ed., *The Cabinet of Dr. Caligari: Texts, Contexts, Histories* (New Brunswick, NJ: Rutgers University Press, 1990); Lotte H. Eisner, *The Haunted Screen: Expressionism in the German Cinema and the Influence of Max Reinhardt* (Berkeley: University of California Press, 1974); Thomas Elsaesser, "Weimar Cinema, Mobile Selves, and Anxious Males: Kracauer and Eisner Revisited," in *Expressionist Film: New Perspectives*, ed. Dietrich Scheunemann (Rochester: Camden House, 2003), 33–72; Hans Janowitz, "*Caligari*: The Story of a Famous Story," in *The Cabinet of Dr. Caligari: Texts, Contexts, Histories*, ed. Mike Budd (New Brunswick, NJ: Rutgers University Press, 1990), 221–40; Anton Kaes, "*The Cabinet of Dr. Caligari*: Expressionism and Cinema," in *Masterpieces of Modernist Cinema* (Bloomington: Indiana University Press, 2006); Vincent LoBrutto, *Becoming Film Literate: The Art and Craft of Motion Pictures* (Westport: Praeger, 2005); David Robinson, *Das Cabinet Des Dr. Caligari* (London: British Film Institute, 1997); Dietrich Scheunemann, "The Double, the

Décor, and the Framing Device: Once More of Robert Wiene's The Cabinet of Dr. Caligari," in Expressionist Film: New Perspectives, ed. Dietrich Scheunemann (Rochester: Camden House Publishing, 2003), 125–56; Kristin, "Dr. Caligari at the Folies-Bergère, or, The Successes of an Early Avant-Garde Film," in The Cabinet of Dr. Caligari: Texts, Contexts, Histories, ed. Budd, 121–69.

My initial and deepest gratitude goes to Ricardo Miguel-Alfonso for his crucial input on this chapter, and for creating another compelling occasion for further collaboration. I also owe special thanks to colleagues in the Department of English at Cornell University, the Department of Cinema, Photography, and Media Arts at Ithaca College, the Department of Philosophy at the College of Cortland, and the Cinema Department at Binghamton University with whom I discussed this and related material during my visiting appointments. Moreover, W. J. T. Mitchell, during his summer as a seminar leader at the School of Criticism and Theory at Cornell University, in 2016, generously shared his reflections on *Caligari*, adduced key secondary literature (pointing me to the work of Friedrich Kittler), and noted relevant films (remarks on Scorsese's *Shutter Island* were especially illuminating). Emily Apter, and fellow participants in her "Thinking in Untranslatables" seminar at the School of Criticism and Theory at Cornell University, in 2017, further enriched scope and depth. Conversations with Stephen Mulhall at "Le Pensée du cinéma: en hommage à Stanley Cavell," convened at Université Paris 1 Panthéon Sorbonne, June 2019, and correspondence, were a crucial aid to reflection on the Bourne series.

2 Siegfried Kracauer, *From Caligari to Hitler: A Psychological History of the German Film* (Princeton, NJ: Princeton University Press, 1947), 67. Hereafter cited parenthetically in the text.

3 Susan Hayward, *Cinema Studies: The Key Concepts*, 4th ed. (London: Routledge, 2013), 193.

4 See David Bordwell, *Narration in the Fiction Film* (Madison: University of Wisconsin Press, 1985), 50–57, 64–73, 77–88, 157–58, 344–46.

5 Noël Carroll, "Theater and the Emotions," in *The Oxford Handbook of Cognitive Literary Studies* (Oxford: Oxford university Press, 2015), 313–28.

6 Such diction and phrasing surely and rightly calls to mind Stanley Cavell's "The Thought of Movies," though I do not mean here to invoke or expound on his remarks there, but instead merely to acknowledge indebtedness by noting a certain kindredness of interest in what we mean by "thought on film," or as he has put it, "the thought of film." See "The Thought of Movies," in *Themes Out of School: Effects and Causes* (San Francisco: North Point Press, 1984), 3–26; see also *The World Viewed: Reflections on the Ontology of Film*, enlarged ed. (Cambridge, MA: Harvard University Press, 1979) and *The Thought of Stanley Cavell and Cinema: Turning Anew to the Ontology of Film a Half-Century after* The World Viewed, ed. David LaRocca (New York: Bloomsbury, 2020).

7   Carroll, "Theater and the Emotions," 313–28; For additional orientation on the relationship between film and emotion, see the exceptional contributions to Carroll's edited volume *Philosophy of Film and Motion Pictures*, ed. Noël Carroll and Jinhee Choi (Oxford: Blackwell, 2006), 21–80, with probing chapters by Carroll, Kendall Walton, Alex Neill, Berys Gaut, and Deborah Knight.
8   For representative works, see Roland Barthes, "Introduction to the Structural Analysis of Narratives" (1966), in *Narrative Theory: Critical Concepts in Literary and Cultural Studies*, vol. I: *Major Issues in Narrative Theory*, ed. Mieke Bal (London: Routledge, 2004), 65–94; Vladimir Propp, *Morphology and the Folktale*, trans. Laurence Scott (Austin: University of Texas Press, 1968); Tzvetan Todorov, "Structural Analysis of Narrative," *Novel* 3 (Fall 1969): 74–76, and *The Poetics of Prose*, trans. Richard Howard (Ithaca, NY: Cornell University Press, 1978); Seymour Chatman, *Story and Discourse: Narrative Structure in Film* (Ithaca, NY: Cornell University Press, 1978); Gérard Genette, *Narrative Discourse: An Essay in Method*, trans. Jane E. Lewin (Ithaca, NY: Cornell University Press, 1983); *On Narrative*, ed. W. J. T. Mitchell (Chicago: University of Chicago Press, 1981); David Bordwell, *Narration in the Fiction Film* (Madison: University of Wisconsin Press, 1985); Edward Branigan, *Narrative Comprehension and Film* (London: Routledge, 1992); and Rick Altman, *A Theory of Narrative* (New York: Columbia University Press, 2008).
9   Carroll, "Theater and the Emotions," 322.
10 Ibid., 323.
11 Ibid.
12 For remarks on empathy in film, see Robert Sinnerbrink, *Cinematic Ethics: Exploring Ethical Experience through Film* (London: Routledge, 2015), especially 89–95; see also my review of this book in *The Review of Politics* 79, no. 1 (Winter 2017): 177–80. For further notes on empathy and empathic projection in relation to literature, philosophy, and cinema, see my chapter "Achilles' Tears: Cavell, the *Iliad*, and Possibilities for the Human," in *Stanley Cavell on Aesthetic Understanding*, ed. Garry Hagberg (New York: Palgrave, 2018).
13 Carroll, "Theater and the Emotions," 324.
14 Ibid., 323–24.
15 Ibid.
16 David Denby, *Great Books: My Adventures with Homer, Rousseau, Woolf, and Other Indestructible Writers of the Western World* (New York: Touchstone, 1996), 424.
17 I hope these remarks on the "frame" (as a figure that is invoked in literary studies and narrative theory as well as in cinema studies and cognitive studies) can be read in conversation with works such as Katherine Young's "Frame and Boundary in the Phenomenology of Narrative," in *Narrative across Media: The Languages of Storytelling*, ed. Marie-Laure Ryan (Lincoln: University of Nebraska Press,

2004), 76–107; and earlier, Gregory Bateson and Jurgen Ruesch, *Communication: The Social Matrix of Psychiatry* (New York: Norton, 1968).

18 For help thinking through the narrative design of *The Thief of Bagdad*, I thank Haaris Naqvi.

19 This observation is indebted to Ibrahim Marazka.

20 For more on film, narrative innovation, metafiction, and what I call "translational hermeneutics," see my "Translating Carlyle: Ruminating on the Models of Metafiction at the Emergence of an Emersonian Vernacular," ed. Kenneth S. Sacks and Daniel Koch, *Religions* 8.8 (2017): 1–26.

21 Of the many works worth noting, I will highlight Peter Gay, *Weimar Culture: The Outsider as Insider* (1968; rpt. New York: Norton, 2001); *German Film and Literature: Adaptations and Transformations*, ed. Eric Rentschler (1986; rpt. London: Routledge, 2012); Eric Rentschler, *The Ministry of Illusion: Nazi Cinema and Its Afterlife* (Cambridge, MA: Harvard University Press, 1996); Noah Isenberg, *Weimar Cinema: An Essential Guide to Classic Films of the Era* (New York: Columbia University Press, 2009); and Anton Kaes, *Shell Shock: Weimar Culture and the Wounds of War* (Princeton, NJ: Princeton University Press, 2009).

22 Lisa Zunshine, "Cognitive Narratology," in *Introduction to Cognitive Cultural Studies*, ed. Zunshine (Baltimore: Johns Hopkins University Press, 2010), 151. See also David Herman, "Toward a Transmedial Narratology," in *Narrative across Media*, 47–75; and *New Perspectives on Narrative and Multimodality*, ed. Ruth Page (New York: Routledge, 2010).

23 See Daniel Yacavone, *Film Worlds: A Philosophical Aesthetics of Cinema* (New York: Columbia University Press, 2015).

24 See also *The Thought of Stanley Cavell and Cinema: Turning Anew to the Ontology of Film a Half-Century after* The World Viewed, ed. David LaRocca (New York: Bloomsbury, forthcoming in 2020).

25 For incisive remarks on the Bourne franchise, see Stephen Mulhall, "The Legacy of Jason Bourne: Identity and the Sinfulness of Origins," in his *On Film*, 3rd ed. (New York: Routledge, 2016).

26 See, for example, *Seeing Wittgenstein Anew*, ed. William Day and Victor J. Krebs (Cambridge: Cambridge University Press, 2010); David LaRocca, "The False Pretender: Deleuze, Sherman, and the Status of Simulacra," *Journal of Aesthetics and Art Criticism* 69, no. 3 (Summer 2011): 321–29; and Burke Hilsabeck, "Seeing Soldiers, Seeing Persons: Wittgenstein, Film Theory, and Charlie Chaplin's *Shoulder Arms*," in *The Philosophy of War Films*, ed. David LaRocca (Lexington: University Press of Kentucky, 2014), 179–204.

27 See my "Performative Inferentialism: A Semiotic Ethics," *Liminalities: A Journal of Performance Studies* 9, no. 1 (2013): 1–26.

10

Reading Minds in Christopher Isherwood's *The Berlin Stories*

Janine Utell

A Camera and a Puzzle

Readers familiar with Christopher Isherwood will be expecting this chapter to begin with the author's most famous statement: "I am a camera." Have no fear; I'll get there. I prefer to defer the fulfillment of this expectation for a moment in service of setting up a different set of theoretical and interpretive priorities from those often encountered in studies of Isherwood's work. Rather than start with the second paragraph of "A Berlin Diary: Autumn 1930" from *Goodbye to Berlin*, I'd like to start with a few lines from its companion text, *Mr. Norris Changes Trains*.[1] Late in the story, our narrator, William Bradshaw, is trying to work out the mysterious occupation of his friend Arthur Norris. He reports:

> Here my reasoning came to an end. It was bounded by guesses and possibilities as vague and limitless as the darkness which enclosed the train. . . . I tried to puzzle backwards, sideways, all ways up.[2]

William does not realize it, but he is about to have the mystery of Mr. Norris cleared up by a leader of the Berlin Communist Party, Ludwig Bayer. As the truth is revealed to him in Bayer's office, William reports:

> With bewildering speed the jig-saw puzzle was fitting itself together in my brain. In a flash another piece was added. . . . The puzzle fitted together perfectly. I could see it all, if I wished to look at it, a compact, vivid picture, at a single glance. (*BS* 167, 169)

My interest here is not the mystery of Mr. Norris (at least not for the moment). What I'm interested in is the narrator's reporting of his own thinking: the metarepresentation of cognitive activity forming part of the work of the narrator, indeed here part of the story itself.³ William performs mind-reading on himself and does the mind-writing that goes along with it, as part of narrating the story of Mr. Norris and the role he, William, plays. The climax of *Mr. Norris Changes Trains* is this instance of revelation, and the mental activity William performs to manage and report it.

What we find upon closer examination of these lines are several interesting components of cognitive activity. First, we see an acknowledgment of the temporal nature of thinking, as it takes place over a span of time, at varying speeds and durations. Next, it is simultaneously bounded and limitless, but its boundedness takes two different forms. William's thinking must be bounded by his own guesswork, by his own awareness (or lack thereof) of the possibilities available to him given his limited cognizance and access to accurate knowledge. Yet, then, it is bounded—made to fit together—by his finally achieving access to epistemological completeness (or so he thinks). Third, thinking takes up space and happens in space. Spatial metaphors are part of William's mind-writing: the processes, according to Peter Rabinowitz, of mental representation that go along with the activity of mind-reading.⁴ The puzzle can be tried "backwards, sideways, all ways up." Another kind of mental work, another metarepresentation, is embedded in the one being narrated, that of making metaphor, which itself is spatialized: "As vague and limitless as the darkness which enclosed the train." Finally, thinking is aspectual, a key point made by Alan Palmer (whose work will be essential throughout this piece). Thinking occurs from a position with a defined perspective: "I could see it all, if I wished to look at it." William's position, via Bayer's revelation, has changed. The aspectual nature of thinking can be understood further through the concept of possible worlds, as the work of Marie-Laure Ryan and David Herman suggest: it is possible, in another version of this story, that William would not see, that he would not wish to look. His disposition, his desire, is revealed via the possibility that other dispositions, other desires, might exist.

These lines permit insight into how we might read minds in Isherwood's fiction of the 1930s. Yet, many astute readers of Isherwood take, critically or not, the second paragraph of "A Berlin Diary: Autumn 1930" in *Goodbye to Berlin* as their frame for reading the author's work:

> I am a camera with its shutter open, quite passive, recording, not thinking. Recording the man shaving at the window opposite and the woman in the kimono washing her hair. Some day, all this will have to be developed, carefully printed, fixed. (*BS* 207; emphasis mine).

In the spirit of the cognitive approach that informs the work of this chapter, I begin with a critique of the "frame" that has led to particular readings of Isherwood, which not only take uncritically the claim "I am a camera" but also ignore the phrase "not thinking." As I hope will become clear, I do this for two reasons. The first should have been made apparent by my opening: Isherwood is most definitely interested in thinking. The second has wider implications for how we read minds in Isherwood's fiction and, more broadly, in late modernist narrative.[5] If we can undo some of the givens, the assumptions, that come with uncritical acceptance of "I am a camera . . . not thinking," then we can read Isherwood more completely in the context of late Modernism, and by doing so further undo some of those givens and assumptions that come with conventional readings of minds in modernist literary texts.

Thinking Isherwood Thinking

David Herman tells us that frames, like schema, represent a static set of expectations or stereotypical knowledge.[6] It is beyond the scope of this chapter to consider how critical readings over time themselves contribute to schema that shape our interpretations of literary texts, and how difficult it might be to dismantle those schema to read differently. But I will suggest that a kind of schema has emerged around reading Isherwood's work of the 1930s, and his autobiographically inflected work more broadly, that has led to a neglect of the interpretive power of the cognitive approach. The focus on recording, apparently unthinkingly, has led readers to miss how Isherwood gets at thinking; and the focus on self-writing—accepting that the diary is Isherwood's preferred form because of the assumption that it is a recording device—has led readers to miss the sociality of minds in Isherwood's work. Finally, as Patricia Waugh has suggested, we maintain a misapprehension of modernist narrative more generally as solipsistic (a point we will return to in a moment).

Not only is Isherwood, or, as the homodiegetic narrator of *Goodbye to Berlin* "Isherwood," not a "camera," but the representation of mind in his fiction is all to the purpose of generating epistemological crisis and doubt. Furthermore, it is meant to represent an active, rather than a passive engagement with the world and others. Such an active engagement with the minds of others, the representation of "enactive minds," in Waugh's words, does not compromise Isherwood's self-writing or autobiographical project; on the contrary, in order to write the self, in order to fully engage with the self-writing project at the core of his fiction, the mind must become the story, and the mind must be read alongside and distributed across and situationally positioned with the minds of others. If we shift the focus away from "seeing," as Palmer proposes, we can refocus our attention on "thinking."[7] Why has this been so challenging for readers of Isherwood? Why take "I am a camera" as the "obligatory starting point" for any examination of Isherwood's work, as "a declaration of authorial method" or a "theoretical manifesto?"[8]

It is not because the author himself has not encouraged his readers to attend to his work differently. In a 1972 interview, David Geherin put the question to Isherwood regarding whether "some critics have put too much emphasis" on "I am a camera" as an articulation of "technique" or intention, to which the novelist replied, "Yes, very much so. What I was simply trying to do was describe my mood at that particular moment."[9] What was an attempt to describe mood—a mental state akin to disposition, emotion, motive, and so on—has been taken up as a literal formal device. While Isherwood may have been trying to represent a mental state in a particular moment in time from a particular position, such as "neurotic withdrawal"[10] or "indifference,"[11] one limited by the date marker at the start of "A Berlin Diary: Autumn 1930," readers have not taken it as such, not taken it as a mental state bounded by time, position, and aspect. One of Isherwood's earliest readers, Carolyn Heilbrun, makes the kind of assertion about his narrative that a cognitive approach allows us to at the very least interrogate:

> It is . . . extraordinary . . . that critics have failed to recognize that Isherwood alone developed the form of the documentary and the particular narrator who makes it possible. Not even Wayne Booth, whose *Rhetoric of Fiction* is devoted to the relationship between the chosen point of narration and the sense of truth and morality conveyed by the story, has seen how Isherwood's first-person dummy makes possible a kind of veracity.[12]

It might be worth pointing out here that interrogating Isherwood's choices from a perspective informed by cognitive approaches to narrative allows us to move beyond the Boothian question of reliability. As should have been fairly clear just from my brief opening example of William Bradshaw, the interesting question is not whether he is reliable; he certainly is not, because there is just so much he does not know and this profoundly affects his judgment both intellectually and ethically. The more interesting questions, for us, are these. How do we read his mind? And, how does he read the minds of others? And, how successful is he at this?

This line of analysis continues through more recent work on Isherwood, similarly invested not only in the documentary impulse but also in its ideological and political implications as well. For instance, Judy Suh, in her work on modernist responses to fascism, sees Isherwood's use of the diary form in *Goodbye to Berlin* (as deployed in the first and final stories) as an ironic commentary, along with the camera-eye and its documentary mode, on the belief that "unmediated truth" is possible; under fascism, these forms cannot respond adequately to the "violent distortions of reality" engendered by political ideology.[13] Thomas Davis is even more explicit in his taking Isherwood's "heralded camera-eye narration" as "bear[ing] strong affinities with the documentary aesthetic of the 1930s, which understood documentary as a combination of description, editing, and narration,"[14] particularly in its attention to everyday life. Both Suh and Davis regard Isherwood's supposed documentary approach in light of the creative effort put forth in arranging, and both critics see Isherwood's camera metaphor as more deeply ironized through the lens (if you will) of late Modernism. Nevertheless, even the acknowledgment that "Christopher Isherwood" can only speak of "himself" as a "camera" as metaphor reminds us that such mental acts cannot be overlooked. We simply cannot let the "not thinking," a seemingly logical conclusion to all of this camera talk, stand. If "Christopher Isherwood" is not a camera, then he is most certainly thinking.

Isherwood, Late Modernism, and Cognitive Narratology

And so is everyone else around him. As with many other texts of late Modernism, *Mr. Norris Changes Trains* and *Goodbye to Berlin* are eminently preoccupied with minds, and the minds of others. In considering *The Berlin Stories* in light of cognitive approaches to modernist and late modernist narrative, we heed Palmer's call to put the "intersubjective first."[15] David James rightly characterizes modernist narrative by its "commitment to representing mental processes ... [to] the social, ethical, and epistemological work of fiction."[16] Like Patricia Waugh, though, he extends the thinking on "mental processes" to allow for the "negotiation between evoking mental states and social situations" that characterizes late modernist narrative fiction.[17] Waugh's work is essential for dismantling the "disabling myth of modernism as the performance of a solipsistic mind," the privileging of "a purely private self."[18] In her call for a rethinking of modernist narrative through cognitive theory, she insists on several key points that will prove to be integral to the work of the rest of this chapter. First among them is that modernist fiction seeks to represent "the perception and constitution of a world through minds that are also constituted in and through that world."[19] Minds are distributed and enacted through situatedness, what Palmer calls mind "beyond the skin."[20] At the same time, the mind is embodied, manifesting "bodily thinking," making analogies and associations and inferences.[21] We saw this, for instance, in William's thinking through his own fitting together of the puzzle of Mr. Norris: making an analogy to the darkness surrounding the train, associating his thought process with a jig-saw puzzle. The mind is "enactive" and "experiencing."[22] For Alan Wilde, the problems raised by such attention to the mind and what it does in, to, and through the world are defining aspects of late Modernism and its epistemological project.[23] So, we should read modernist narrative beyond the privileging of interiority, internalism, and solipsism; be thus attentive not only to the working of the mind but also to the working of the mind in the world with others; and thereby gain a deeper engagement with late modernist narrative, preoccupied as it is with social thinking, with the mind-reading and -writing that happens with and through others, and with the epistemological implications and crises engendered therein.

The two texts that comprise *The Berlin Stories* read together provide a compelling case for a cognitive approach to Isherwood, and a cognitive approach to late Modernism more broadly. A brief summary follows for those who might be less familiar. *Mr. Norris Changes Trains* is narrated by William Bradshaw, an educated Englishman in his mid-twenties generally taken for a gentleman. He is in Berlin teaching English, lodging at the boarding house of Fräulein Schroeder. He shares these characteristics with the "Christopher Isherwood" narrator of *Goodbye to Berlin*, although in the latter it is clear that "Chris," or "Herr Issyvoo," as he is called affectionately by Frl. Schroeder, is also a would-be novelist (in "Sally Bowles" he is working on a novel; in "The Landauers" he has published one, the actual Isherwood novel *All the Conspirators* [1928], which according to "Chris" has sold a mere five copies). In *Mr. Norris Changes Trains*, William befriends Arthur Norris on the train to Berlin; over the two years' span of the novel they become close, as William witnesses Arthur's debauchery, his debts, his predilections for cosmetics and sado-masochistic sexual practices (particularly once Arthur's debts necessitate his moving into Frl. Schroeder's boarding house, thus becoming William's neighbor). The two get involved in the Communist Party, Arthur takes a number of mysterious trips to Paris and is blackmailed by his secretary Schmidt, and William becomes the object of erotic interest by a one Baron von Pregnitz. The story comes to a head when William is asked to accompany von Pregnitz to Switzerland under the guise of a ski weekend; in reality, Arthur has been spying on the communists in Berlin to contacts in Paris, and William is being used as a decoy for a meeting von Pregnitz is having with one of those contacts so that the Baron can share government secrets.

Goodbye to Berlin has a much less dramatic plot. In fact, it might be said to not have a "plot" at all, as those who emphasize the fragmentary, arbitrary, and diary-like nature of the text might.[24] The collection is framed by two stories tagged "diary," although they lack the self-revelation over specifically bounded temporalities one expects to see in diaries. The "Berlin diaries" at the beginning and end of *Goodbye to Berlin* are not storying the self, but rather "storying the world."[25] The rest of the text consists of a series of stories focused on "Christopher's" relationship with particular, even singular, people: with Sally, a nightclub singer who is a bit of a gold-digger and winds up pregnant in "Sally Bowles"; with Peter, a wealthy Englishman infatuated with a working-class Berlin teenager named Otto Nowak in "On Ruegen Island"; with Otto, who returns to the Isherwood stage along with his family, in "The Nowaks"; and with Natalia, his student, and Bernhard, her cousin and a delicate soul, both scions of the Jewish family that owns a major department store in Berlin in "The Landauers." These relationships manifest themselves in the stories each singular person relays to "Chris" about themselves and their lives. The conclusion of *Goodbye to Berlin* has "Christopher" leaving the city as the Nazis' rise to power and the catastrophic outcomes of that development are made clear. The anxious conclusion to *Goodbye to Berlin*, with its air of ominous anticipation as well as its appearance on the cusp of the Second World War, helps us position the text within late Modernism.

Isherwood's Storyworlds: Our Men in Berlin

It is my feeling that *Goodbye to Berlin*, a plot of revelation, will help us establish Isherwood's interest in the social, enactive mind, and how this interest shapes his narrative and its "moments," to use Rabinowitz's term, from a more theoretical standpoint. *Mr. Norris Changes Trains*, a more straightforward plot of resolution, allows us to see social minds in action.[26] I would like to suggest that the storyworlds of both are contiguous, if not continuous, and further this contiguity is revealed if one considers Isherwood's texts from a cognitive approach. In his introduction to *The Berlin Stories*, Armistead Maupin suggests that the narrators are the same, Bradshaw/Isherwood, with "his eye" "always turned towards the Others."[27] I do not think this is quite or entirely accurate, and I do not think the contiguity of the storyworlds is dependent on the narrators being the same. To insist on the necessity of the narrators being the same for the storyworlds to be contiguous, even continuous, gives so much weight to the perspective of the narrator that it perhaps contributes to us missing other aspects of storyworld. It is true that the tone, emerging from the disposition as well as the position, of each narrator is different, and they approach mind-reading in rather different ways. William is often inclined to share that he is "mystified," while "Christopher" is often being told how much he understands—"I expect you understand," says Sally (*BS* 280)—or treated implicitly as though he does, even though he often asserts that he does not. At the same time, however, "Christopher" sees how much he does not know through his relationships with others, such as Bernhard Landauer. It is worth noting, too, that just because mental acts are not made manifest by speech or direct reporting does not mean they are not present from the point of view of "the whole mind," as noted by Palmer. In other words, the mental states of "Herr Issyvoo" or "Christopher" are represented in ways other than direct reporting, while direct reporting is often key to reading William's mind (even as it reveals his own failures in reading the minds of others).

Nevertheless, while what the two narrators say and how they say it might differ, what they see is not—and how they think about it and with and through whom is, I think, not, and this is important for any claim about the storyworlds of the two texts. Palmer, in explaining how the storyworld is aspectual, writes that "like the real world, it is different depending on the various aspects under which it is viewed. Its characters can only ever experience it from a particular perceptual and cognitive aspect at any one time."[28] The two texts that comprise *The Berlin Stories* present different perceptual and cognitive aspects across two related storyworlds. The five concepts necessary for reading mental processes in the construction of storyworlds as defined by David Herman can be helpful here, as we will find some similarities along with some moments of disjuncture: positioning, embodiment, situationalizing, emotion discourse, and qualia.[29]

In the case of both of Isherwood's narrators, certain elements of positioning hold steady: their Englishness, their political inclinations, their ambiguous sexuality and attractiveness to others. Each, to return to Alan Wilde's comments on the epistemology of late Modernism, inhabits the surface, seeing across it while also supposing there is more below it that cannot be seen, or can be known only in its incompleteness. Each Isherwood narrator inhabits the intersection of multiple storylines of which they can only have an incomplete understanding, yet each plays the role in those stories they have been assigned. A common refrain across both novels is other characters telling the Isherwood narrator that he always knows just what to say or just what to do. These include moments such as when Sally Bowles finds out she's been jilted by a lover and "Chris" suggests they have Prairie Oysters, a disgusting-sounding concoction of raw egg and Worcester sauce particularly favored by Sally for some reason: "How marvellous you are, Chris! You always think of just the right thing" (BS 247); or Arthur Norris's comments to William along the lines of "You're always so philosophical" (BS 77), or, "With your customary consideration for my feelings, you help me over the most painful part of the story" (BS 110). What one sees when one takes these as a pattern is that these characters are often expressing appreciation for the Isherwood narrator's ability to deflect from more painful probing of their mental or emotional states, even as he is acknowledging them and more or less accurately reporting them.

Isherwood attends to the embodiment of minds more so than readers have credited, something that becomes more apparent as we shift focus toward "bodily thinking."[30] Here are a few examples:

From *Goodbye to Berlin*:

> He [Otto Nowak] began to run along the beach [away from Peter, with whom he is quarrelling] towards the teacher and her children, very gracefully displaying his figure to the best possible advantage. (BS 296)

> Berlin is a skeleton which aches in the cold: it is my own skeleton aching. (BS 389)

From *Mr. Norris Changes Trains*:

> I sighed. I gave him up. I smiled. (BS 176)

> I blushed. It was astonishing what a cad he could make me feel. Hadn't I, after all, misunderstood him? Hadn't I misjudged him? Hadn't I, in some obscure way, behaved very badly? (BS 188)

> The whole city lay under an epidemic of discreet, infectious fear. I could feel it, like influenza, in my bones. (BS 193)

We might take the two examples that come last, toward the conclusions of each novel, to begin. In each case, the bones, the skeleton, are analogies for emotions and mental states. In addition, these examples are social. The metaphor depends on beginning with the city itself—Berlin, "the whole city"—and then moves inward to the individual—"my own." While interiority is certainly a component of the expression of a mental state, it is not the sole component, and the sociality of the experience is essential to the working of the analogy: the skeleton and its bones are, after all, connected (as those familiar with "Dem Bones" will recall).[31] Our other examples are part of Isherwood's attention to the sociality of minds, too. In the depiction of Otto running down the beach—toward a female teacher with whom he is carrying on a flirtation in part to deepen his rift with Peter, and away from that jealous infatuated would-be suitor (and the voyeuristic "Chris")—Isherwood uses the body to (a) represent Otto's mental state by way of his attempt to "display," to perform his status as object of desire in order to antagonize Peter and (b) suggest an ambivalence in "Chris's" own less-than-articulated response to Otto: "gracefully." The adverb is a qualifier of "Chris's" perception of Otto and suggests a disposition toward his physical appeal. Bodily responses also cue us to think about mental responses, particularly in the examples from *Mr. Norris Changes Trains*. These two moments occur after William has found out the truth about Arthur being a spy, and we are given insight into his thinking about Arthur by way of a sigh and a smile. Without the direct report of thought, we can read William's mind through these bodily manifestations. William's blush as he is seeing Arthur off on the train that will eventually take him out of Germany, away from the police hunting him for his espionage activity, is accompanied by direct thought report. What is interesting about this series of questions, however, is its occurrence after it has been made clear to William that, yes, he had misunderstood, he had misjudged—but all of that is removed to the past once he gains the necessary knowledge from Bayer about Arthur's treason. The clearing up of misunderstanding and misjudging actually causes William to ask whether or not he had misunderstood and misjudged, well after to do so would make any sense. The effect of this is to lead the reader to "read" the blush more ambiguously.

Minds in Isherwood are distributed, rather than localized, internal, or individual: "Instead of being abstract, individualistic, and constant across all contexts, thinking in its most basic form is grounded in particular situations, socially distributed, and domain specific."[32] One of the contributing factors to the sense that Isherwood's texts construct contiguous storyworlds is the distribution of thought across recurring characters. Two characters in particular, Frl. Schroeder and Fritz Wendel, are significant in their role in creating social spaces—we might think of them as heterotopia—where Berlin denizens gather, where discourse accumulates, where material reality is experienced. The narrator William who introduces Frl. Schroeder to Arthur is different from the narrator "Chris" who introduces Frl. Schroeder to Sally Bowles, but the Frl. Schroeder is the same, and she responds to each of those characters similarly: with unwavering hospitality and unswerving admiration for what she perceives to be their glamour. On the other hand, it is Fritz Wendel who introduces both William and "Chris" to the wider world of Berlin and all that entails: its demi-monde, its pornographic escapades, its debauched nightlife. Fritz's preferred bar, the Troika, is to one element of sociality in Isherwood's Berlin as Frl. Schroeder's house is to another.

A further element essential to the positioning of William and "Chris" that is also key to the presentation of emotion discourse in the novels is their ability to manage the needs—the emotional neediness—of others. These affects conjure a kind of reciprocal emotional response on the part of the two narrators to which perhaps they themselves hitherto had not had access. Peter J. Rabinowitz notes that acts of mind-reading are complicated by, among other things, "emotional valence."[33] We will return to his other complications when we consider each of Isherwood's novels in turn in the latter part of this chapter, but for the moment it seems worth making the general statement that a cognitive approach to Isherwood's narrative allows for much greater attention to emotion discourse and affects than the general insistence on "detachment" and "indifference" might suggest.

As we shall see in our further discussion of *Goodbye to Berlin*, other characters' emotional needs are fulfilled by telling "Christopher" their stories. In his reporting of these stories, and his reporting of his own responses, we see engagement with the minds of others that can be precarious and not wholly complete or successful. Here, an example will suffice to show how the fulfillment of the emotional needs of others through storytelling can prompt emotion discourse on the part of our narrator "Chris":

From *Goodbye to Berlin*:

> Because I am not as he [Bernhard Landauer] is, because I am the opposite of this, and would gladly share my thoughts and sensations with forty million people if they cared to read them, I half admire Bernhard but also half dislike him. (*BS* 362)

This is, incidentally, another shared quality between our two narrators—the willingness to share thoughts and sensations—although paradoxically much less of either narrative is given over to the reporting of said thoughts and sensations, except insofar as those thoughts and sensations pertain to thoughts and sensations prompted by the thoughts and sensations of others.

Here we see "Chris" comparing himself to Bernhard; and defining his own sense of self and the thoughts and sensations comprising that self; and the relation of others to that self, those thoughts and sensations, by way of that comparison. This strikes me as an instance of Waugh's "enactive" mind doing its work of positioning itself in the world and in its social situatedness. In addition, Bernhard's sharing or not sharing is what leads "Christopher" to be emotionally disposed one way or another toward him, or rather both ways in his characteristic ambivalence; but when Bernhard does share, "Christopher's" response is yet another instance of emotion discourse: "Oh dear, I sighed to myself, shall I ever get to the bottom of these people, shall I ever understand them? The mere act of thinking about the Landauers' psychic make-up overcame me, as always, with a sense of absolute, defeated exhaustion" (*BS* 368). Here emotion discourse meets several other of the concepts we have already explored: an embodiment of mind (exhaustion), the distribution of thought across others ("shall I ever get to the bottom of these people?"), along with the direct reporting of mind work by the narrator. It also illustrates Herman's concept of qualia, by demonstrating for us "Christopher's" subjective experience of others emerging as a result of their telling of their own subjective experiences.

Arthur Norris's neediness presents itself differently; he tells William the story of his delicate childhood and present trials as a way to prompt pity, and he characterizes himself to William thusly: "Mine is a sensitive nature. I react immediately to my surroundings. When the sun shines on me, I expand. To see me at my best, you must see me in my proper setting. A good table. A good cellar. Art. Music. Beautiful things. Charming and witty society. Then I begin to sparkle. I am transformed" (*BS* 51). This serves to illustrate, again, our final concept from Herman, qualia. What we see in this passage is Arthur's subjective experience of the world, no matter how markedly different it is from the narrative world he finds himself in: the dingy, impoverished, sordid world of 1930s Berlin, the world of both novels shaping the qualia of all of Isherwood's characters. Arthur insists, to William, on the distinctness of his qualia. Here William reports Arthur's disquisition on himself and how he sees himself in the world, grounded in and responding to the material reality of his experience. William responds accordingly throughout the novel.

William's perception of Arthur, guided by Arthur's reporting of his perception of Arthur himself, leads William to see himself, and to speak of his emotional attachment to Arthur as constitutive of that view of himself:

From *Mr. Norris Changes Trains*:

> Stage by stage I was building up a romantic background for Arthur, and was jealous lest it should be upset.... I was, I flattered myself, more profound, more humane, an altogether subtler connoisseur of human nature than they [other friends, like Helen Pratt the journalist and Fritz Wendel, warning him that Arthur is shady].... I wanted to imagine him as a glorified being; audacious and self-reliant, reckless and calm. All of which, in reality, he only too painfully and obviously wasn't. (*BS* 39–40)

A closer analysis of this passage and its embedded metarepresentations, to draw on a concept from the work of Lisa Zunshine, will reveal the tack we take to read William's mind with regard to Arthur, as well as the ways in which William's own mind-reading is incomplete:[34]

a) Stage by stage: the working of William's mind over time: thinking occurs in time, as a process;

b) I was building up a romantic background for Arthur: thinking occurs as a result of specific situations and the participation in particular storylines; by being brought into Arthur's storyline, William is now part of it, and the storyline is now contributing to William's shaping of his own storyline; William also reports how he characterizes the background he is "building" for Arthur, a qualia that may or may not speak to William's judgment as narrator and as a character;

c) was jealous lest it should be upset: William articulates the emotion discourse that is now part of his experience of Arthur, Arthur's story, and William's own role in that story; he also indicates causality: when his other friends question his relationship with Arthur, it prompts a mental and emotional response;

d) I was, I flattered myself . . . I wanted to imagine: direct reporting of two mental states, one embedded in the other; first, William perceives himself to be a connoisseur of human nature, and second, he sees he is flattering himself on this count;

e) I wanted to imagine him. . . . All of which, in reality, he only too painfully and obviously wasn't: William here reports the contrast between how he wants to imagine Arthur (not how he does, but how he wants to, revealing a gap even in his own consciousness, not just a gap between imagination and reality) and how Arthur really is, thereby getting at two versions of subjective experience: how he imagines Arthur, and how he perceives Arthur in reality; the qualifier "painfully" indicates emotional state or disposition on the part of William prompted by Arthur, and the qualifier "obviously" indicates William's epistemological relationship to his own perception.

However: let us pause on "obviously" for a moment, for therein lies the rub. William sees that "obviously" Arthur is not "audacious and self-reliant, reckless and calm"; I think it would be safe to say that up to a point the reader shares this assessment (although once we, like William, learn the truth about Arthur, it would not be too far a stretch to suggest that he is in fact both audacious and reckless). But the "obviously" stems from what Menakhem Perry has called "the primacy effect": "What we encounter first in a text will decisively shape our subsequent conceptualization of the textual world."[35] We have seen Arthur the way William sees him, and so if we agree with William on the "obviously," it is because that is how we have encountered Arthur up to this point. Furthermore, once we know that William is wrong, we can only look back at the "obviously" and wonder how obvious anything about the story truly is: how successful, really, has William been at what Zunshine calls the "ascribing" of "states of mind based on observable action, or explaining behavior in terms of thoughts, feelings, beliefs, desires"?[36] Because we arrive at the point where we have to question the "obviously," we must further arrive at the point where we must question reality as William is experiencing it. And this is a further, and my final, point of contiguity in the storyworlds of *The Berlin Stories*. At the conclusion to *Goodbye to Berlin*, "Chris" says, "No. Even now I can't altogether believe that any of this has really happened" (*BS* 410). The subjective experience of the storyworld and its others can only lead to epistemological crisis.

For the remainder of this chapter, we will consider some very specific complications to the processes of mind-reading that manifest themselves in Isherwood's fiction, leading to the kinds of epistemological and ontological crises that characterize late modernist narrative. First, we will return to the storytelling moments in *Goodbye to Berlin* and consider the extent to which reciprocity—or the failure thereof—generates what Karin Kukkonen has called the "precarious[ness] of the successful collaboration of minds."[37] Then, we will look more closely at the ways the dynamic between occlusion and sincerity in *Mr. Norris Changes Trains* leads to the varieties of epistemological crises to which we have already alluded. The minds of others—and the knowledge and experience of those minds—come to be seen as core preoccupations of modernist and late modernist fiction, even as they are also a site of complication, confusion, and crisis.

Goodbye to Berlin: Embedded Narratives, Reciprocity, and the Crisis of the Collaboration of Minds

The move to read Isherwood through the metaphor of the camera has led many to see the embedded narratives in *Goodbye to Berlin*—those of Sally Bowles, Peter Wilkinson, and Bernhard Landauer—as portraits; moreover, these portraits are seen to shape, through autobiographical practice, Isherwood's own versions of himself. Rose Kamel, for one, sees Isherwood "filming" these characters "in prose," a strategy that Kamel argues generates a kind of "ontological reciprocity between the narrator and his characters."[38] It is worth pointing out, however, that in the stories "Sally Bowles," "On Ruegen Island," and "The Landauers," as has already been suggested, there exists a decided lack of ontological reciprocity: "Christopher" reports the stories of these figures as a way to tell the story of his own mind, and that story is one of separateness. Recall his words regarding Bernhard, "Shall I ever get to the bottom of these people?" (*BS* 368). If we use Palmer's idea of the embedded narrative to define these "set pieces," the stories of Sally, Peter, and Bernhard become the story of "Christopher's" social mind working through what he is being told.[39] This narrative is not as fragmented as it might appear; rather, the narrator attempts to portray a coherent vision of the minds of the people he meets—the coherent vision they themselves have crafted as a way to storyline their own lives. These characters have constructed and then shared their stories, and in "Chris" sharing them, they develop explanatory power for those telling them as well as for our narrator seeking to understand his own mind in relation to the minds of others.

At the same time these embedded narratives show the socially distributed nature of minds; however, they also show a lack of reciprocity, to draw on one of Rabinowitz's "complications."[40] We might take the telling and reporting of the embedded narrative of Peter Wilkinson in "On Ruegen Island" as exemplary. The telling and reporting begin with an interestingly tagged moment of attributive discourse: "In the Bavarian café, where the band makes a noise like Hell unchained, Peter bawled into my ear the story of his life" (*BS* 283). The verb "bawled" is revealing of a slightly negative disposition toward this event, and "the story of his life" suggests that a deliberate process of storylining has (a) occurred and (b) is visible to "Chris" as interlocutor. The story proceeds with no intervention or interleaved commentary from "Chris"—and no reciprocity. Peter's telling ends with the moment of encounter with Otto, bringing his storyline into the narrative present, on Ruegen with "Chris." Once "Chris" has the knowledge of the story, his interactions with Peter consist of noticing the latter's jealousy toward Otto, and reporting it to the reader: "I noticed that Otto glanced at the poster wistfully, and that Peter had seen him do this" (*BS* 288; emphasis mine). The embedded metarepresentation here gets at a triangulation of views among the three men and the varying attribution of mental state—all of this made newly possible by the distributed nature of minds in a kind of sharing that is nevertheless not entirely reciprocal.

Mr. Norris Changes Trains: Occlusion, Sincerity, and Epistemological Crisis

William Bradshaw approaches the work of telling the story of Arthur Norris in entirely good faith, and according to the preferences we expect from narrative situations. Indeed, he seems to approach the narrative situation of Arthur himself with a clear understanding and expectations of those preferences. Manfred Jahn suggests we can use Jackendoff's preferences to understand how narrators fit information into frames. Thus we prefer to assume the following: that information is "relevant"; that the narrator "believes" what is being communicated; and that the information is of the right amount and in the proper order.[41] William has a heightened preference for assuming that what he is being told is true, and communicates accordingly. However, it is this very sincerity, another of Rabinowitz's complications, that leads to occlusion.[42] William is completely sincere in how he goes about the narrative, and he buys Arthur's performance of sincerity, which makes it very easy for Mr. Norris to occlude, and for William to report an occluded narrative without even realizing it.

Let us return to William's unwitting participation in Arthur's scheme to involve Baron von Pregnitz in espionage by bringing them all to Switzerland. The scheme revolves around getting von Pregnitz into the hands of Arthur's contact, whose alias is "Margot." William discovered the name by opening some of Arthur's telegrams at Frl. Schroeder's, and so believes Arthur when he tells William that he is serving as a go-between for the Baron in a potential business deal with a Paris glass-works. William accepts this, preferring to assume all of Arthur's information is relevant, orderly, and believable. From there, he begins to imagine who this "Margot" might be, and when he spots a likely candidate—a rather brutal-looking Frenchman—at the Swiss ski resort, he is able to fit this nefarious-seeming visitor right into the frame he has created by participating in Arthur's tale:

> I felt a curious thrill pass through my nervous system; antagonistic, apprehensive, expectant... I had frequently pictured... I had imagined... My imagination had been altogether too timid; I hadn't dreamed of anything so authentic, so absolutely, immediately convincing. Nobody's intuition could be at fault here. I was as certain of his identity as if I'd known him for years. (*BS* 147; emphasis mine)

Leaving aside the comic revelation that the brutish Frenchman is in fact not "Margot" but instead the author of a series of cheap pornographic novels favored by none other than Fritz Wendel, we can see here that William's sincere belief in Arthur's story leads him to participate in the occlusion of the truth. He seems to understand the workings of his mind emerging from what he believes to be unfaulty perception, and writes that mind-reading accordingly. William's own imagination, his filling in the narrative frame provided by Arthur, his collaboration in the construction of this particular storyworld, leads him to utmost certainty. And therein lies the epistemological crisis with which we began.

Isherwood's Berlin is made of story, of singular individuals writing themselves and others through story. This storylining is essential to who they are, but it does not come without complications. Stories can be used to show the work of minds, and that work often involves hiding one's mind from oneself and others. It involves knowing and not knowing. Above all, *The Berlin Stories* as a whole shows us the essential role attending to mind plays in the making of a storyworld, and what can be revealed if we expand our understanding of modernist narrative minds.

Notes

1. *Mr. Norris Changes Trains* and *Goodbye to Berlin* are published together as *The Berlin Stories*. Originally *Mr. Norris Changes Trains* (published in the United States under the title *The Last of Mr. Norris*) was published in 1935 and *Goodbye to Berlin* was published in 1939, after several of the stories comprising that latter volume were published separately by Virginia and Leonard Woolf's Hogarth Press. The stories that make up *Goodbye to Berlin* are: "A Berlin Diary: Autumn 1930," "Sally Bowles," "On Ruegen Island," "The Nowaks," "The Landauers," and "A Berlin Diary: Winter 1932–33." See Thomas Davis, *The Extinct Scene: Late Modernism and Everyday Life* (New York: Columbia University Press, 2016) for an overview of the composition, publication, and critical reception of the works.
2. Christopher Isherwood, *The Berlin Stories* (New York: New Directions, 2008), 163. Hereafter cited in the text as BS. *Mr. Norris Changes Trains* and *Goodbye to Berlin* are published together as *The Berlin Stories*.
3. Lisa Zunshine, *Why We Read Fiction: Theory of Mind and the Novel* (Columbus: Ohio State University Press, 2006), 47.
4. Peter J. Rabinowitz, "Toward a Narratology of Cognitive Flavor," in *The Oxford Handbook of Cognitive Literary Studies*, ed. Lisa Zunshine (Oxford: Oxford University Press, 2015), 88.
5. The term "late Modernism" is somewhat contested, but I happen to accept it and will use it throughout, especially with reference to Isherwood's fiction of the 1930s. Late Modernism is generally meant to refer to work produced after the high-water marks of the 1920s, often with reference to the context of fascism, war, and global imperialism (Kristin Bluemel in *Intermodernism: Literary Culture in Mid-Twentieth-Century Britain* [Edinburgh: Edinburgh University Press, 2009] has also coined the term "intermodernism" to refer to this period and its texts, coming as it does after Modernism and before postmodernism). It is critically characterized by its changing modes of experimentation along with a pivot toward realism (see Tyrus Miller, *Late Modernism: Politics, Fiction, and the Arts between the Wars* [Berkeley: University of California Press, 1999] and Davis, *The Extinct Scene*); by the alienation and anxiety that comes with anticipating war (see Paul Saint-Amour, *Tense Future: Modernism, Total War, Encyclopedic Form* [Oxford: Oxford University Press, 2015]); and by new forms of political commitment manifesting in alternative formal choices (see Rebecca L. Walkowitz, *Cosmopolitan Style: Modernism beyond the Nation* [New York: Columbia University Press, 2006]).
6. David Herman, *Story Logic: Problems and Possibilities of Narrative* (Lincoln: University of Nebraska Press, 2002), 89.
7. Alan Palmer, *Fictional Minds* (Lincoln: University of Nebraska Press, 2002), 48.

8   David P. Thomas, "'Goodbye to Berlin': Refocusing Isherwood's Camera," *Contemporary Literature* 13 (1972): 44–55.

9   *Mr. Norris Changes Trains* is narrated by William Bradshaw, a first-person overt homodiegetic figure (some consider the name "William Bradshaw" as evidence that the narrator is autobiographically inflected, given they are Isherwood's middle names); *Goodbye to Berlin* is narrated by "Christopher Isherwood," a first-person overt homodiegetic figure who has generated critical controversy due to his clear manifestation as a persona of the author. In this same interview with Geherin, Isherwood said,

"I felt the story could only be told from the point of view of myself as the narrator. The reason being that I couldn't really project myself into anybody else and tell the story through his or her eyes. . . . I don't really trust my ability to know what anything looks like through anybody else's eyes anyhow under any circumstance in life whatsoever. . . . I began to realize that the person who tells the story is also a character in the story." (David Geherin, "An Interview with Christopher Isherwood," *Journal of Narrative Technique* 2.3 [1972]: 74–75).

Katherine Bucknell has written extensively on the relationship between this narrative persona/character and the author himself. While it is beyond the scope of this chapter to engage with this critical conversation (interested though I am in extending Palmer's work on fictional minds beyond the third-person narrator to the work of the first person), I do want to point out that Isherwood is describing the creative—and cognitive—process of generating a narrative persona, not writing an autobiography; and he is also very explicit about the problem of other minds in narrative ("I don't really trust my ability to know what anything looks like through anybody else's eyes anyhow under any circumstance in life whatsoever"). This problem of knowing is at the core of his work with other minds, as well as a significant preoccupation of much late modernist narrative. See Katherine Bucknell, "Who Is Christopher Isherwood?" in *The Isherwood Century*, ed. James Berg and Chris Freeman (Madison: University of Wisconsin Press, 2001), 13–30.

10 Thomas, " 'Goodbye to Berlin': Refocusing Isherwood's Camera," 52.

11 Judy Suh, "Christopher Isherwood and Virginia Woolf: Diaries and Fleeting Impressions of Fascism," *Modern Language Studies* 38 (2008): 57.

12 Carolyn Heilbrun, *Christopher Isherwood* (New York: Columbia University Press, 1970), 19.

13 Suh, "Christopher Isherwood and Virginia Woolf," 57–58.

14 Davis, *The Extinct Scene*, 94.

15 Palmer, *Fictional Minds*, 5.

16 Davis James, "Modernist Narratives: Revisions and Rereadings," in *The Oxford Handbook of Modernisms*, ed. Peter Brooker et al. (Oxford: Oxford University Press, 2010), 89.
17 Patricia Waugh, "Thinking in Literature: Modernism and Contemporary Neuroscience," in *The Legacies of Modernism: Historicizing Postwar and Contemporary Fiction*, ed. David James (Cambridge: Cambridge University Press, 2012), 100.
18 Waugh, "Thinking in Literature," 76.
19 Ibid.," 79.
20 Palmer, *Fictional Minds*, 157.
21 Ibid., 80.
22 Ibid., 87, 92. See James Harker, "'Laura Was Not Thinking': Cognitive Minimalism in Sylvia Townsend Warner's Lolly Willowes," *Studies in the Novel* 46 (2014): 44–62, for an application of Waugh's work to Sylvia Townsend Warner's *Lolly Willowes* (1926), another important but less studied early twentieth-century text.
23 Alan Wilde, "Surfacings: Reflections on the Epistemology of Late Modernism," *boundary* 2.8 (1980): 210–11.
24 See Suh, "Christopher Isherwood and Virginia Woolf," 46; Davis, *The Extinct Scene*, 94; and Richard Johnstone, *The Will to Believe: Novelists of the Nineteen-Thirties* (Oxford: Oxford University Press, 1982), 113.
25 David Herman, *Storytelling and the Sciences of Mind* (Cambridge, MA: MIT Press, 2013), 264.
26 For plots of revelation versus plots of resolution, see Seymour Chatman, *Story and Discourse: Narrative Structure in Fiction and Film* (Ithaca, NY: Cornell University Press, 1978).
27 Armistead Maupin, Introduction to *The Berlin Stories*, by Christopher Isherwood, ix.
28 Alan Palmer, "Storyworlds and Groups," in *Introduction to Cognitive Cultural Studies*, ed. Liza Zunshine (Baltimore: Johns Hopkins University Press, 2010), 182.
29 David Herman, "Narrative Theory after the Second Cognitive Revolution," in *Introduction to Cognitive Cultural Studies*, ed. Zunshine, 161–62.
30 Waugh, "Thinking in Literature," 80.
31 Inspired by lines from Ezekiel, this well-known spiritual begins, "Toe bone connected to the foot bone / Foot bone connected to the heel bone / Heel bone connected to the ankle bone," and so on.
32 Herman, "Narrative Theory after the Second Cognitive Revolution," 166.
33 Rabinowitz, "Toward a Narratology of Cognitive Flavor," 88.
34 Lisa Zunshine, "Theory of Mind and Experimental Representations of Fictional Consciousness," in *Introduction to Cognitive Cultural Studies*, ed. Zunshine, 204–7.

35 Quoted in Monika Fludernik, *The Fictions of Language and the Language of Fictions* (London: Routledge, 1993), 926.
36 Lisa Zunshine, "Theory of Mind and Cultural Historicism," in *Introduction to Cognitive Cultural Studies*, ed. Zunshine, 117.
37 Karin Kukkonen, "When Social Minds Get Into Trouble," *Orbis Litterarum* 71 (2016): 307–27.
38 Rose Kamel, "'Unravelling One's Personal Myth': Christopher Isherwood's Autobiographical Strategies," *Biography* 5.2 (1982): 169, 165.
39 Palmer, *Fictional Minds*, 183–85.
40 Rabinowitz, "Toward a Narratology of Cognitive Flavor," 88–89.
41 Quoted in Manfred Jahn, "Frames, Preferences, and the Reading of Third-Person Narratives: Towards a Cognitive Narratology," *Poetics Today* 18 (1997): 447; emphasis mine.
42 Rabinowitz, "Toward a Narratology of Cognitive Flavor," 88–89.

Notes on Editor and Contributors

Editor

Ricardo Miguel-Alfonso is Associate Professor of American Studies and Literary Theory at the University of Castilla-La Mancha, Spain. He is the author of *El romanticismo en Estados Unidos y la idea de la literatura* (*American Romanticism and the Idea of Literature* [Madrid: Verbum, 2018]) and has recently coedited with David LaRocca *A Power to Translate the World: New Essays on Emerson and International Culture* (Dartmouth, 2015). He is the author of journal essays and book chapters on such figures as Robert Coover, Lydia Sigourney, Ralph Waldo Emerson, and Nathaniel Hawthorne, and has also translated into Spanish Emerson's *Essays* and George Santayana's *Reason in Art*, among others. He is currently working on a book manuscript on Emerson and modern disenchantment.

Contributors

José A. Álvarez-Amorós is Professor of English Literature and Criticism at the University of Alicante (Spain), a position he formerly held at the University of Corunna (Spain) from 1995 to 1999. He now teaches history of English and American criticism and postgraduate courses in literary theory and narrative analysis. His essays on diverse aspects of Anglo-American literature, literary theory, and criticism have appeared in *Style*, *Comparative Literature*, *Language Forum*, *Studia Neophilologica*, *Studies in Short Fiction*, *Journal of Narrative Theory*, *English Studies* (Nijmegen), several Spanish journals, *Festschriften*, and a wide variety of collective works.

Marco Caracciolo received a PhD in Comparative Literature from the University of Bologna in 2012, and has held fellowships in Hamburg, Groningen, and Freiburg since then. He is currently an Alexander von Humboldt postdoctoral researcher at the University of Freiburg, with a joint appointment at the Freiburg Institute for Advanced Studies and the English Department. During his PhD he was a visiting scholar at University College London and the Ohio State University (Project Narrative). His work explores the phenomenology of narrative, or the structure of the experiences afforded by literary fiction and other narrative media. He is also interested in the dynamics of interpretation and in engaging with characters, especially those we perceive as "strange" or deviant (narrating animals, serial killers, cyborgs). He has published articles in journals such as *Poetics Today*, *Narrative*, *New Literary History*, and *Phenomenology and the Cognitive Sciences*. He is the author of an introduction to cognitive literary studies in Italian (with Marco Bernini; *Letteratura e scienze cognitive*, Carocci, 2013) and of *The Experientiality of Narrative: An Enactivist Approach* (De Gruyter, 2014). His third book, coauthored with psychologist Russ Hurlburt, is titled *A Passion for Specificity: Confronting Inner Experience in Literature and Science* (Ohio State, 2016).

José Ángel García-Landa is a tenured professor of English at the University of Zaragoza, Spain. He has coedited a Longman critical reader on *Narratology* and the volumes *Gender, I-deology* and *Semiosphere of Narratology*. He is the author of *Samuel Beckett y la Narración Reflexiva* (Zaragoza, 1992) of *Acción, Relato, Discurso: Estructura de la ficción narrativa* (Salamanca, 1998), and of more than a hundred papers, book chapters, and blogs. He has been the editor of *Miscelánea: A Journal of English and American Studies* and is currently editing *A Bibliography of Literary Theory, Criticism and Philology* (at http://bit.ly/abiblio).

Garry L. Hagberg is the James H. Ottaway Professor of Philosophy and Aesthetics at Bard College, and has in recent years also held a chair in the School of Philosophy at the University of East Anglia. Author of numerous papers at the intersection of aesthetics and the philosophy of language, his books include *Meaning and Interpretation: Wittgenstein, Henry James, and Literary Knowledge*, and *Art as Language: Wittgenstein, Meaning, and Aesthetic Theory* (Cornell, 1995). His *Describing Ourselves: Wittgenstein and Autobiographical Consciousness* appeared with Oxford University Press in 2008. His edited collections include *Art and Ethical Criticism* (Blackwell, 2008), *A Companion to the Philosophy of Literature* (with Walter Jost, Wiley-Blackwell, 2010), and *Fictional Characters, Real Problems: The Search for Ethical Content in Literature* (Oxford, 2016). He is also the editor of the journal *Philosophy and Literature*. He is presently writing a new book on the contribution literary experience makes to the formation of self and sensibility, *Living in Words: Literature, Autobiographical Language, and the Composition of Selfhood*.

Patrick Colm Hogan is Board of Trustees Distinguished Professor of English at the University of Connecticut, where he is also part of the Cognitive Science Program and the Asian and Asian American Studies Institute, among others. He has written extensively on literary and narrative theory, cognitive science and the emotions, and literary universals. His latest publications include *Ulysses and the Poetics of Cognition* (Routledge, 2014), *Beauty and Sublimity* (Cambridge, 2016), *Literature and Emotion* (Routledge, 2017), and *Sexual Identities: A Cognitive Literary Study* (Oxford, 2018).

David LaRocca is the author, editor, or coeditor of ten books, including *The Thought of Stanley Cavell and Cinema: Turning Anew to the Ontology of Film a Half-Century after The World Viewed*, *The Philosophy of Charlie Kaufman*, *The Philosophy of War Films*, and *The Philosophy of Documentary Film: Image, Sound, Fiction, Truth* as well as *Emerson's English Traits and the Natural History of Metaphor*, Stanley Cavell's *Emerson's Transcendental Etudes*, *Estimating Emerson: An Anthology of Criticism from Carlyle to Cavell*, *The Bloomsbury Anthology of Transcendental Thought: From Antiquity to the Anthropocene*, and *A Power to Translate the World: New Essays on Emerson and International Culture* (co-edited with Ricardo Miguel-Alfonso). He has served as Visiting Assistant Professor in the Cinema Department at Binghamton University, Visiting Assistant Professor in the Department of Philosophy at the State University of New York College at Cortland, Visiting Scholar in the Department of English at Cornell University, and Lecturer in Screen Studies in the Department of Cinema, Photography, and Media Arts at the Roy H. Park School of Communications at Ithaca College. Educated at Buffalo, Berkeley, Vanderbilt, and Harvard, he was also Harvard's Sinclair Kennedy Traveling Fellow in the United Kingdom and has participated in a National Endowment for the Humanities Institute, a workshop with Abbas Kiarostami, Werner Herzog's Rogue Film School, and The School of Criticism and Theory at Cornell University.

Jukka Mikkonen is a postdoctoral fellow at the School of Social Sciences and Humanities at the University of Tampere. His publications include *The Cognitive Value of Philosophical Fiction* (Bloomsbury, 2013) as well as several articles in scholarly journals.

Paul Sheehan is an associate professor in the Department of English at Macquarie University (Sydney, Australia). He is the author of *Modernism,*

Narrative and Humanism (Cambridge, 2002) and *Modernism and the Aesthetics of Violence* (Cambridge, 2013). Prof. Sheehan is also the coeditor of "The Uses of Anachronism" (2012), a special issue of *Textual Practice*, and "Post-Archival Beckett: Genre, Process, Value," a special issue of the *Journal of Beckett* Studies (2017). He has recently published essays on Joyce and encryption, Einstein and literary modernism, posthuman bodies, and zoopoetics. His current project is an international collaboration entitled "Transnational Coetzee."

Janine Utell is Professor and Chair of English at Widener University in Chester, Pennsylvania. Her research focuses on the study of nineteenth- and twentieth-century narratives of couplehood and intimate life, with a broader interest in the application of narrative theory and postmodern ethics to literary, visual, and digital texts. She is the author of *James Joyce and the Revolt of Love: Marriage, Adultery, Desire* (Palgrave, 2010) and *Engagements with Narrative* (Routledge, 2015), and is currently developing a potential project for the Modern Language Association on teaching modernist women writers. She has also published or has articles forthcoming on film, life writing, and modernist studies in *Journal of Modern Literature, College Literature, Life Writing, Literature/Film Quarterly*, and *James Joyce Quarterly*. Utell is the editor for the journal *The Space Between: Literature and Culture 1914–1945*.

Index

Abbott, H. Porter   107 n.50
Affective empathy   120, 133, 137, 138, 141, 142, 143, 147–51, 184
Alber, Jan   24–5, 28 n.23, 28 n.24, 30 n.42–8
Alicke, Mark   154 n.31
Altman, Rick   203 n.8
Anderson, Benedict   155 n.34
Anderson, Lanier   23, 30 n.36, 30 n.37, 30 n.38
Apter, Emily   199
Aristotle   3
Aron, Arthur   155 n.32
Associacionist philosophy   160–1
Auerbach, Erich   20, 28 n.21
Austen, Jane   157, 200
Aute, Luis Eduardo   130 n.34

Banfield, Ann   28 n.17
Barnden, John   35–6, 50 n.22–4, 50 n.26
Barth, John   3
Barthes, Roland   1, 14 n.1, 203 n.8
Bateson, Gregory   204 n.17
Beach, Joseph Warren   105 n.16
Bergson, Henri   19, 112, 128 n.12
Bersani, Leo   177 n.56
Bickerton, Derek   128 n.16
Biebuyck, Benjamin   50 n.35
Bluemel, Kristin   222 n.5
Bonds, Diane S.   177 n.51
Bordwell, David   202 n.4, 203 n.8
Borges, Jorge Luis   3
Bradley, Margaret   154 n.25
Brecht, Bertolt   vii
Brentatno Franz   33
Briggs, Julia   128 n.13, 128 n.14, 131 n.36
Brontë, Emily   127, 129 n.23, 130 n.28
Brooks, Peter   106 n.34, 168, 177 n.54, 177 n.55
Bruner, Jerome   3, 14 n.5, 15 n.15, 24, 30 n.40
Bucknell, Katherine   223 n.9

Budd, Mike   201 n.1
Burke, Kenneth   128 n.6
Burn, Stephen J.   49 n.15
Butte, George   170, 177 n.62

Cameron, Sharon   104, 108 n.57, 174 n.5
Cano, Christine   177 n.52, 177 n.53
Capra, Frank   193
Caracciolo, Marco   15 n.8, 51 n.49
Carew, Thomas   128 n.17
Carroll, Noël   181, 183, 184, 190, 202 n.5, 203 n.7, 203 n.9, 203 n.10, 203 n.11, 203 n.13, 203 n.14, 203 n.15
Cartesianism   10, 11, 31–4
Cave, Terence   2, 14 n.3
Cavell, Stanley   191, 202 n.6
Cervantes, Miguel de   3
Chalmers, David J.   51 n.48
Charon, Joel M.   128 n.6
Chatman, Seymour   107 n.45, 203 n.8
Chopin, Kate   32, 37–40, 41, 50 n.33
Churchland, Paul M.   49 n.6
cognitive frames   25–6
Cohen, Simon Baron   131 n.37
Cohn, Dorrit   18, 23, 27 n.6, 29 n.35, 107 n.45, 128 n.11
Conrad, Joseph   105 n.2, 167
Cooley, Charles H.   129 n.18
Coover, Robert   3
Cormier, Harvey   174 n.4
Cortázar, Julio   3
Costall, Alan   152 n.2
Culler, Jonathan   98, 107 n.44
Culpeper, Jonathan   106 n.36
Cummings, E. E.   117, 129 n.19
Currie, Gregory   19, 27 n.10, 30 n.49
Curtis, Richard   193

Damasio, Antonio   49 n.14, 51 n.50
Danius, Sara   163, 176 n.30
Darío, Rubén   vii
Davidson, Arnold E.   106 n.36

Davis, Rebecca 152 n.11
Davis, Thomas 209, 222 n.1, 223 n.14, 224 n.24
Day, William 198, 200, 204 n.26
Debenedetti, Giacomo 41, 51 n.36
DeKoven, Marianne 12, 16 n.30, 38, 50 n.32
Denby, David 184, 203 n.16
Derrida, Jacques 199
Descombes, Vincent 163, 176 n.31
Devos, Thierry 153 n.14
Dickens, Charles 97, 193
Doherty, Martin 152 n.6
Dokic, Jérôme 130 n.26

Eagleton, Terry 67–8, 80 n.7, 80 n.8, 176 n.28
Ebbinghäus, Hermann 175 n.15
Edel, Leon 86, 105 n.3, 105 n.4
Eisner, Lotte 201 n.1
Eliot, George 157, 158, 160
Eliot, T. S. vii, 43, 51 n.43
Elsaesser, Thomas 201 n.1
enactivism 4–5
epiphany 111

Fadiman, Clifton 81 n.13
Fauconnier, Gilles 129 n.22
Faulkner, William 167
Felski, Rita 176 n.22
Fitzgerald, F. Scott 167
Flaubert, Gustave 37
Fludernik, Monika 18, 24, 27 n.8, 28 n.25, 30 n.41, 175 n.18, 225 n.35
Ford, Ford Madox 167
Frattarola, Angela 153 n.19
Freud, Sigmund 19, 117, 159, 162, 174 n.6, 175 n.9, 176 n.26

Gang, Joshua 27 n.16
Gard, Roger 105 n.12
Gay, Peter 204 n.21
Gazzaniga, Michael 153 n.17
Geherin, David 208, 223 n.9
Geismar, Maxwell 105 n.18, 106 n.35
Gentner, Dedre 35–6, 50 n.20, 50 n.21
Gibson, James J. 2
Gibson, John 6, 15 n.11
Gilbert, Daniel 153 n.12

Gilbert, Sandra M. 121
Ginzburg, Lydia 166, 177 n.48
Goethe, Johann W. von vii
Golgi, Camillo vii
Gondry, Michel 183
Goodkin, Richard E. 166, 177 n.45
Goodman, Nelson 190
Gottschall, Jonathan 2, 14 n.2
Grudin, Jonathan 35–6, 50 n.20, 50 n.21
Gubar, Susan 121
Gutsell, J. N. 153 n.15

Haffey, Kate 109, 127 n.2, 127 n.3, 127 n.4
Hagberg, Garry 80 n.4, 80 n.6, 80 n.9, 82 n.14, 83 n.16
Hain, G. 153 n.17
Hamburger, Kate 18, 27 n.5
Hammond, Meghan 152 n.7, 154 n.28
Harker, James 224 n.22
Hayes, Kevin J. 105 n.9
Hayward, Susan 202 n.3
Heilbrun, Carolyn 208, 223 n.12
Heilmann, Ann 50 n.31
Hemingway, Ernest 103
Herman, David 1, 5, 10–11, 15 n.10, 15 n.12, 15 n.22, 15 n.23, 15 n.24, 15 n.25, 18, 19, 27 n.4, 27 n.13, 27 n.15, 31–5, 48 n.1, 48 n.3, 48 n.4, 107 n.52, 175 n.10, 204 n.22, 206, 207, 222 n.6, 224 n.25, 224 n.29, 224 n.32
Hilsabeck, Burke 204 n.26
Hintikka, Jaakko 28 n.17
Hoffman, Martin 152 n.3
Hogan, Patrick Colm 1, 5, 15 n.9, 15 n.16, 133, 152 n.5, 153 n.13, 154 n.30
Holland, John 153 n.16
Hume, David 118–19

ideology 5–6, 162, 176 n.24, 209
inwardness 10, 11, 19, 31, 39, 40, 43, 54, 60, 61, 76, 157, 158, 214
Isenberg, Noah 204 n.21
Isherwood, Christopher 205–21, 222 n.1, 222 n.2
Isle, Walter 105 n.18

Jahn, Manfred 225 n.41
James, David 209, 224 n.16

James, Henry   8, 14, 67–75, 78, 80 n.5, 80 n.10, 80 n.11, 81 n.12, 82 n.15, 85–105, 105 n.5, 105 n.7, 105 n.8, 112, 157, 158, 160
James, William   19, 33, 49 n.13
Jameson, Fredric   157, 174 n.1, 176 n.29
Janowitz, Hans   187, 201 n.1
Jiménez, Juan Ramón   vii
Johnson, Mark   33, 49 n.17, 50 n.28
Johnstone, Richard   224 n.24
Joyce, James   9, 28 n.20, 29 n.35, 112, 116, 170

Kaes, Anton   201 n.1
Kamel, Rose   225 n.38
Kaplan, Sydney   152 n.10
Kaufman, Charlie   183, 198
Kawabata, Yasunari   vii
Kearns, Michael   37, 50 n.25, 50 n.29, 50 n.30
Keats, John   119
Keestra, Machiel   153 n.17
Kermode, Frank   82 n.16
Kierkegaard, Søren   67, 69
Kittler, Friedrich   188
Klage, Ludwig   199
Klimecki, Olga   153 n.17
Krakauer, Siegfried   179–90, 192, 197–201, 202 n.2
Krebs, Victor J.   204 n.26
Kukkonen, Karin   218, 225 n.37
Kurnick, David   106 n.24, 106 n.28

Lakoff, George   33, 36, 49 n.17, 50 n.28, 171, 172, 178 n.68
Lamarque, Peter   2, 28 n.26, 29 n.30, 29 n.31, 29 n.32, 29 n.33, 30 n.39, 30 n.49
Lametti, Daniel   129 n.24
Lang, Fritz   188
Lang, Peter   154 n.25
LaRocca, David   202 n.6, 203 n.12, 204 n.20, 204 n.26, 204 n.27
Larrain, Jorge   176 n.24
late modernism   222 n.5
Latour, Bruno   176 n.22
Lee, Hermione   109, 127 n.1, 128 n.8, 130 n.32

Leech, Geoffrey   105 n.42
Leslie, Alan   177 n.60
Leudar, Ivan   152 n.2
Leverage, Paula   152 n.4
Lewes, George Henry   158
Lloyd, Dan   152 n.11
LoBrutto, Vincent   201 n.1
Locke, John   55–9, 70, 79 n.1
Lodge, David   4, 15 n.7
Lubbock, Percy   89, 105 n.17, 107 n.39
Luckhurst, Nikola   169, 177 n.57

McCabe, Susan   33, 49 n.11
McCarey, Leo   194
McEwan, Ian   48
McHale, Brian   18, 27 n.2
Mach, Ernst   19, 33
Mäkelä, Maria   29 n.34
Martens, Gunther   50 n.35
Martí, José   vii
Martin, Kirsty   33, 40 n.12
Marx, Karl   162, 163
Matz, Jesse   15 n.21, 48 n.2
Maupassant, Guy de   37
Maupin, Armistead   27, 212, 224
Mayer, Carl   187
Mead, George Herbert   110, 111, 127 n.5, 128 n.6, 129 n.18
Meisel, Perry   28 n.17
Menary, Richard   51 n.47
metaphor   34–7
Mikkonen, Jukka   30 n.50
Miller, Tyrus   222 n.5
Mimesis   vii, 26
Mitchell, W. J. T.   203 n.8
Moby-Dick   115, 167
Moers, Ellen   130 n.29
Moi, Toril   130 n.30
Montaigne, Michel de   166
Morton, Timothy J.   48, 51 n.52
Moses, Omri   13, 16 n.32

Nardone, Natalie   155 n.32
New Criticism   112
Nicholson-Weir, Rebecca   154 n.20
Nietzsche, Friedrich   162, 163, 176 n.25
Nigro, Frank G.   177 n.51
Noë, Alva   49 n.7
Nolan, Jonathan   180, 186

Oatley, Keith 154 n.27, 154 n.29, 163, 170, 176 n.33, 177 n.63
Olsen, Stein H. 22, 28 n.26, 29 n.30, 29 n.31, 29 n.33
Owen, Elizabeth 106 n.24

Painter, George D. 175 n.13
Palmer, Alan 1, 9–10, 15 n.19, 15 n.20, 18, 19, 27 n.3, 27 n.11, 27 n.12, 27 n.14, 97, 105 n.1, 106 n.38, 107 n.40, 107 n.41, 107 n.47, 108 n.56, 152 n.8, 175 n.16, 190, 191, 193, 200, 206, 208, 210, 222 n.7, 223 n.15, 224 n.20, 225 n.39
Pavel, Thomas 9, 15 n.17
Perosa, Sergio 106 n.18, 106 n.29
Perry, Menahem 218
Pippin, Robert B. 79 n.3
Plato 186, 187
Pollard-Gott, Lucy 106 n.38
Popova, Yana 3, 14 n.4, 15 n.6
Postlethwaite, Diana 174 n.2
Powers, Richard 48
Prinz, Jesse J. 49 n.8
Propp, Vladimir 203 n.8
Proust, Marcel 112, 159–74, 175 n.20, 176 n.35–41, 176 n.43, 177 n.44, 177 n.46, 177 n.61, 178 n.64–7, 178 n.72, 178 n.73

Quigley, Megan 28 n.17

Rabinowitz, Peter J. 193, 200, 206, 211, 215, 219, 220, 222 n.4, 224 n.33, 225 n.40, 225 n.42
Ramón y Cajal, Santiago viii
Ratcliffe, Matthew 38, 50 n.34
realism 3, 77, 158, 159, 174, 222 n.5
Reber, Arthur S. 49 n.19
Rentschler, Eric 204 n.21
Ribot, Théodule 160, 175 n.12
Richardson, Brian 1
Richardson, Dorothy 112, 134, 135, 138–50, 152 n.7
Ricoeur, Paul 162, 163, 175 n.22, 176 n.23
Rivière, Jacques 173
Robinson, David 201 n.1
Robinson, Howard 31, 49 n.5

Rohrer, Tim 49 n.16
Rozin, Paul 154 n.26
Ruesch, Juergen 204 n.17
Ryan, Judith 33, 49 n.9, 49 n.10, 174 n.8
Ryan, Marie-Laure 18, 27 n.7, 51 n.39, 107 n.38, 206

Second World War 9
Saccone, Eduardo 41, 51 n.37
Saint-Amour, Paul 222 n.5
Sander, Dvaid 154 n.22
Sapolsky, Robert 154 n.23, 154 n.24
Sass, Louis 177 n.50
Schenkler, Bary 155 n.33
Scheunemann, Dietrich 201 n.1
Scorsese, Martin 186
Semino, Elena 51 n.44
Shakespeare, William 128 n.15
Shattuck, Roger 165, 166, 176 n.42, 177 n.49
Sheehan, Paul 9, 15 n.18
Short, Michael H. 107 n.42
Shyamalan, M. Night 186
Sinnerbrink, Robert 203 n.12
social pragmatism 110
Stein, Gertrude 9, 11–12, 15 n.26, 15 n.27, 15 n.28, 16 n.29
Sternberg, Meir 107 n.46
Sterne, Laurence 3, 24, 116
Stimpson, Catherine R. 130 n.30
stream of consciousness 19, 46, 95, 97, 116, 125, 135, 196
Suh, Judy 223 n.11, 223 n.13, 224 n.24

Taine, Hippolyte 161, 175 n.14, 175 n.15
Talmy, Leonard 43, 51 n.42
Taussig, Michael 161, 175 n.19
Taylor, Charles 128 n.9
Taylor, Julie 33, 49 n.12
theory of mind (ToM) 19, 27 n.9, 96, 103, 133–8, 141, 144, 145, 149, 151, 153 n.19, 160, 161, 163, 169, 173
Thomas, David 223 n.8, 223 n.10
Thompson, Kristine 201
Tintner, Adeline 106 n.21, 106 n.27
Todorov, Tzvetan 203 n.8
Tomasello, Michael 129 n.21
Tozzi, Federigo 32, 41–3, 44, 51 n.38

Trexler, Adam   51 n.53
Turner, Mark   36, 129 n.22

Uspensky, Boris   106 n.32, 107 n.51, 107 n.53

Varela, Francisco   51 n.51
Veidt, Conrad   185, 186
Vermeule, Blakey   153 n.18
Vuilleumier, Patrik   153, 154 n.27

Wales, Katie   152 n.9
Walkowitz, Rebecca   222 n.5
Walton, Kendall   22, 28 n.28, 29 n.29
Warner, Sylvia Townsend   224 n.22
Waugh, Patricia   209, 224 n.17, 224 n.18, 224 n.19, 224 n.30
Wheeler, Kathleen M.   16 n.31
Wiene, Robert   179, 180, 181
Wilde, Alan   210, 212, 224 n.23
Wimmer, Heinz   177 n.59

Winnicott, D. W.   131 n.37
Wittgenstein, Ludwig   14, 53, 54, 59–66, 68, 69, 70, 76, 78, 79, 79 n.2, 198
Wollaeger, Mark   140, 154 n.21
Woolf, Virginia   8, 14, 20, 21–2, 23, 25, 27 n.1, 28 n.18, 28 n.19, 28 n.22, 32, 44–7, 48, 51 n.46, 109–31, 158, 165, 167, 174 n.7, 222 n.1

Yacavone, Daniel   190, 204 n.23
Young, Katherine   302 n.17

Zemeckis, Robert   193
Zola, Émile   32, 159
Zunshine, Lisa   1, 7, 15 n.14, 19, 23, 27 n.9, 106 n.37, 107 n.38, 107 n.54, 134 n.1, 152 n.4, 175 n.11, 190, 198–200, 204 n.22, 217, 222 n.3, 224 n.34, 225 n.36
Zwaan, Rolf A.   51 n.41

www.ingramcontent.com/pod-product-compliance
Lightning Source LLC
Chambersburg PA
CBHW052035300426
44117CB00012B/1824